Taste of Home ULTIMATE
5 INGREDIENT COOKBOOK

TASTE OF HOME BOOKS • RDA ENTHUSIAST BRANDS, LLC • MILWAUKEE, WI

Visit us at **tasteofhome.com** for other
Taste of Home books and products.

International Standard Book Number:
979-8-88977-018-3

Content Director: Mark Hagen
Creative Director: Raeann Thompson
Senior Editor: Christine Rukavena
Editor: Hazel Wheaton
Senior Art Director: Courtney Lovetere
Senior Print Publication Designer:
Jogesh Antony
Deputy Editor, Copy Desk: Ann Walter
Copy Editors: Suchismita Ukil, Rayan
Naqash
Contributing Copy Editor: Pam Grandy

Cover Photography:
Photographer: Mark Derse
Set Stylists: Melissa Franco, Stacey Genaw
Food Stylist: Sue Draheim

Pictured on front cover:
Bean Burritos, p. 102

Pictured on title page:
Crispy Baked Chicken Thighs, p. 131

Printed in China
1 3 5 7 9 10 8 6 4 2

**RAVIOLI LASAGNA,
PAGE 115**

HOW DO YOU COUNT TO 5?

You'll notice throughout this book that some recipe lists run longer than five lines. That's because there are a few items we don't include in our five-ingredient counts. These are essentials that are so basic we feel comfortable assuming every kitchen always has them on hand. What are they? There are five items on the list, some of which you can customize as you wish.

1. WATER

2. SALT When we say "salt," we're referring to traditional table salt, and we don't count it. Many cooks regularly use kosher salt instead, preferring it for its more predictable "pinch" measure—feel free to do so. If a recipe calls for kosher salt, sea salt or another specialty salt, we'll name it specifically and include it in our count.

3. PEPPER Black pepper is a go-to kitchen staple, and we don't count it. However, if a recipe demands freshly cracked black pepper, we will name it and count it. Cracked pepper gives the freshest flavor, but not everyone owns a pepper mill.

4. OIL Two oils make our "don't count" list: canola oil and regular olive oil. Canola oil doesn't have a strong flavor and has a high smoke point, which makes it ideal for frying, sauteing and baking. Regular olive oil adds a hint of fruity flavor and can be used for light sauteing and roasting, and for dressings and sauces. Extra virgin olive oil, on the other hand, has more specialized uses due to its low smoke point and will be specified (and counted!) when it's needed for a recipe.

5. OPTIONAL INGREDIENTS We also don't include optional items when counting ingredients. We view these items as suggestions—either as garnishes or as complements—but they aren't necessary to make the recipe work, so you can easily leave them out. And, you can always swap them for your own preferred finishing touches.

CONTENTS

SHORT ON TIME?

Keep an eye out for these handy icons to help you quickly identify recipes that fit your schedule.

Fast-fix dishes are table-ready in 30 minutes (or less!)—so they're perfect for your busiest nights.

Freezer-friendly recipes include instructions for freezing and reheating so you can make them in advance.

MANGO SMOOTHIES,
PAGE 24

BREAKFAST & BRUNCH

MANGO SMOOTHIES
1. Pineapple Juice
2. Mangoes
3. Banana
4. Yogurt
5. Honey

**MAKEOVER
HASH & EGGS**

CHEDDAR BACON GRITS

In the South, grits can be served plain with a little butter or loaded with extras—my recipe has bacon, cheddar and green chiles.
—*Amanda Reed, Nashville, TN*

- -

TAKES: 30 min.
MAKES: 12 servings

- 8 cups water
- 2 cups uncooked old-fashioned grits
- 1 tsp. salt
- ¼ tsp. paprika
- 2 cups shredded white cheddar cheese
- 5 bacon strips, cooked and crumbled
- 1 can (4 oz.) chopped green chiles
  Sliced green onions, optional

1. In a 6-qt. stockpot, bring water to a boil. Slowly stir in grits, salt and paprika. Reduce heat; cook, covered, 15-20 minutes or until thickened, stirring occasionally.
2. Reduce heat to low. Stir in cheese, bacon and chiles until cheese is melted. If desired, sprinkle with green onions.
¾ CUP 199 cal., 8g fat (4g sat. fat), 22mg chol., 418mg sod., 24g carb. (0 sugars, 1g fiber), 7g pro.

MAKEOVER HASH & EGGS

Loaded with red potatoes and corned beef, our lightened-up version of the diner classic delivers fresh flavors with a healthy dose of fiber.
—*Taste of Home Test Kitchen*

- -

TAKES: 30 min.
MAKES: 4 servings

- 1 large onion, chopped
- 1 Tbsp. canola oil, divided
- 6 medium red potatoes (about 1½ lbs.), cut into ½-in. cubes
- ¼ cup water
- 3 pkg. (2 oz. each) thinly sliced deli corned beef, coarsely chopped
- ¼ tsp. pepper
- 4 large eggs
  Additional pepper, optional

1. In a large nonstick skillet, saute onion in 2 tsp. oil until tender. Stir in potatoes and water. Bring to a boil. Reduce heat; cover and simmer for 15-20 minutes or until potatoes are tender. Stir in corned beef and pepper; heat through.
2. Meanwhile, in a large nonstick skillet, fry eggs in the remaining 1 tsp. oil as desired. Season with additional pepper if desired. Serve with corned beef hash.
1 EGG WITH 1 CUP HASH 301 cal., 12g fat (3g sat. fat), 239mg chol., 652mg sod., 31g carb. (4g sugars, 4g fiber), 18g pro. **DIABETIC EXCHANGES** 2 starch, 2 medium-fat meat, ½ fat.

CHEDDAR
BACON GRITS

STUFFED HAM &
EGG BREAD

STUFFED HAM & EGG BREAD

My son Gus is a lover of all things ham and eggs, so I created this comforting stuffed bread with him in mind. I added tomatoes to the recipe, and he still gives it a big thumbs-up.
—*Karen Kuebler, Dallas, TX*

PREP: 25 min. • **BAKE:** 20 min.
MAKES: 8 servings

- 2 tsp. canola oil
- 1 can (14½ oz.) diced tomatoes, drained
- 6 large eggs, lightly beaten
- 2 cups chopped fully cooked ham
- 1 tube (11 oz.) refrigerated crusty French loaf
- 2 cups shredded sharp cheddar cheese

1. Preheat oven to 400°. In a large nonstick skillet, heat oil over medium heat. Add the tomatoes; cook and stir until juices are evaporated, 12-15 minutes. Add beaten eggs; cook and stir until thickened and no liquid egg remains, 3-4 minutes. Remove from heat; stir in ham.
2. Unroll dough onto a greased baking sheet. Sprinkle cheese lengthwise down half of dough to within 1 in. of edges. Top with the egg mixture. Fold the dough over filling, pinching to seal; tuck ends under.
3. Bake until deep golden brown, 17-20 minutes. Cut into slices.
1 PIECE 321 cal., 17g fat (7g sat. fat), 188mg chol., 967mg sod., 22g carb. (3g sugars, 1g fiber), 22g pro.

CHEDDAR-HAM OVEN OMELET

CHEDDAR-HAM OVEN OMELET

We had a family reunion for 50 relatives from the U.S. and Canada, and it took four pans of this hearty omelet to feed the whole crowd. Fresh fruit and an assortment of muffins helped round out our brunch menu.
—*Betty Abrey, Imperial, SK*

PREP: 15 min.
BAKE: 40 min. + standing
MAKES: 12 servings

- 16 large eggs
- 2 cups 2% milk
- 2 cups shredded cheddar cheese
- ¾ cup cubed fully cooked ham
- 6 green onions, chopped

1. Preheat oven to 350°. In a large bowl, whisk eggs and milk. Stir in cheese, ham and onions. Pour into a greased 13x9-in. baking dish.
2. Bake, uncovered, until a knife inserted in the center comes out clean, 40-45 minutes. Let stand 10 minutes before cutting.
1 PIECE 208 cal., 14g fat (7g sat. fat), 314mg chol., 330mg sod., 4g carb. (3g sugars, 0 fiber), 15g pro.

DID YOU KNOW?

Buying bagged shredded cheese is convenient, but shredding your own is more economical—plus, it melts better because it's pure cheese. Bagged cheese often contains additives to prevent shreds from sticking together.

MARMALADE FRENCH TOAST SANDWICHES

MARMALADE FRENCH TOAST SANDWICHES

I change up these warm, filling sandwiches by using sweet or savory jellies depending on my mood. Try adding some hot pepper jelly when you want a little sizzle in the morning.
—Danielle Loring, Lewiston, ME

TAKES: 25 min.
MAKES: 6 servings

- 1 container (8 oz.) whipped cream cheese
- 12 slices sourdough bread
- ¾ cup orange marmalade
- 4 large eggs, room temperature
- 2 Tbsp. 2% milk
  Maple syrup, optional

1. Spread the cream cheese over 6 slices of bread; top with marmalade and remaining slices of bread. In a shallow bowl, whisk eggs and milk.
2. Heat a large greased cast-iron skillet or griddle over medium heat. Dip both sides of sandwiches into the egg mixture. Place the sandwiches in skillet; cook until golden brown, 2-3 minutes on each side. Serve with maple syrup if desired.

1 SANDWICH 447 cal., 16g fat (9g sat. fat), 151mg chol., 628mg sod., 65g carb. (28g sugars, 2g fiber), 13g pro.

HOME FRIES

HOME FRIES

When I was little, my dad and I would get up early on Sundays and make these for the family. The rest of the gang would be awakened by the tempting aroma.
—Teresa Koide, Manchester, CT

PREP: 25 min.
COOK: 15 min./batch.
MAKES: 8 servings

1 lb. bacon, chopped
8 medium potatoes (about 3 lbs.), peeled and cut into ½-in. pieces
1 large onion, chopped
1 tsp. salt
½ tsp. pepper

1. In a large skillet, cook chopped bacon over medium-low heat until crisp. Remove bacon from pan with a slotted spoon; drain on paper towels. Reserve the bacon drippings.

2. Working in batches, add ¼ cup bacon drippings, potatoes, onion, salt and pepper to pan; toss to coat. Cook and stir over medium-low heat until potatoes are golden brown and tender, 15-20 minutes, adding more drippings as needed. Stir in the cooked bacon; serve immediately.

1 CUP 349 cal., 21g fat (8g sat. fat), 33mg chol., 681mg sod., 31g carb. (3g sugars, 2g fiber), 10g pro.

MEAL IN A MUFFIN PAN

STRAWBERRY-LIME QUINOA PARFAITS

When I serve quinoa with strawberries and Key lime pie yogurt, friends scrape the bottom of the parfait glass to get every delectable bite.
—*Be Jones, Brunswick, MO*

PREP: 10 min.
COOK: 15 min. + chilling
MAKES: 4 servings

- 1   cup water
- ½   cup quinoa, rinsed
- 2   tsp. grated lime zest
- 4   containers (6 oz. each) Key lime pie-flavored yogurt
- 2⅔ cups sliced fresh strawberries
- ½   cup flaked coconut

1. In a small saucepan, bring water to a boil. Add quinoa. Reduce heat; simmer, covered, 12-15 minutes or until liquid is absorbed. Remove from heat; fluff with a fork. Stir in lime zest; refrigerate 30 minutes.
2. Layer ⅓ cup yogurt, ⅓ cup strawberries, ¼ cup quinoa mixture and 1 Tbsp. coconut into 4 parfait glasses. Repeat layers.
1 PARFAIT 341 cal., 8g fat (5g sat. fat), 9mg chol., 123mg sod., 60g carb. (43g sugars, 4g fiber), 11g pro.

MEAL IN A MUFFIN PAN

This meal-in-a-pan is ideal for busy weekday mornings. I just add fresh fruit and beverages for a complete breakfast.
—*Michelle Plumb, Montrose, CO*

PREP: 20 min. • **BAKE:** 15 min.
MAKES: 6 servings

- 1   can (15 oz.) corned beef hash
- 6   large eggs
     Salt and pepper to taste
- 1   pkg. (8½ oz.) cornbread/ muffin mix

1. Preheat oven to 400°. Grease a 12-cup muffin pan. Divide hash among 6 cups; firmly press onto the bottoms and all the way up the sides to form shells. Break 1 egg into each shell; season with salt and pepper. Mix muffins according to package directions. Spoon the batter into the remaining 6 cups.
2. Bake 15-20 minutes or until muffins are golden brown and eggs are set.
1 EGG CUP AND 1 CORN MUFFIN
377 cal., 18g fat (7g sat. fat), 243mg chol., 717mg sod., 36g carb. (9g sugars, 3g fiber), 17g pro.

STRAWBERRY-LIME
QUINOA PARFAITS

CHORIZO SALSA OMELET

Just a few ingredients jazz up a basic omelet and make it delish!
—Taste of Home *Test Kitchen*

- -

TAKES: 20 min. • **MAKES:** 1 serving

1 Tbsp. butter
3 large eggs
3 Tbsp. water
⅛ tsp. salt
⅛ tsp. pepper
¼ cup cooked chorizo or sausage
2 Tbsp. chunky salsa

1. In a small nonstick skillet, melt butter over medium-high heat. Whisk the eggs, water, salt and pepper. Add egg mixture to skillet (mixture should set immediately at edges).
2. As eggs set, push cooked edge toward center, letting uncooked portion flow underneath. When the eggs are set, spoon chorizo and salsa on 1 side; fold other side over filling. Slide omelet onto a plate.
1 OMELET 588 cal., 48g fat (19g sat. fat), 727mg chol., 1568mg sod., 3g carb. (2g sugars, 0 fiber), 34g pro.

DID YOU KNOW?

Chorizo is a coarsely ground fresh or smoked pork sausage that has Mexican, Spanish and Portuguese origins. Traditionally flavored with paprika or chili powder, which gives it its reddish color, chorizo is often used in egg dishes, soups, casseroles and a variety of Mexican dishes.

CHEESY HASH BROWN BAKE

CHEESY HASH BROWN BAKE

Prepare this cheesy dish ahead of time for less stress on brunch day. You'll love it!
—Karen Burns, Chandler, TX

- -

PREP: 10 min. • **BAKE:** 40 min.
MAKES: 10 servings

1 pkg. (30 oz.) frozen shredded hash brown potatoes, thawed
2 cans (10¾ oz. each) condensed cream of potato soup, undiluted
2 cups sour cream
2 cups shredded cheddar cheese, divided
1 cup grated Parmesan cheese
  Sliced green onions, optional

1. Preheat oven to 350°. In a large bowl, combine potatoes, soup, sour cream, 1¾ cups cheddar cheese and Parmesan cheese. Place in a greased 3-qt. baking dish. Sprinkle with remaining ¼ cup cheddar cheese.
2. Bake, uncovered, until the casserole is bubbly and cheese is melted, 40-45 minutes. Let stand 5 minutes before serving. If desired, sprinkle with green onions.
½ CUP 305 cal., 18g fat (12g sat. fat), 65mg chol., 554mg sod., 21g carb. (3g sugars, 1g fiber), 12g pro.
ZIPPY HASH BROWN BAKE
Substitute pepper jack cheese for the cheddar cheese; omit the Parmesan cheese.
NACHO HASH BROWN BAKE
Substitute 1 can (10¾ oz.) condensed cream of celery soup and 1 can (10¾ oz.) condensed nacho cheese soup for the potato soup. Instead of cheddar cheese, try a Mexican cheese blend and omit the Parmesan cheese.

BERRY-FILLED DOUGHNUTS

Four ingredients are all you will need for this sure-to-be-popular treat. Friends and family will never guess that refrigerated buttermilk biscuits are the base for these golden, jelly-filled doughnuts.
—*Ginny Watson, Broken Arrow, OK*

TAKES: 25 min.
MAKES: 10 doughnuts

Oil for deep-fat frying
2 tubes (6 oz. each) small refrigerated flaky biscuits (5 count)
½ cup seedless strawberry jam
¾ cup confectioners' sugar

1. In an electric skillet or deep fryer, heat oil to 350°. Separate biscuits; press each to flatten slightly. Fry biscuits, a few at a time, until golden brown, 1-1¼ minutes on each side. Drain on paper towels.
2. Cut a small hole in the tip of a pastry bag; insert a small pastry tip. Fill bag with jam. With a small knife, pierce a hole into the side of each doughnut; fill with jam.
3. Toss with confectioners' sugar. Serve warm.

1 DOUGHNUT 190 cal., 7g fat (1g sat. fat), 0 chol., 360mg sod., 30g carb. (17g sugars, 0 fiber), 2g pro.

BERRY-FILLED DOUGHNUTS

RISE & SHINE PARFAIT

Start your day with a smile. This fruit, yogurt and granola parfait is so easy to make. You can also use whatever favorite fresh fruit is in season and looking best at the supermarket.
—*Diana Laskaris, Chicago, IL*

TAKES: 15 min.
MAKES: 4 servings

- 4 cups fat-free vanilla yogurt
- 2 medium peaches, chopped
- 2 cups fresh blackberries
- ½ cup granola without raisins or Kashi Go Lean Crunch cereal

Layer half the yogurt, peaches, blackberries and granola into 4 parfait glasses. Repeat layers.

1 PARFAIT 259 cal., 3g fat (0 sat. fat), 7mg chol., 6mg sod., 48g carb. (27g sugars, 7g fiber), 13g pro.

★ ★ ★ ★ ★ **READER REVIEW**

"A brilliant way to start the day and so quick to prepare—it was very filling too. Love it!"
—BONITO15, TASTEOFHOME.COM

RISE & SHINE PARFAIT

MINI HAM & CHEESE
FRITTATAS

MINI HAM & CHEESE FRITTATAS

I found this recipe a few years ago and made some little changes to it. I'm diabetic, and it fits into my low-carb and low-fat diet. Every time I serve a brunch, the frittatas are the first to disappear, and nobody knows they are low in fat!
—Susan Watt, Basking Ridge, NJ

- -

PREP: 15 min. • **BAKE:** 25 min.
MAKES: 8 servings

6 large eggs
4 large egg whites
2 Tbsp. fat-free milk
¼ tsp. salt
¼ tsp. pepper
3 Tbsp. minced fresh chives
¾ cup cubed fully cooked ham (about 4 oz.)
1 cup shredded fat-free cheddar cheese

1. Preheat oven to 375°. In a bowl, whisk the first 5 ingredients until blended; stir in chives. Divide ham and cheese among 8 muffin cups coated with cooking spray. Top with egg mixture, filling cups three-fourths full.

2. Bake until a knife inserted in the center comes out clean, 22-25 minutes. Carefully run a knife around sides to loosen.

1 MINI FRITTATA 106 cal., 4g fat (1g sat. fat), 167mg chol., 428mg sod., 2g carb. (1g sugars, 0 fiber), 14g pro. **DIABETIC EXCHANGES** 2 medium-fat meat.

ZUCCHINI FRITTATA

ZUCCHINI FRITTATA

When we travel by car, I make the frittata the night before, stuff slices into pita bread in the morning and microwave for 1-2 minutes. I wrap them in a towel so down the road we can enjoy a still-warm breakfast!
—Carol Blumenberg, Lehigh Acres, FL

- -

TAKES: 20 min.
MAKES: 2 servings

3   large eggs
¼   tsp. salt
1   tsp. canola oil
½   cup chopped onion
1   cup coarsely shredded zucchini
½   cup shredded Swiss cheese
    Coarsely ground pepper, optional

1. Preheat oven to 350°. Whisk together eggs and salt.
2. In an 8-in. ovenproof skillet coated with cooking spray, heat oil over medium heat; saute onion and zucchini until onion is crisp-tender. Pour in egg mixture; cook until almost set, 5-6 minutes. Sprinkle with cheese.
3. Bake, uncovered, until cheese is melted, 4-5 minutes. If desired, sprinkle with pepper.
1 SERVING 261 cal., 18g fat (8g sat. fat), 304mg chol., 459mg sod., 7g carb. (3g sugars, 1g fiber), 18g pro.

BACON EGG CUPS

This breakfast dish is a fresh take on the classic bacon-and-eggs combo. Make sure to use ovenproof bowls when baking!
—*Carol Forcum, Marion, IL*

- -

PREP: 20 min. • **BAKE:** 20 min.
MAKES: 2 servings

- 4   bacon strips
- 4   large eggs
- ⅓   cup half-and-half cream
- ⅛   tsp. pepper
- ½   cup shredded cheddar cheese
- 2   green onions, chopped

1. In a small skillet, cook bacon over medium heat until cooked but not crisp. Remove to paper towels to drain; keep warm.
2. In a small bowl, whisk 2 eggs, cream and pepper. Wrap 2 bacon strips around the inside edge of each of two 8-oz. ramekins or custard cups coated with cooking spray.
3. Sprinkle each with half the cheese and onions. Divide egg mixture between ramekins. Break 1 egg into each ramekin. Sprinkle with remaining cheese and onion. Bake at 350° until the eggs are completely set, 18-22 minutes.

1 SERVING 380 cal., 28g fat (14g sat. fat), 486mg chol., 521mg sod., 5g carb. (3g sugars, 0 fiber), 24g pro.

BACON EGG CUPS TIPS

Can I make these ahead of time? If you're keeping them in the refrigerator, you can make them up to 3 days in advance. You can also freeze them: Place on a baking sheet until frozen, and then transfer to an airtight freezer container. Use within 3 months for best results. Reheat in a microwave for a perfect on-the-go breakfast.

Why are mine rubbery? Eggs can get rubbery when they're overcooked. Keep an eye on the clock for best results. Also, a spongy texture could be the result of overmixing your eggs, which adds too much air.

Why did mine deflate? If your egg cups went flat, they may have baked for too long. Otherwise, cooling them too quickly can also result in sunken centers. Try cooling your egg cups inside their ramekins to keep them from collapsing.

BACON
EGG CUPS

MAPLE
PANCAKES

MAPLE PANCAKES

Our family looks forward to tapping maple trees in March, and then enjoying pure maple syrup year-round. This is just one of the recipes I like to make that has maple syrup as an ingredient.
—*Mary Colbath, Concord, NH*

TAKES: 30 min.
MAKES: 6 servings

- 3 cups all-purpose flour
- 4½ tsp. baking powder
- 1½ tsp. salt
- 3 large eggs, room temperature
- 2¼ cups 2% milk
- ⅓ cup canola oil
- 3 Tbsp. maple syrup
  Optional: Additional maple syrup, butter and fresh blueberries

1. In a large bowl, combine the flour, baking powder and salt. In another bowl, whisk eggs, milk, oil and syrup; stir into the dry ingredients just until blended.
2. Preheat griddle over medium heat. Lightly grease griddle. Pour batter by ¼ cupfuls onto griddle; cook until bubbles on top begin to pop and bottoms are golden brown. Turn; cook until second side is golden brown (pancakes will be thin).
3. Serve with additional maple syrup, butter and blueberries as desired.

3 PANCAKES 445 cal., 17g fat (3g sat. fat), 100mg chol., 1031mg sod., 59g carb. (11g sugars, 2g fiber), 13g pro.

APPLE SPICE SYRUP

APPLE SPICE SYRUP

This syrup has just the right sweetness to complement your favorite pancakes or waffles. The spicy apple flavor is terrific for an autumn breakfast or for whenever you'd like something a bit different.
—*Renae Moncur, Burley, ID*

TAKES: 10 min. • **MAKES:** 1¾ cups

- ¼ cup packed brown sugar
- 2 Tbsp. cornstarch
- ¼ tsp. ground allspice
- ⅛ tsp. ground nutmeg
- 1¾ cups apple juice or cider

In a saucepan, combine brown sugar, cornstarch, allspice and nutmeg; mix well. Add juice or cider. Cook; stir over medium heat until syrup is bubbly and slightly thickened.

3 TBSP. 53 cal., 0 fat (0 sat. fat), 0 chol., 4mg sod., 13g carb. (11g sugars, 0 fiber), 0 pro.

GOLDEN BUTTERMILK
WAFFLES

GOLDEN BUTTERMILK WAFFLES

You'll hear nothing but cheering from family or friends when you stack up these golden waffles for breakfast! My clan regularly requests this morning mainstay.
—*Kim Branges, Grand Canyon, AZ*

TAKES: 25 min.
MAKES: 16 waffles (4 in.)

1¾ cups all-purpose flour
1   tsp. baking powder
1   tsp. baking soda
½   tsp. salt
2   large eggs, room temperature
2   cups buttermilk
⅓   cup canola oil
     Optional: Sliced fresh strawberries, strawberry syrup and whipped cream

1. In a large bowl, combine flour, baking powder, baking soda and salt. In another bowl, beat eggs; add buttermilk and oil. Stir into dry ingredients just until combined.

2. Bake in a preheated waffle maker according to manufacturer's directions until golden brown. If desired, serve with sliced fresh strawberries, syrup and whipped cream.
2 WAFFLES 223 cal., 11g fat (2g sat. fat), 56mg chol., 435mg sod., 24g carb. (4g sugars, 1g fiber), 6g pro.

DUTCH HONEY SYRUP

I grew up on a farm where a big breakfast was an everyday occurrence. Still, it was a special treat when Mom served this scrumptious syrup with our pancakes.
—*Kathy Scott, Lingle, WY*

TAKES: 15 min. • **MAKES:** 2 cups

- 1 cup sugar
- 1 cup corn syrup
- 1 cup heavy whipping cream
- 1 tsp. vanilla extract

In a saucepan, combine sugar, corn syrup and cream. Bring to a boil over medium heat; boil for 5 minutes or until slightly thickened, stirring occasionally. Stir in vanilla. Serve warm over pancakes, waffles or French toast.

2 TBSP. 158 cal., 6g fat (3g sat. fat), 20mg chol., 31mg sod., 29g carb. (23g sugars, 0 fiber), 0 pro.

★ ★ ★ ★ ★ **READER REVIEW**

"This is an excellent syrup. It's great on ice cream too. We've used rice syrup to make it a little healthier. It gives it a delicious caramel taste."

—BRAVABEAR, TASTEOFHOME.COM

DUTCH HONEY SYRUP

LEMON & CORIANDER GREEK YOGURT

You'll be surprised how easy it is to make homemade Greek yogurt. Flavored with lemon and coriander, it's simply amazing.
—Taste of Home *Test Kitchen*

PREP: 5 min. + chilling
COOK: 20 min. + standing
MAKES: about 3 cups

- 2 qt. pasteurized whole milk
- 2 Tbsp. plain yogurt with live active cultures
- 2 tsp. grated lemon zest
- 1 tsp. ground coriander
  Honey, optional

1. In a Dutch oven, heat milk over medium heat until a thermometer reads 200°, stirring occasionally to prevent milk from scorching. Remove from heat; let stand until a thermometer reads 112°-115°, stirring occasionally. (If desired, place pan in an ice-water bath for faster cooling.)
2. Whisk 1 cup warm milk into the yogurt until smooth; return all to pan, stirring gently. Stir in lemon zest and coriander. Transfer the mixture to warm, clean jars, such as 1-qt. canning jars.
3. Cover jars; place in oven, turn on oven light to keep mixture warm, about 110°. Let stand, undisturbed, 6-24 hours or until yogurt is set, tilting jars gently to check. (Yogurt will become thicker and more tangy as it stands.)
4. Cover; refrigerate until cold. Store in refrigerator up to 2 weeks. If desired, serve with honey.
½ CUP 203 cal., 11g fat (6g sat. fat), 33mg chol., 142mg sod., 16g carb. (16g sugars, 0 fiber), 10g pro.

MANGO SMOOTHIES

Treat yourself to this yummy blend of mango, pineapple, banana and honey. The yogurt makes it rich and creamy, but a serving has only 2 grams of fat!
—Taste of Home *Test Kitchen*

TAKES: 10 min.
MAKES: 2 servings

- ½ cup unsweetened pineapple juice
- 2 cups frozen chopped peeled mangoes
- ½ medium ripe banana
- ½ cup reduced-fat plain yogurt
- 1 Tbsp. honey

In a blender, combine all the ingredients; cover and process until smooth. Pour into chilled glasses; serve immediately.
1 CUP 237 cal., 2g fat (1g sat. fat), 4mg chol., 48mg sod., 56g carb. (47g sugars, 4g fiber), 5g pro.

MANGO SMOOTHIES

BREAKFAST WRAPS

We like quick and simple morning meals during the week, and these wraps can be prepped ahead of time. With just a minute in the microwave, breakfast is ready to go.

—*Betty Kleberger, Florissant, MO*

TAKES: 15 min.
MAKES: 4 servings

- 6 large eggs
- 2 Tbsp. 2% milk
- ¼ tsp. pepper
- 1 Tbsp. canola oil
- 1 cup shredded cheddar cheese
- ¾ cup diced fully cooked ham
- 4 flour tortillas (8 in.), warmed

1. In a small bowl, whisk the eggs, milk and pepper. In a large skillet, heat oil. Add egg mixture; cook and stir over medium heat until eggs are completely set. Stir in cheese and ham.

2. Spoon egg mixture down the center of each tortilla; roll up.

FREEZE OPTION Wrap cooled egg wraps in foil or parchment and store in a freezer container. To use, thaw in refrigerator overnight. Remove foil or parchment; wrap in a moist paper towel. Microwave on high until heated through, 30-60 seconds. Serve immediately.

1 WRAP 436 cal., 24g fat (10g sat. fat), 364mg chol., 853mg sod., 28g carb. (1g sugars, 0 fiber), 25g pro.

PIZZA BREAKFAST WRAPS
Prepare recipe as directed, replacing cheddar cheese and ham with mozzarella cheese and cooked sausage. Serve with warm marinara sauce on the side.

PULLED PORK BREAKFAST WRAPS Prepare recipe as directed, replacing cheddar cheese and ham with smoked Gouda cheese and precooked pulled pork. Serve with warm barbecue sauce on the side.

SWEET BROILED GRAPEFRUIT

I was never a fan of grapefruit until I had it broiled at a restaurant—it was so tangy and delicious! I finally got the recipe and now I make it often for my whole family.
—*Terry Bray, Auburndale, FL*

TAKES: 15 min. • **MAKES:** 2 servings

- 1 large grapefruit
- 2 Tbsp. butter, softened
- 2 Tbsp. sugar
- ½ tsp. ground cinnamon

1. Preheat broiler. Cut grapefruit crosswise in half; if desired, cut a thin slice from the bottom of each to level. Cut around each grapefruit section to loosen fruit. Top with butter. Mix sugar and cinnamon; sprinkle over fruit.
2. Place on a baking sheet. Broil 4 in. from heat until the sugar is bubbly.
½ GRAPEFRUIT 203 cal., 12g fat (7g sat. fat), 31mg chol., 116mg sod., 26g carb. (24g sugars, 2g fiber), 1g pro.

SWEET BROILED GRAPEFRUIT

HOMEMADE
STRAWBERRY SYRUP

HOMEMADE STRAWBERRY SYRUP

This recipe is a spinoff of my dad's homemade syrup. Our son requests it with fluffy pancakes whenever he and his family come to visit.
—*Nancy Dunaway, Springfield, IL*

TAKES: 20 min.
MAKES: about 2½ cups

- 1 cup sugar
- 1 cup water
- 1½ cups mashed unsweetened strawberries

In a saucepan, bring sugar and water to a boil. Gradually add strawberries; return to a boil. Reduce heat; simmer, uncovered, 10 minutes, stirring occasionally. Serve over pancakes, waffles or ice cream.

2 TBSP. 43 cal., 0 fat (0 sat. fat), 0 chol., 0 sod., 11g carb. (11g sugars, 0 fiber), 0 pro.

TEST KITCHEN TIP

If you prefer a thicker syrup, the simplest way to adjust this recipe is to increase the simmering time to 15 minutes. Keep the temperature to a low simmer, and keep an eye on your pan so you don't burn the syrup. Be aware that the syrup will thicken a bit further as it cools.

Alternatively, you can thicken the syrup with a slurry of water and cornstarch in a 1:1 ratio. Stir about 1 Tbsp. slurry into the hot syrup and simmer for 5 minutes, stirring occasionally.

BACON BREAKFAST PIZZA

Pizza for breakfast? Yes, please! I used to make this for my morning drivers when I worked at a pizza delivery place. It's an easy rise-and-shine recipe that quickly became a hit!
—*Cathy Shortall, Easton, MD*

TAKES: 30 min.
MAKES: 8 servings

- 1 tube (13.8 oz.) refrigerated pizza crust
- 2 Tbsp. olive oil, divided
- 6 large eggs
- 2 Tbsp. water
- 1 pkg. (3 oz.) bacon bits
- 1 cup shredded Monterey Jack cheese
- 1 cup shredded cheddar cheese

1. Preheat oven to 400°. Unroll and press dough onto bottom and ½ in. up sides of a greased 15x10x1-in. pan. Prick thoroughly with a fork; brush with 1 Tbsp. oil. Bake until lightly browned, 7-8 minutes.
2. Meanwhile, whisk together the eggs and water. In a nonstick skillet, heat remaining 1 Tbsp. oil over medium heat. Add eggs; cook and stir just until thickened and no liquid egg remains. Spoon over crust. Sprinkle with bacon bits and cheeses.
3. Bake until cheese is melted, 5-7 minutes.
1 PIECE 352 cal., 20g fat (8g sat. fat), 169mg chol., 842mg sod., 24g carb. (3g sugars, 1g fiber), 20g pro.

CHOCOLATE PEANUT BUTTER OVERNIGHT OATS

Soon after I discovered overnight oats I decided to create a recipe with my favorite sugary combo: chocolate and peanut butter. Overnight oats are a perfect breakfast for busy mornings.
—Anna Bentley, Swanzey, NH

PREP: 10 min. + chilling
MAKES: 1 serving

- ½ cup old-fashioned oats
- ⅓ cup chocolate or plain almond milk
- 1 Tbsp. baking cocoa
- 1 Tbsp. creamy peanut butter, warmed
- 1 Tbsp. maple syrup
  Miniature dairy-free semisweet chocolate chips, optional

In a small container or Mason jar, combine the oats, milk, cocoa, peanut butter and maple syrup. Seal; refrigerate overnight. Top with additional peanut butter and mini chocolate chips if desired.
½ CUP 346 cal., 13g fat (2g sat. fat), 0 chol., 121mg sod., 53g carb. (21g sugars, 6g fiber), 10g pro.

UPSIDE-DOWN BACON PANCAKE

Make a big impression when you present one family-sized bacon pancake. The brown sugar adds sweetness that complements the salty bacon. If you can fit more bacon in the skillet and want to add more, go for it!
—Mindie Hilton, Susanville, CA

PREP: 10 min.
BAKE: 20 min. + cooling
MAKES: 6 servings

- 6 bacon strips, coarsely chopped
- ¼ cup packed brown sugar
- 2 cups complete buttermilk pancake mix
- 1½ cups water
  Optional: Maple syrup and butter

1. In a large cast-iron or other ovenproof skillet, cook bacon over medium heat until crisp. Remove bacon to paper towels with a slotted spoon. Remove drippings, reserving 2 Tbsp. in pan. Return bacon to the pan; sprinkle with brown sugar.
2. In a small bowl, combine the pancake mix and water just until moistened. Pour into pan.
3. Bake at 350° until a toothpick inserted in the center comes out clean, 18-20 minutes. Cool for 10 minutes before inverting onto a serving plate. Serve warm, with maple syrup and butter if desired.
1 PIECE 265 cal., 9g fat (3g sat. fat), 12mg chol., 802mg sod., 41g carb. (13g sugars, 1g fiber), 6g pro.

UPSIDE-DOWN BACON PANCAKE

CREAMY
BAKED EGGS

CLASSIC BURRATA TOAST

Burrata toast is a culinary blank canvas. The rich and creamy cheese goes well with both sweet and savory toppings, so add your favorites for a quick snack or a satisfying appetizer.
—Taste of Home *Test Kitchen*

TAKES: 5 min. • **MAKES:** 1 serving

- 1 slice hearty bread, toasted
- 1 tsp. extra virgin olive oil
- 2 oz. burrata cheese (about ¼ cup)
- ⅛ tsp. sea salt
  Dash freshly ground pepper

Spread toast with olive oil. Spread burrata over toast. Sprinkle with salt and pepper. If desired, drizzle with additional olive oil.

1 PIECE 264 cal., 17g fat (9g sat. fat), 40mg chol., 448mg sod., 14g carb. (3g sugars, 1g fiber), 12g pro.

STRAWBERRY BASIL BURRATA TOAST Top burrata with 2 sliced fresh strawberries. Drizzle with 1 tsp. balsamic glaze. Sprinkle with chopped fresh basil, salt and pepper.

ROASTED CHERRY TOMATO BURRATA TOAST Toss ½ cup cherry tomatoes with ½ tsp. olive oil. Roast on a rimmed baking sheet at 400° until tomatoes begin to burst, about 10 minutes. Spread tomatoes over burrata; sprinkle with salt and pepper.

AVOCADO BURRATA TOAST Top burrata with ¼ medium ripe sliced avocado. Drizzle with additional 1 tsp. olive oil; sprinkle with salt and pepper.

APRICOT ALMOND BURRATA TOAST Top burrata with 2 tsp. apricot preserves. Sprinkle with 2 tsp. toasted sliced almonds, salt and pepper.

CREAMY BAKED EGGS

My husband loves eggs prepared in any way. This recipe is simple but special, and every time the eggs come out just as he likes them. If you like soft yolks, cook the eggs for 9 minutes; for firmer yolks, cook for about 11 minutes.
—Macey Allen, Green Forest, AR

TAKES: 25 min.
MAKES: 8 servings

- ¼ cup half-and-half cream
- 8 large eggs
- 1 cup shredded Jarlsberg cheese
- 2 Tbsp. grated Parmesan cheese
- ¼ tsp. salt
- ⅛ tsp. pepper
- 2 green onions, chopped

1. Preheat oven to 400°. Pour cream into a greased cast-iron or other ovenproof skillet. Gently break 1 egg into a small bowl; slip into skillet. Repeat with remaining eggs. Sprinkle with cheeses, salt and pepper.

2. Bake until the egg whites are completely set and yolks begin to thicken but are not hard, 10-12 minutes. Top with green onions; serve immediately.

1 BAKED EGG 135 cal., 9g fat (4g sat. fat), 200mg chol., 237mg sod., 2g carb. (1g sugars, 0 fiber), 11g pro.

BISCUITS &
SAUSAGE GRAVY

BISCUITS & SAUSAGE GRAVY

This is an old southern recipe that I've adapted. It's the kind of hearty breakfast that will warm you right up.
—*Sue Baker, Jonesboro, AR*

TAKES: 15 min. • **MAKES:** 2 servings

¼ lb. bulk pork sausage
2 Tbsp. butter
2 to 3 Tbsp. all-purpose flour
¼ tsp. salt
⅛ tsp. pepper
1¼ to 1⅓ cups whole milk
Warm biscuits

In a small skillet, cook sausage over medium heat until no longer pink, 3-5 minutes, breaking into crumbles; drain. Add butter and heat until melted. Add the flour, salt and pepper; cook and stir until blended. Gradually add the milk, stirring constantly. Bring to a boil; cook and stir until thickened, about 2 minutes. Serve with biscuits.

¾ CUP 337 cal., 27g fat (14g sat. fat), 72mg chol., 718mg sod., 14g carb. (8g sugars, 0 fiber), 10g pro.

TEST KITCHEN TIP
You can make this gravy gluten free by eliminating the flour. To thicken the gravy, use cornstarch or arrowroot—about 1 Tbsp. for every cup of liquid in the recipe. Mix the agent with an equal amount of water to create a slurry and add it to the pan. Whisk continuously over high heat until the agent is well incorporated and the gravy starts to thicken. Serve with gluten-free biscuits.

CHICKEN SAUSAGE PATTIES

CHICKEN SAUSAGE PATTIES

Enjoy the taste of homemade breakfast sausage without the guilt. This hearty recipe used ground chicken in place of regular pork sausage for a lighter spin on the favorite breakfast fare.
—*Mary Webb, Longwood, FL*

TAKES: 25 min. • **MAKES:** 2 servings

2 Tbsp. chopped onion
¾ tsp. plus 2 tsp. olive oil, divided
½ cup grated peeled tart apple
1 Tbsp. minced fresh sage or ¾ tsp. rubbed sage
¼ tsp. salt
⅛ tsp. pepper
Dash ground cinnamon
¼ lb. ground chicken or turkey

In a nonstick skillet, saute onion in ¾ tsp. oil until crisp-tender. Add apple; cook until tender, about 5 minutes. Let stand until cool enough to handle. Stir in seasonings. Crumble chicken over apple mixture; mix lightly but thoroughly. Shape into four ½-in.-thick patties. In a skillet, cook patties in remaining oil over medium heat until juices run clear.

2 PATTIES 159 cal., 11g fat (2g sat. fat), 38mg chol., 329mg sod., 7g carb. (5g sugars, 1g fiber), 9g protein. **DIABETIC EXCHANGES** 2 lean meat, ½ fruit.

CORNFLAKE-COATED
CRISPY BACON

CORNFLAKE-COATED CRISPY BACON

I have loved my aunt's crispy-coated bacon ever since I was a child. Now I have shared the super simple recipe with my own children. We still enjoy a big panful every Christmas morning—and on many other days throughout the year!
—Brenda Severson, Norman, OK

- -

PREP: 20 min. • **BAKE:** 25 min.
MAKES: 9 servings

- ½ cup evaporated milk
- 2 Tbsp. ketchup
- 1 Tbsp. Worcestershire sauce
  Dash pepper
- 18 bacon strips (1 lb.)
- 3 cups crushed cornflakes

1. Preheat oven to 375°. In a large bowl, combine the milk, ketchup, Worcestershire sauce and pepper. Add bacon strips, turning to coat. Dip strips in crushed cornflakes, patting to help coating adhere.
2. Place bacon on 2 racks; place each rack on an ungreased 15x10x1-in. baking pan. Bake until golden and crisp, 25-30 minutes, rotating pans halfway through baking.
2 BACON STRIPS 198 cal., 7g fat (3g sat. fat), 20mg chol., 547mg sod., 26g carb. (4g sugars, 0 fiber), 8g pro.

HOT FRUIT & SAUSAGE

HOT FRUIT & SAUSAGE

Pineapple, brown sugar and cinnamon make plain pork sausage links extra tasty. And the banana slices really complement the sausage. This dish makes any breakfast special.

—Marian Peterson, Wisconsin Rapids, WI

- -

TAKES: 10 min.
MAKES: 6 servings

1 pkg. (12 oz.) uncooked pork sausage links
¾ cup pineapple tidbits
2 Tbsp. brown sugar
Pinch ground cinnamon
1 medium firm banana, sliced

In a large cast-iron or other heavy skillet, cook sausage according to package directions; drain. Add pineapple, brown sugar and cinnamon; heat through. Stir in banana just before serving.

1 SERVING 261 cal., 18g fat (6g sat. fat), 47mg chol., 736mg sod., 14g carb. (12g sugars, 1g fiber), 11g pro.

TEST KITCHEN TIP
If you prefer, you can substitute maple syrup for the brown sugar and cinnamon. You can also try adding other spices like cardamom, ginger, nutmeg or cloves.

EASY BREAKFAST CASSEROLE

Make this casserole over the weekend and save leftovers to eat during the week. It reheats really well in the microwave, so you can have a hearty breakfast ready in just minutes.
—Taste of Home *Test Kitchen*

- -

PREP: 20 min. • **BAKE:** 50 min.
MAKES: 8 servings

- 1   lb. bulk pork sausage
- 1   pkg. (30 oz.) frozen shredded hash brown potatoes, thawed
- 1½ cups shredded cheddar cheese, divided
- ½   tsp. salt
- ¼   tsp. pepper
- 8   large eggs
- 2   cups 2% milk

1. Preheat the oven to 350°. In a large skillet, cook sausage over medium heat until no longer pink, 5-7 minutes, breaking into crumbles; drain. In a large bowl, combine hash browns, sausage, 1 cup cheese, salt and pepper. In another large bowl, whisk eggs and milk until blended; stir into potato mixture. Spoon into a greased 13x9-in. baking dish.
2. Bake, uncovered, until a knife inserted in center comes out clean, 45-50 minutes. Sprinkle with remaining ½ cup cheese. Bake until cheese is melted, 2-3 minutes.
1 PIECE 418 cal., 26g fat (11g sat. fat), 244mg chol., 752mg sod., 24g carb. (4g sugars, 2g fiber), 22g pro.

EASY RHUBARB SAUCE

EASY RHUBARB SAUCE

Celebrate spring with the sweet-tart taste of rhubarb in this simple sauce. I enjoy it on toast, English muffins and pancakes, but it's equally decadent drizzled on pound cake or ice cream.
—*Jackie Hutshing, Sonoma, CA*

- -

TAKES: 20 min. • **MAKES:** 1¼ cups

- ⅓   cup sugar
- ¼   cup water
- 2¼ cups sliced fresh or frozen rhubarb
- 1   tsp. grated lemon zest
- ⅛   tsp. ground nutmeg

1. In a small saucepan, bring sugar and water to a boil. Add rhubarb; cook and stir until rhubarb is tender and mixture is slightly thickened, 5-10 minutes. Remove from the heat; stir in lemon zest and nutmeg. Serve warm or chilled over pancakes, crepes, pound cake or ice cream. Refrigerate leftovers.
NOTE If using frozen rhubarb, measure rhubarb while still frozen, then thaw completely. Drain in a colander, but do not press liquid out.
¼ CUP 64 cal., 0 fat (0 sat. fat), 0 chol., 2mg sod., 16g carb. (14g sugars, 1g fiber), 1g pro.

BASIC CREPES

This simple crepe recipe is a winner, and works well with both sweet and savory fillings (including the rhubarb sauce on the opposite page!). Make the batter at least 30 minutes ahead so the flour can absorb all the moisture before you start cooking.
—Taste of Home *Test Kitchen*

- -

PREP: 10 min. + chilling
COOK: 20 min. • **MAKES:** 20 crepes

  4   large eggs
1½ cups 2% milk
  1   cup all-purpose flour
1½ tsp. sugar
 ⅛ tsp. salt
  8   tsp. butter
      Optional: Powdered sugar
      or whipped cream

1. In a small bowl, whisk eggs and milk. In another bowl, mix flour, sugar and salt; add to egg mixture and mix well. Refrigerate, covered, 1 hour.
2. Melt 1 tsp. butter in an 8-in. nonstick skillet over medium heat. Stir batter. Fill a ¼-cup measure halfway with batter; pour into center of pan. Quickly lift and tilt pan to coat bottom evenly. Cook until top appears dry; turn crepe over and cook until bottom is cooked, 15-20 seconds longer. Remove to a wire rack. Repeat with remaining batter, adding butter to skillet as needed. When cool, stack crepes between pieces of waxed paper or paper towels. Serve with a dusting of powdered sugar, a dollop of whipped cream, and/or the topping of your choice.
1 CREPE 61 cal., 3g fat (2g sat. fat), 43mg chol., 50mg sod., 6g carb. (1g sugars, 0 fiber), 3g pro.
CREAMY STRAWBERRY FILLING: In a large bowl, beat 1 pkg. (8 oz.) softened cream cheese, 1¼ cups confectioners' sugar, 1 Tbsp. lemon juice, 1 tsp. grated lemon zest and ½ tsp. vanilla extract until smooth. Fold in 2 cups each sliced fresh strawberries and whipped cream. Spoon about ⅓ cup filling down the center of 14 crepes; roll up. Garnish with additional sliced berries. MAKES: 7 servings.
BANANA FILLING: In a small skillet, bring ⅔ cup sugar, ⅔ cup orange juice, ½ cup butter and 4 tsp. grated orange zest to a boil. Remove from the heat. Peel 6 medium firm bananas and cut in half lengthwise. Add to orange sauce; cook over medium heat until heated through, about 1 minute. Place 1 banana half in center of 12 crepes; roll up. Place seam side down on a plate; drizzle with orange sauce. MAKES: 6 servings.

BASIC CREPES

BACON-WRAPPED SCALLOPS
PAGE 48

SNACKS, APPETIZERS & BEVERAGES

BACON-WRAPPED SCALLOPS

1. Bacon Strips
2. Sea Scallops
3. Parsley

Plus: Salt, Pepper, Olive Oil

APRICOT
ICE CREAM SODA

CHAMPION CHICKEN PUFFS

My guests peel rubber getting to the table to munch on these chicken puffs. The tender bites are made with hassle-free refrigerated crescent rolls and a flavorful chicken and cream cheese filling.
—*Amber Kimmich, Powhatan, VA*

- -

TAKES: 30 min.
MAKES: 32 servings

- 4 oz. cream cheese, softened
- ½ tsp. garlic powder
- ½ cup shredded cooked chicken
- 2 tubes (8 oz. each) refrigerated crescent rolls

1. Preheat oven to 375°. In a small bowl, beat cream cheese and garlic powder until smooth. Stir in chicken.
2. Unroll crescent dough; separate into 16 triangles. Cut each in half lengthwise, forming 2 triangles. Place 1 tsp. chicken mixture in the center of each. Fold short side over filling; press sides to seal and roll up.
3. Place 1 in. apart on greased baking sheets. Bake until golden brown, 12-14 minutes. Serve warm.
1 PUFF 67 cal., 4g fat (1g sat. fat), 6mg chol., 119mg sod., 6g carb. (2g sugars, 0 fiber), 2g pro.

APRICOT ICE CREAM SODA

This recipe came from my husband's aunt, who was born in the early 1900s. It's a delightful drink for hot Texas summers.
—*Joan Hallford,*
North Richland Hills, TX

- -

PREP: 20 min. + freezing
MAKES: 4 servings

- 2 cans (15 oz. each) apricot halves, drained
- ⅔ cup sugar
- 2 Tbsp. lemon juice
- 1 cup heavy whipping cream, whipped
- 2 cups chilled ginger ale

1. Press apricots through a fine-mesh strainer into a bowl; discard skin and pulp. Stir sugar and lemon juice into apricot puree. Gently fold in whipped cream. Transfer to a 8-in. square dish. Freeze until firm, about 6 hours or overnight.
2. Divide ice cream among 4 glasses; top with ginger ale. Serve immediately.
1 ICE CREAM SODA 554 cal., 22g fat (14g sat. fat), 68mg chol., 34mg sod., 92g carb. (88g sugars, 3g fiber), 3g pro.

CHAMPION
CHICKEN PUFFS

CHICKEN & BACON ROLL-UPS

CHICKEN & BACON ROLL-UPS

My children like these roll-ups so much that they ask for them every day for lunch during the summer. Whenever I have leftover chicken or turkey breast, this is a delicious way to use it up.
—*Patricia Nieh, Portola Valley, CA*

- -

PREP: 20 min. + chilling
MAKES: 4 dozen

1   can (9¾ oz.) chunk white chicken, drained
1   carton (8 oz.) spreadable garden vegetable cream cheese
1   cup salsa, divided
4   pieces ready-to-serve fully cooked bacon, crumbled
6   flour tortillas (8 in.), room temperature

Mix chicken, cream cheese, ½ cup salsa and bacon; spread over tortillas. Roll up tightly; wrap. Refrigerate at least 1 hour. Just before serving, unwrap and cut tortillas into 1-in. slices. Serve with remaining salsa.
1 PIECE 43 cal., 2g fat (1g sat. fat), 4mg chol., 100mg sod., 4g carb. (0 sugars, 0 fiber), 3g pro.

★ ★ ★ ★ ★ **READER REVIEW**

"I made these for my granddaughter's graduation party and got rave reviews—plus multiple requests for the recipe! Everybody loved them!"

—VICKY985, TASTEOFHOME.COM

STRAWBERRY TOMATO SALSA

STRAWBERRY TOMATO SALSA

Here's a sweet and tangy salsa that's miles away from the spicy version people expect. Serve it as an appetizer with tortilla chips for scooping, or make it part of the main event and spoon it over chicken or pork.
—*Amy Hinkle, Topeka, KS*

- -

TAKES: 25 min. • **MAKES:** 6 cups

2   pints cherry tomatoes, quartered
1   pint fresh strawberries, chopped
8   green onions, chopped
½   cup minced fresh cilantro
6   Tbsp. olive oil
2   Tbsp. balsamic vinegar
½   tsp. salt

In a large bowl, combine cherry tomatoes, strawberries, green onions and cilantro. In a small bowl, whisk oil, vinegar and salt; gently stir into tomato mixture. Refrigerate until serving.
¼ CUP 41 cal., 4g fat (0 sat. fat), 0 chol., 53mg sod., 3g carb. (2g sugars, 1g fiber), 0 pro.

PARISIAN SIPPING
CHOCOLATE

PARISIAN SIPPING CHOCOLATE

One of my fondest memories of Paris is sipping a cup of thick, dark hot chocolate at one of the patisseries there. Parisian hot chocolate is velvety smooth, rich and decadent, and almost the consistency of a molten chocolate bar. It is meant to be sipped slowly and savored. I bought Parisian espresso cups so we could enjoy this at home.
—Darlene Brenden, Salem, OR

- -

TAKES: 15 min.
MAKES: 2 servings

⅔ cup 2% milk
2 Tbsp. heavy whipping cream
1 tsp. brown sugar
½ tsp. confectioners' sugar
⅛ tsp. instant espresso powder, optional
2 oz. dark chocolate candy bar, chopped
   Optional: Whipped cream and chocolate shavings

1. In a small saucepan, heat milk, cream, brown sugar, confectioners' sugar and, if desired, espresso powder over medium heat until bubbles form around sides of pan. Remove from heat.

2. Whisk in dark chocolate until melted. Serve in mugs with whipped cream and chocolate shavings, if desired.
½ CUP 226 cal., 16g fat (10g sat. fat), 27mg chol., 43mg sod., 24g carb. (22g sugars, 2g fiber), 5g pro.

TEST KITCHEN TIP
Adding espresso powder intensifies the chocolate flavor, but you may substitute coffee power or omit it altogether.

SUN-DRIED TOMATO GOAT CHEESE EMPANADAS

I created this appetizer because I entertain a lot and wanted something simple but special. People like these empanadas so much! I always make extra.
—*Lynn Scully, Rancho Santa Fe, CA*

- -

PREP: 1 hour • **BAKE:** 15 min.
MAKES: about 1½ dozen

- 1 Tbsp. olive oil
- 1 medium sweet onion, halved and thinly sliced
- 1 log (4 oz.) fresh goat cheese, crumbled
- ¼ cup finely chopped oil-packed sun-dried tomatoes, drained
  Dough for a single-crust pie (9 in.) or 1 sheet refrigerated pie crust

1. In a large skillet, heat oil over medium heat. Add onion; cook, stirring, 4-5 minutes or until softened. Reduce heat to medium-low; cook, stirring occasionally, 30-40 minutes or until deep golden brown. Remove from heat.
2. Let cool slightly. Gently stir in goat cheese and tomatoes. Preheat oven to 400°.
3. On a lightly floured surface, roll dough to ¼-in. thickness. Cut with a floured 3-in. round biscuit cutter. Place circles 2 in. apart on baking sheets. Place 1 heaping tsp. of filling on 1 side of each circle. Brush edges of pastry with water; fold circles in half. With a fork, press edges to seal. Bake until golden brown, 15-20 minutes.
1 EMPANADA 99 cal., 7g fat (4g sat. fat), 18mg chol., 98mg sod., 8g carb. (0 sugars, 0 fiber), 2g pro.

DOUGH FOR SINGLE-CRUST PIE
Combine 1¼ cups all-purpose flour and ¼ tsp. salt; cut in ½ cup cold butter until crumbly. Gradually add 3-5 Tbsp. ice water, tossing with a fork until dough holds together when pressed. Cover and refrigerate 1 hour.

HOMEMADE TORTILLA CHIPS

I make these tortilla chips to serve with roasted tomatillo salsa. They have a little heat from the chipotle. If you prefer, omit the chipotle and just sprinkle with salt after frying. Try adding a squeeze of lime to your chips right before serving for a tajin flavor.
—*David Ross, Spokane Valley, WA*

- -

TAKES: 25 min.
MAKES: 4 servings

- ¾ tsp. salt
- ½ tsp. ground chipotle pepper
- 10 corn tortillas (6 in.)
  Canola or corn oil for deep-fat frying

1. In a small bowl, mix salt and chipotle powder. Cut each tortilla into 4 wedges. In an electric skillet, heat 1 in. oil to 350°. Fry tortilla wedges, several at a time, 2-3 minutes on each side or until golden brown. Drain on paper towels.
2. Transfer chips to a large bowl; sprinkle with salt mixture and gently toss to coat.
10 CHIPS 183 cal., 8g fat (1g sat. fat), 0 chol., 479mg sod., 27g carb. (1g sugars, 4g fiber), 3g pro.

SUN-DRIED TOMATO GOAT CHEESE EMPANADAS

PALOMA

PALOMA

Soon after I learned about this cocktail, I brought the ingredients to a family dinner at my parents'. The next time we got together, my dad had the fixings set out and ready to go.
—*Ian Cliffe, Milwaukee, WI*

- -

TAKES: 5 min. • **MAKES:** 1 serving

Dash salt
1½ oz. tequila
½ oz. lime juice
½ cup grapefruit soda or sparkling peach citrus soda
Lime wedge

In a highball glass filled with ice, combine salt, tequila and lime juice. Top with soda. Garnish with lime.

1 SERVING 148 cal., 0 fat (0 sat. fat), 0 chol., 163mg sod., 14g carb. (13g sugars, 0 fiber), 0 pro.

TEST KITCHEN TIP
Not sure where to find grapefruit soda? Two of the easiest to find are Fresca (the original flavor is grapefruit) and Jarritos (often found in the ethnic foods aisle). Other brands to try Izze, Sanpellegrino, Ting and Whole Foods' pink grapefruit.

BUFFALO RANCH
POPCORN

SOUTHERN PIMIENTO CHEESE SPREAD

Pimiento cheese is the ultimate Southern comfort food. We serve it as a dip for crackers, chips and celery or slather it on burgers and hot dogs.
—*Eileen Balmer, South Bend, IN*

PREP: 10 min. + chilling
MAKES: 1¼ cups

- 1½ cups shredded cheddar cheese
- 1 jar (4 oz.) diced pimientos, drained and finely chopped
- ⅓ cup mayonnaise
  Assorted crackers

Combine cheese, pimientos and mayonnaise. Refrigerate for at least 1 hour. Serve with crackers.
2 TBSP. 116 cal., 11g fat (4g sat. fat), 21mg chol., 144mg sod., 1g carb. (0 sugars, 0 fiber), 4g pro.

CUCUMBER GIN SMASH

It doesn't get more refreshing than this gin cocktail. If you like your drinks on the sweet side, top yours off with lemon-lime soda instead of club soda.
—Taste of Home *Test Kitchen*

TAKES: 5 min. • **MAKES:** 1 serving

- 1 tsp. sugar
- 2 slices cucumber
- 4 basil sprigs
- 2 oz. gin
  Club soda

Muddle sugar, cucumber and basil in an old-fashioned glass. Add gin and crushed ice. Top with club soda and stir.
1 SERVING 146 cal., 0 fat (0 sat. fat), 0 chol., 1mg sod., 5g carb. (4g sugars, 0 fiber), 0 pro.

BUFFALO RANCH POPCORN

This zippy blend is sure to spice up your favorite snack. It's perfect for game time, movie time, or as a special after-school treat.
—*Joyce McCarthy, Sussex, WI*

TAKES: 10 min. • **MAKES:** 4 qt.

- 16 cups popped popcorn
- 3 Tbsp. Buffalo wing sauce
- 2 Tbsp. butter, melted
- ⅛ tsp. cayenne pepper
- 1 Tbsp. ranch salad dressing mix
  Additional cayenne pepper

Place popcorn in a large bowl. In a small bowl, combine Buffalo wing sauce, butter and cayenne; drizzle over popcorn, 1 Tbsp. at a time, and toss to coat. Sprinkle with dressing mix and additional cayenne to taste; toss to coat. Serve immediately.
1 CUP 82 cal., 6g fat (2g sat. fat), 4mg chol., 395mg sod., 6g carb. (0 sugars, 1g fiber), 1g pro.

SAVORY PARTY BREAD

EFFORTLESS EGG ROLLS

Egg rolls are such a cinch with this recipe, you'll wonder why you haven't been making them all along! Look for a good dipping sauce on the Asian aisle in your supermarket.
—*Angel Randol, Apple Valley, CA*

TAKES: 30 min.
MAKES: 10 egg rolls

- ½ lb. bulk pork sausage
- 2½ cups frozen stir-fry vegetable blend, thawed and chopped
- 1 Tbsp. teriyaki sauce
- 10 egg roll wrappers
  Oil for frying

1. In a large skillet, cook sausage and vegetables over medium heat until meat is no longer pink; drain. Stir in teriyaki sauce.
2. Place 3 Tbsp. sausage mixture in center of one egg roll wrapper. (Keep the remaining wrappers covered with a damp paper towel until ready to use.) Fold bottom corner over filling. Fold sides toward center over filling. Moisten remaining corner with water; roll up tightly to seal. Repeat.
3. In an electric skillet, heat 1 in. of oil to 375°. Fry egg rolls in batches or until golden brown, 3-4 minutes on each side. Drain on paper towels.
1 EGG ROLL 244 cal., 14g fat (2g sat. fat), 11mg chol., 349mg sod., 23g carb. (1g sugars, 2g fiber), 5g pro.

SAVORY PARTY BREAD

It's impossible to stop nibbling on warm pieces of this cheesy, oniony loaf. The bread fans out for a fun presentation.
—*Kay Daly, Raleigh, NC*

PREP: 10 min. • **BAKE:** 25 min.
MAKES: 8 servings

- 1 unsliced round loaf sourdough bread (1 lb.)
- 1 lb. Monterey Jack cheese
- ½ cup butter, melted
- ½ cup chopped green onions
- 2 to 3 tsp. poppy seeds

1. Preheat oven to 350°. Cut bread widthwise into 1-in. slices to within ½ in. of bottom of loaf. Repeat cuts in opposite direction. Cut cheese into ¼-in. slices; cut slices into small pieces. Place cheese in cuts in bread.

2. In a small bowl, mix butter, green onions and poppy seeds; drizzle over bread. Wrap in foil; place on a baking sheet. Bake for 15 minutes. Unwrap; bake until cheese is melted, about 10 minutes longer.
1 SERVING 481 cal., 31g fat (17g sat. fat), 91mg chol., 782mg sod., 32g carb. (1g sugars, 2g fiber), 17g pro.

TEST KITCHEN TIP
For a variation, substitute Swiss cheese, a 4½-oz. jar of sliced mushrooms (drained) and ¼ tsp. garlic powder for the Monterey Jack, green onions and poppy seeds. Experiment further by trying different cheeses (like smoked Gouda and Brie) and seasonings, and adding meaty mix-ins like bacon, diced salami or ham.

EFFORTLESS
EGG ROLLS

TRADITIONAL POPCORN BALLS

Having an old-fashioned popcorn ball will make you feel like a kid again. You'll find one batch of this sweet treat goes a long way.
—*Cathy Karges, Hazen, ND*

TAKES: 20 min.
MAKES: 20 servings

- 7 qt. popped popcorn
- 1 cup sugar
- 1 cup light corn syrup
- ¼ cup water
- ¼ tsp. salt
- 3 Tbsp. butter
- 1 tsp. vanilla extract
  Food coloring, optional

1. Place popcorn in a large baking pan; keep warm in a 200° oven.
2. In a heavy saucepan, combine sugar, corn syrup, water and salt. Cook over medium heat until a candy thermometer reads 235° (soft-ball stage).
3. Remove from heat. Add butter, vanilla extract and, if desired, food coloring; stir until butter is melted. Immediately pour over popcorn and stir until evenly coated.
4. When mixture is cool enough to handle, quickly shape into 3-in. balls, dipping hands into cold water as needed to prevent sticking.

NOTE We recommend you test your candy thermometer before each use by bringing water to a boil; the thermometer should read 212°. Adjust your recipe temperature up or down based on your test.

1 POPCORN BALL 177 cal., 6g fat (2g sat. fat), 5mg chol., 203mg sod., 31g carb. (18g sugars, 2g fiber), 1g pro.

BACON-WRAPPED SCALLOPS

BACON-WRAPPED SCALLOPS

Sweet, tender scallops and salty, savory bacon make the perfect combination in this easy recipe that brings new elegance to bacon-wrapped appetizers.
—*Taste of Home Test Kitchen*

TAKES: 25 min.
MAKES: 4 servings

- 8 bacon strips
- 16 sea scallops (about 2 lbs.), side muscles removed
- ¼ tsp. salt
- ¼ tsp. pepper
- 2 tsp. olive oil
  Chopped fresh parsley
  Seafood cocktail sauce, optional

1. Place bacon in a large nonstick skillet. Cook over medium heat, until partially cooked but not crisp. Remove to paper towels to drain. Cut bacon strips lengthwise in half.
2. Wrap a halved bacon strip around each scallop; secure with a toothpick. Sprinkle with salt and pepper.
3. Wipe skillet clean if necessary. Add oil; heat over medium-high heat. In batches, add scallops; cook 3-4 minutes on each side or until scallops are firm and opaque. Discard toothpicks. Sprinkle with parsley. If desired, top with additional salt and pepper and serve with seafood cocktail sauce.

4 SCALLOPS 258 cal., 10g fat (3g sat. fat), 71mg chol., 1327mg sod., 8g carb. (0 sugars, 0 fiber), 33g pro.

TAJIN LIMEADE

Tajin is a blend of chili peppers, salt and lime. I sprinkle it on a lot of food, but I've found it's really delicious in limeade.

—*Amanda Phillips, Portland, OR*

PREP: 20 min. + freezing
MAKES: 8 servings

3 Tbsp. Tajin seasoning, divided
1 cup plus 1 Tbsp. sugar, divided
4 cups water, divided
3 cups fresh lime juice
Lime wedges

1. Sprinkle 2 Tbsp. Tajin seasoning evenly in the bottom of 2 ice cube trays (16 ice cubes each). Fill with water and freeze.

2. In a saucepan, stir together 1 cup sugar and 1 cup water over medium-high heat. Bring to a boil, stirring frequently, until sugar dissolves. Remove from heat and let cool until room temperature.

3. In a large pitcher or bowl, stir together lime juice, sugar mixture and remaining 3 cups water. On a small plate, combine remaining 1 Tbsp. Tajin seasoning and 1 Tbsp. sugar. Moisten rims of 8 tall glasses with lime wedges; dip rims in Tajin mixture. Place 3-4 Tajin-spiced ice cubes in each glass; fill with limeade. If desired, garnish with additional lime wedges.

1 CUP 126 cal., 0 fat (0 sat. fat), 0 chol., 749mg sod., 34g carb. (28g sugars, 0 fiber), 0 pro.

TAJIN LIMEADE TIPS

What is Tajin spice?
Tajin spice is a seasoning mix made of dried chili peppers (a blend of chiles de arbol, guajillo and pasilla peppers), dehydrated lime and salt.

How long does Tajin limeade last? It typically lasts for about a week in the refrigerator.

How else can I use Tajin seasoning? Try adding it to the rim of other mixed drinks, like your favorite margarita recipes. You can also use Tajin as a spice rub for meats, or sprinkle it over fresh mango or cucumbers (with some lime juice) to make a healthy, flavorful snack.

TAJIN LIMEADE

SCARLET SIPPER

This sweet, tart and slightly fizzy drink is a favorite for gatherings at our church. The bright color sets a festive tone.

—*Amber Goolsby, Geneva, AL*

- -

TAKES: 5 min.
MAKES: 12 servings (2¼ qt.)

4 cups cranberry-apple juice, chilled
1 cup orange juice, chilled
¼ cup lemon juice, chilled
1 liter ginger ale, chilled
   Optional: Fresh cranberries and orange and lemon wedges

In a pitcher, combine juices; stir in ginger ale. Serve over ice. If desired, garnish with cranberries and orange and lemon wedges.
¾ CUP 91 cal., 0 fat (0 sat. fat), 0 chol., 8mg sod., 23g carb. (21g sugars, 0 fiber), 0 pro.

TEST KITCHEN TIP
You can transform this into an adults-only beverage by using a hard lemonade in the mix, or by using a bottle of sparkling wine—prosecco or cava—in place of the ginger ale.

SCARLET SIPPER

HAM & BRIE
PASTRIES

HAM & BRIE PASTRIES

Growing up, I loved pocket
pastries. Now with a busy family,
I need quick bites, and my spin
on the classic ham and cheese
delivers at snack or supper time.
—*Jenn Tidwell, Fair Oaks, CA*

- -

TAKES: 30 min.
MAKES: 16 pastries

1	sheet frozen puff pastry, thawed
⅓	cup apricot preserves
4	slices deli ham, quartered
8	oz. Brie cheese, cut into 16 pieces

1. Preheat oven to 400°. On a
lightly floured surface, unfold
puff pastry. Roll pastry to a
12-in. square; cut into sixteen
3-in. squares. Place 1 tsp.
preserves in center of each
square; top with ham, folding
as necessary, and cheese.
Overlap 2 opposite corners
of pastry over filling; pinch
tightly to seal.
2. Place pastries on a parchment-
lined baking sheet. Bake until
golden brown, 15-20 minutes.
Cool on pan 5 minutes before
serving. If desired, serve with
additional apricot preserves.

FREEZE OPTION Freeze cooled
pastries in a freezer container,
separating layers with waxed
paper. To use, reheat pastries
on a baking sheet in a preheated
400° oven until heated through.
1 APPETIZER 144 cal., 8g fat (3g
sat. fat), 17mg chol., 192mg sod.,
13g carb. (3g sugars, 1g fiber),
5g pro.

GARLIC BLUE CHEESE DIP

This thick, creamy dip is my
mother's recipe and a family
favorite for ringing in the season.
It also makes a tasty substitute
for mayonnaise on chicken and
turkey sandwiches.
—*Lillian Nardi, Richmond, CA*

- - - - - - - - - - - - - - - - - - - -

TAKES: 10 min.
MAKES: About 1½ cups

½   cup milk
1   pkg. (8 oz.) cream cheese,
    cubed
1   cup (4 oz.) crumbled
    blue cheese
2   garlic cloves, peeled
    Assorted vegetables or
    crackers

In a blender, combine milk, cream
cheese, blue cheese and garlic;
cover and process until blended.

If desired, top with additional
crumbled blue cheese just before
serving. Serve with vegetables or
crackers.
2 TBSP. 113 cal., 10g fat (6g sat. fat),
31mg chol., 218mg sod., 1g carb.
(1g sugars, 0 fiber), 4g pro.

EASY SMOKED SALMON

A magazine featured this recipe years ago, and it's still my favorite way to serve salmon. Just add crackers for a super simple yet elegant appetizer.
—*Norma Fell, Boyne City, MI*

- -

PREP: 10 min. + marinating
BAKE: 35 min. + chilling
MAKES: 16 servings

- 1 salmon fillet (about 2 lbs.)
- 2 Tbsp. brown sugar
- 2 tsp. salt
- ½ tsp. pepper
- 1 to 2 Tbsp. liquid smoke
  Optional: Capers and lemon slices

1. Place salmon, skin side down, in an 11x7-in. baking pan coated with cooking spray. Sprinkle with brown sugar, salt and pepper. Drizzle with liquid smoke. Cover and refrigerate for 4-8 hours.
2. Drain salmon, discarding liquid. Bake, uncovered, at 350° until fish flakes easily with a fork, 35-45 minutes. Cool to room temperature. Cover and refrigerate for 8 hours or overnight. If desired, serve with capers and lemon slices.

1½ OZ. COOKED SALMON 95 cal., 5g fat (1g sat. fat), 28mg chol., 324mg sod., 2g carb. (2g sugars, 0 fiber), 10g pro.

SMOKED SALMON TIPS

What kind of salmon should I use to make this recipe? Although you can use any type of salmon, we find that varieties with high oil content work best, such as king (chinook), coho or sockeye salmon. The high fat content creates a rich flavor and contributes to the buttery texture of the smoked fish. Use skin-on salmon for this recipe; the skin provides a buffer between the hot pan and the delicate flesh, keeping the salmon juicy as it cooks. If you use skinless salmon fillets, keep a close eye on them so they don't overcook and dry out.

How else can I smoke salmon? You can use an outdoor smoker or a grill with soaked wood chips to cook the salmon at temperatures between 250° to 350°. Salmon can also be cold smoked at lower temperatures, typically below 90°. Cold smoking will not cook the salmon, so it needs to be cured with salt so it's safe to eat.

How should I serve this? This smoked salmon is a fantastic main course paired with fresh salad, potatoes, roasted veggies or grains like quinoa or couscous. It can also be incorporated into pasta dishes, used in wraps or sandwiches, folded into scrambled eggs for breakfast, added to salads or used as a topping for pizza.

EASY SMOKED SALMON

FRESH PEACH LEMONADE

Looking for a new twist on lemonade? Fresh peaches lend a fruity flavor to this summertime must-have.
—*Joan Hallford,*
North Richland Hills, TX

- -

TAKES: 20 min.
MAKES: 5 servings

- 4 cups water, divided
- 2 medium peaches, chopped
- 1 cup sugar
- ¾ cup lemon juice
- 1 medium lemon, sliced
  Mint sprigs, optional

1. In a small saucepan, bring 2 cups water, peaches and sugar to a boil. Reduce heat; cover and simmer 5-7 minutes or until peaches are tender. Remove from heat. Cool. Strain, discarding peach skins.
2. In a large pitcher, combine peach mixture, lemon juice and remaining 2 cups water. Add lemon slices and garnish with mint if desired. Serve over ice.
1 CUP 182 cal., 0 fat (0 sat. fat), 0 chol., 1mg sod., 48g carb. (44g sugars, 1g fiber), 0 pro.

SAVORY CUCUMBER SANDWICHES

Italian salad dressing easily flavors this simple snack. You can also omit the bread and serve the spread as a dip with cucumbers or other veggies.
—*Carol Henderson,*
Chagrin Falls, OH

- -

PREP: 15 min. + chilling
MAKES: 3 dozen

- 1 pkg. (8 oz.) cream cheese, softened
- ½ cup mayonnaise
- 1 envelope Italian salad dressing mix
- 36 slices snack rye bread
- 1 medium cucumber, sliced
  Snipped fresh dill, optional

1. In a small bowl, combine cream cheese, mayonnaise and salad dressing mix. Refrigerate 1 hour.
2. Just before serving, spread over each slice of rye bread; top each with a cucumber slice. If desired, sprinkle with dill.
1 SANDWICH 62 cal., 5g fat (2g sat. fat), 7mg chol., 149mg sod., 4g carb. (1g sugars, 0 fiber), 1g pro.

TEST KITCHEN TIP

These sandwiches can be assembled a few hours in advance to save time right before serving. Serve on a buffet with other summer appetizers and a pitcher of homemade lemonade.

SAVORY CUCUMBER SANDWICHES

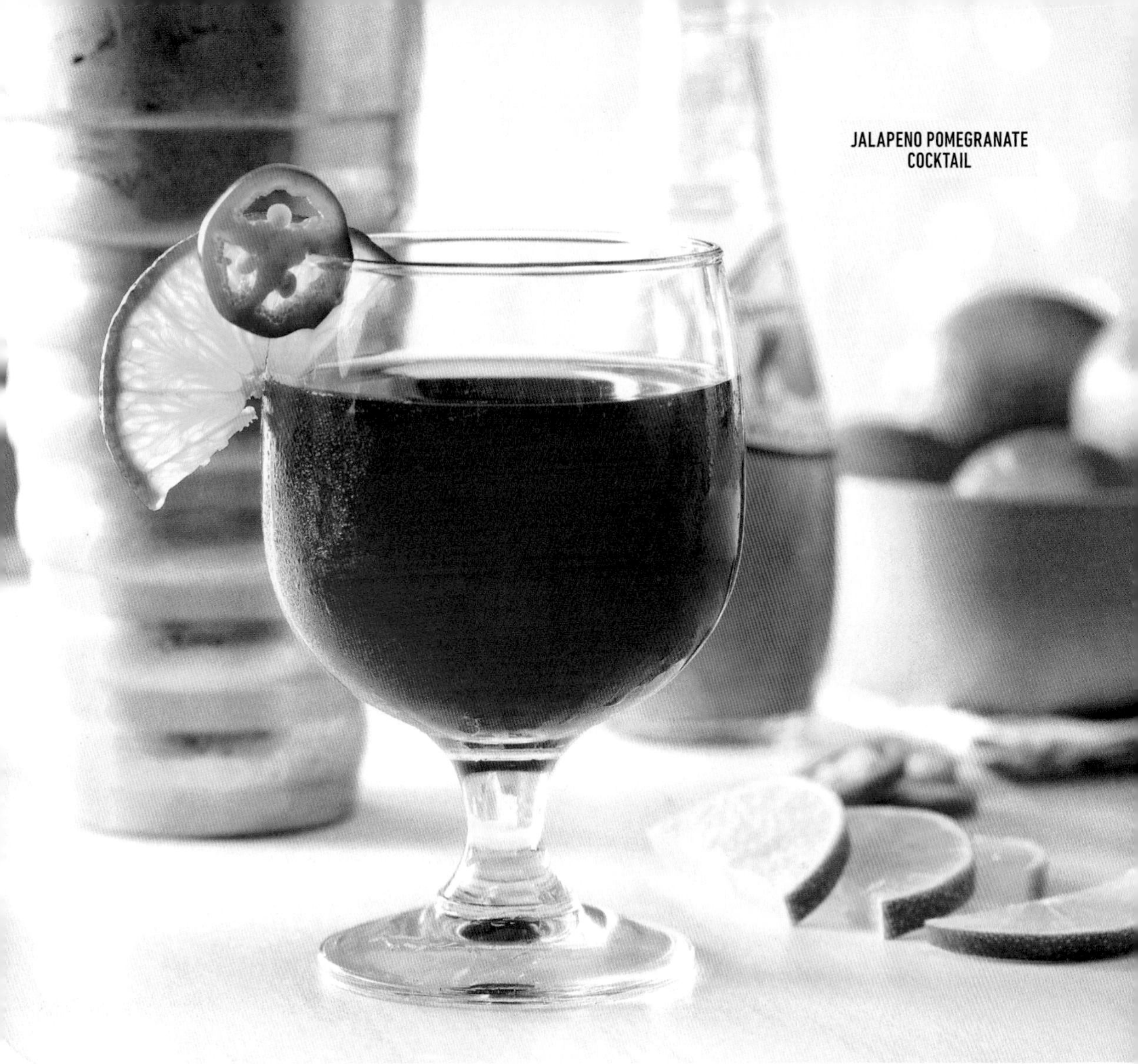

JALAPENO POMEGRANATE COCKTAIL

JALAPENO POMEGRANATE COCKTAIL

This spicy and sweet sipper gives you a little fix of jalapeno flavor minus the heat. Start a couple of days ahead to flavor the vodka.
—Melissa Rodriguez, Van Nuys, CA

PREP: 10 min. + chilling
MAKES: 8 servings

- 2 jalapeno peppers, halved lengthwise and seeded
- 1½ cups vodka
- 6 to 8 cups ice cubes
- 3 cups pomegranate juice
- 3 cups Italian blood orange soda, chilled
- Lime wedges

1. For jalapeno vodka, place jalapenos and vodka in a glass jar or container. Refrigerate, covered, 2-3 days to allow flavors to blend. Strain before using.
2. For each serving, fill cocktail shaker three-fourths full with ice. Add 3 oz. pomegranate juice and 1½ oz. jalapeno vodka; cover and shake until condensation forms on outside of shaker, 10-15 seconds. Strain into a cocktail glass; top with 3 oz. soda. Serve with lime wedges.

NOTE Wear disposable gloves when cutting hot peppers; oils can burn skin. Avoid touching your face.

1 CUP 184 cal., 0 fat (0 sat. fat), 0 chol., 12mg sod., 22g carb. (22g sugars, 0 fiber), 0 pro.

CHEESE-STUFFED
CHERRY TOMATOES

CHEESE-STUFFED CHERRY TOMATOES

We grow plenty of cherry tomatoes, so my husband and I handpick enough for these easy appetizers. This is one of our favorite recipes, and it's impossible to eat just one.
—Mary Lou Robison, Greensboro, NC

PREP: 15 min. + chilling
MAKES: 1 dozen

1   pint cherry tomatoes
1   pkg. (4 oz.) crumbled feta cheese
½   cup finely chopped red onion
½   cup olive oil
¼   cup red wine vinegar
1   Tbsp. dried oregano
    Salt and pepper to taste

1. Cut a thin slice off the top of each tomato. Scoop out and discard pulp. Invert tomatoes onto paper towels to drain. Combine cheese and onion; spoon into tomatoes.
2. In a small bowl, whisk oil, vinegar, oregano, salt and pepper. Spoon over tomatoes. Cover and refrigerate 30 minutes or until ready to serve.
1 TOMATO 111 cal., 11g fat (2g sat. fat), 5mg chol., 93mg sod., 2g carb. (1g sugars, 1g fiber), 2g pro.

★ ★ ★ ★ ★ **READER REVIEW**

"For every get-together my friends beg me to bring these. They're a bit labor intensive but worth it. If you like tomatoes, you and your guests will love these."
—AMCHEFCRAIG, TASTEOFHOME.COM

EASY PUPPY CHOW

EASY PUPPY CHOW

This easy version of everyone's favorite sweet-salty snack mix uses a whole box of cereal, so there's less messy measuring. And there's enough to feed a hungry crowd.
—Taste of Home *Test Kitchen*

TAKES: 15 min. + standing
MAKES: 13 cups

1   box (12 oz.) Corn Chex
2   cups semisweet chocolate chips
¾   cup creamy peanut butter
⅓   cup butter, cubed
3   cups confectioners' sugar

1. Pour cereal into a large bowl. In a large microwave-safe bowl, combine chocolate chips, peanut butter and butter. Microwave on high 30 seconds. Stir gently. Continue microwaving on high, stirring every 30 seconds, until melted and blended. Pour over cereal; gently stir to coat.
2. In batches, place confectioners' sugar in a large airtight container, add cereal mixture, close container and shake until well coated. Spread cereal on a baking sheet. Let stand until set. Store in airtight containers.
½ CUP 229 cal., 10g fat (5g sat. fat), 6mg chol., 146mg sod., 35g carb. (23g sugars, 2g fiber), 3g pro.

CREAMY DEVILED EGGS

These deviled eggs are nicely flavored with a tang of mustard and a spark of sweetness from pickle relish. We served them at my daughter's wedding reception.
—*Barbara Towler, Derby, OH*

PREP: 1 hour + chilling
MAKES: 6 dozen

36 hard-boiled large eggs
1 pkg. (8 oz.) cream cheese, softened
1½ cups mayonnaise
⅓ cup sweet pickle relish
⅓ cup Dijon mustard
¾ tsp. salt
¼ tsp. pepper
    Optional: Paprika and fresh parsley

1. Slice eggs in half lengthwise; remove yolks and set yolks and whites aside.
2. In a large bowl, beat cream cheese until smooth. Add mayonnaise, relish, mustard, salt, pepper and yolks; mix well. Stuff or pipe mixture into egg whites. If desired, garnish with paprika and parsley. Refrigerate until serving.

2 FILLED EGG HALVES 172 cal., 15g fat (4g sat. fat), 222mg chol., 254mg sod., 2g carb. (1g sugars, 0 fiber), 7g pro.

GREEK OLIVE TAPENADE

Welcome to an olive lover's dream. Mix olives with freshly minced garlic, parsley and a few drizzles of olive oil to have the ultimate in Mediterranean bliss.
—*Lisa Sojka, Rockport, ME*

TAKES: 25 min.
MAKES: 16 servings (about 2 cups)

2 cups pitted Greek olives, drained
3 garlic cloves, minced
3 Tbsp. olive oil
1½ tsp. minced fresh parsley
    Toasted baguette slices

In a food processor, pulse olives with garlic until finely chopped. Add oil and parsley; pulse until combined. Serve with toasted baguette slices.

2 TBSP. TAPENADE 71 cal., 7g fat (1g sat. fat), 0 chol., 277mg sod., 2g carb. (0 sugars, 0 fiber), 0 pro.

GREEK OLIVE TAPENADE

CHOCOLATE MOCHA
DUSTED ALMONDS

CHOCOLATE MOCHA DUSTED ALMONDS

I love to make recipes with nuts. These are chocolaty with a hint of coffee—elegant and addictive! I give them away as gifts; I've even made them for wedding favors.
—*Annette Scholz, Medaryville, IN*

PREP: 20 min. + chilling
MAKES: 12 servings

- 1 cup dark chocolate chips
- 2 cups toasted whole almonds
- ¾ cup confectioners' sugar
- 3 Tbsp. baking cocoa
- 4½ tsp. instant coffee granules

1. Microwave chocolate chips, covered, at 50% power, stirring once or twice, until melted, 3-4 minutes. Stir until smooth. Add almonds; mix until coated.
2. Meanwhile, combine remaining ingredients. Transfer almonds to sugar mixture; toss to coat evenly. Spread over a waxed paper-lined baking sheet.
3. Refrigerate until chocolate is set. Store in an airtight container in refrigerator.
NOTE To toast nuts, bake in a shallow pan in a 350° oven for 5-10 minutes or cook in a skillet over low heat until lightly browned, stirring occasionally.

3 TBSP. (ABOUT 17 ALMONDS)
270 cal., 19g fat (5g sat. fat), 0 chol., 12mg sod., 25g carb. (19g sugars, 4g fiber), 7g pro.

TEST KITCHEN TIPS
Like spice? Add ½ tsp. ground chipotle pepper or chili powder.

Try this with any kind of nut. Just make sure you toast them first to bring out all their flavor.

SWISS POTATO PUFFS

Encourage guests to mingle by serving these cute little morsels. They're transportable, mess-free and easy to eat in a few bites.
—*Myra Innes, Auburn, KS*

PREP: 20 min. • **BAKE:** 20 min.
MAKES: about 3 dozen

1⅓ cups water
¼ cup butter, cubed
½ tsp. salt
¾ cup all-purpose flour
¼ cup mashed potato flakes
3 large eggs
1 cup shredded Gruyere or Swiss cheese

1. In a large saucepan, bring water, butter and salt to a boil. Remove from heat.
2. Combine flour and potato flakes; slowly stir into pan. Cook and stir over medium heat until a smooth ball forms. Remove from heat. Add eggs, 1 at a time, beating well after each addition. Continue beating until mixture is smooth and shiny. Stir in cheese.
3. Drop by tablespoonfuls 2 in. apart onto greased baking sheets. Bake at 375° for 18-22 minutes or until golden brown.

1 POTATO PUFF 37 cal., 2g fat (1g sat. fat), 22mg chol., 53mg sod., 2g carb. (0 sugars, 0 fiber), 2g pro.

GARLIC TOMATO BRUSCHETTA

I drew inspiration from my grandma's recipe for this garden-fresh bruschetta. It's a perfect party appetizer, but you can also serve it alongside your favorite Italian entree.

—Jean Franzoni, Rutland, VT

- -

PREP: 30 min. + chilling
MAKES: 2 dozen

- ¼ cup olive oil
- 3 Tbsp. chopped fresh basil
- 3 to 4 garlic cloves, minced
- ½ tsp. salt
- ¼ tsp. pepper
- 4 medium tomatoes, diced
- 2 Tbsp. grated Parmesan cheese
- 1 loaf (1 lb.) unsliced French bread

1. In a large bowl, combine oil, basil, garlic, salt and pepper. Add tomatoes and toss gently. Sprinkle with Parmesan cheese. Refrigerate at least 1 hour.

2. Bring to room temperature before serving. Slice bread into 24 pieces; toast under broiler until lightly browned. Top with tomato mixture. Serve immediately.

1 PIECE 77 cal., 3g fat (0 sat. fat), 0 chol., 172mg sod., 11g carb. (1g sugars, 1g fiber), 2g pro. **DIABETIC EXCHANGES** ½ starch, ½ fat.

BRUSCHETTA TIPS

What kind of olive oil should I use for this recipe? Because there are so few ingredients in this recipe, each flavor really shines through, so make sure you're using high-quality olive oil. You can use either regular or extra-virgin olive oil—because you don't have to cook or heat the oil you don't have to worry about smoke point and can concentrate on fresh flavor.

What variations can I make with this? If you want your bruschetta to have a bite, add 2 Tbsp. minced seeded jalapeno peppers and 2 tsp. balsamic vinegar to the mixture. For creaminess, spread ricotta on the toast before putting the tomatoes on top.

Can I make this bruschetta ahead of time? Make the tomato mixture a few hours ahead of time if you really want the flavors to meld together before serving. Prep it any further in advance than that, though, and the tomatoes will get too juicy. Note: You'll need to use a slotted spoon to scoop the mixture onto the toast slices regardless.

GARLIC TOMATO BRUSCHETTA

LEMON-GARLIC
HUMMUS

LEMON-GARLIC HUMMUS

Whipping up this smooth and creamy bean dip requires just five ingredients. It's a delicious part of our family's Christmas Eve party every year.
—*Kris Capener, Ogden, UT*

TAKES: 10 min. • **MAKES:** 1½ cups

- ¾ cup olive oil
- 2 cups canned garbanzo beans or chickpeas, rinsed and drained
- 3 Tbsp. lemon juice
- 2 tsp. minced garlic
- ½ tsp. salt
  Pita bread wedges or assorted fresh vegetables

In a food processor, combine oil, beans, lemon juice, garlic and salt; cover and process until smooth. Transfer to a small bowl. Serve with pita wedges or vegetables.
¼ CUP 324 cal., 29g fat (3g sat. fat), 0 chol., 309mg sod., 14g carb. (2g sugars, 3g fiber), 3g pro.

★ ★ ★ ★ ★ **READER REVIEW**

"This hummus is so light and refreshing! I used less oil; only about ¼ cup. I just drizzle it into the processor until I get the consistency I like. I liked the simplicity and the fresh, clean taste!"

—RLLEWIS7, TASTEOFHOME.COM

PIZZA PINWHEELS

PIZZA PINWHEELS

These little treats taste a lot like a rolled up pizza. With crispy pepperoni and lots of mozzarella and Parmesan, what's not to love?
—*Dorothy Smith, El Dorado, AR*

TAKES: 25 min.
MAKES: 8 appetizers

- 1 tube (13.8 oz.) refrigerated pizza crust
- 1 cup shredded part-skim mozzarella cheese
- ¼ cup grated Parmesan cheese
- 1 cup chopped pepperoni (about 64 slices)
- ½ cup spaghetti sauce, warmed, optional

1. Preheat oven to 400°. On a lightly floured surface, roll dough into a 16x10-in. rectangle. Sprinkle with cheeses and pepperoni.
2. Roll up jelly-roll style, starting with a long side. Cut into 2-in. slices. Place cut side down in a greased 15x10x1-in. baking pan; lightly press down to flatten.
3. Bake 8-10 minutes or until golden brown. Serve with spaghetti sauce if desired.
1 PINWHEEL 265 cal., 13g fat (5g sat. fat), 26mg chol., 776mg sod., 24g carb. (3g sugars, 1g fiber), 12g pro.

CHEESE CRISPIES

❄ CHEESE CRISPIES

For years I've taken these crispy, crunchy snacks to work. They get high marks from everybody in the teachers lounge.
—*Eileen Ball, Cornelius, NC*

PREP: 20 min. + chilling
BAKE: 15 min./batch
MAKES: 4 dozen

- 1 cup unsalted butter, softened
- 2½ cups shredded extra-sharp cheddar cheese
- 2 cups (250 grams) all-purpose flour
- ¾ tsp. salt
- ½ tsp. cayenne pepper
- 2½ cups Rice Krispies
  Pecan halves, optional

1. In a large bowl, beat butter and cheese until blended. In another bowl, whisk flour, salt and cayenne; gradually beat into cheese mixture. Stir in Rice Krispies. If necessary, turn onto a lightly floured surface and knead 4-6 times, forming a stiff dough.
2. Divide dough in half; shape each half into a 7-in. log. Wrap; refrigerate at least 1 hour or up to 2 days.
3. Preheat oven to 350°. Unwrap logs and cut crosswise into ¼-in. slices. Place slices 1 in. apart on parchment-lined baking sheets. If desired, top each slice with a pecan half. Bake until edges are golden brown, 14-16 minutes. Remove from pans to wire racks to cool.

FREEZE OPTION Freeze wrapped logs in an airtight container. To use, unwrap frozen logs and cut into slices. Bake as directed.

1 CRACKER 87 cal., 6g fat (4g sat. fat), 17mg chol., 92mg sod., 6g carb. (0 sugars, 0 fiber), 2g pro.

KETTLE CORN

KETTLE CORN TIPS

How can I stop the sugar from burning? Popcorn only pops in really hot oil, and sugar burns easily at higher temperatures—therein lies the kettle corn dilemma! The remedy? Hold off on adding your sugar. Stir the popcorn and oil together over medium heat first. As the oil gets hotter (a kernel or two may pop), carefully add the sugar, stir, then cover. It also helps to keep the pot continuously moving, so shake vigorously as the popcorn pops.

How big of a pot do I need for this recipe? We recommend using at least a 4½-qt. Dutch oven. In general, a wide pot is best, so that all the kernels can be as immersed as possible in the oil as it heats.

How can I tell when the popcorn is done? When there are a couple of seconds between pops, your kettle corn is done. Remove from the heat and uncover. There may be several unpopped kernels, but that's much better than a whole scorched batch!

How should I store kettle corn? Keep kettle corn in an airtight tin or canister at room temperature. It should last for handy snacking for several days—but we think it's too tasty to last that long!

KETTLE CORN

If one of the reasons you go to fairs is to satisfy your craving for kettle corn, you'll get the same wonderful salty-sweet taste at home with this recipe. Now you can indulge whenever the mood strikes you.
—*Jenn Martin, Sebago, ME*

- -

TAKES: 15 min. • **MAKES:** 3 qt.

½ cup popcorn kernels
¼ cup sugar
3 Tbsp. canola oil
2 to 3 Tbsp. butter, melted
½ tsp. salt

1. In a Dutch oven over medium heat, cook popcorn, sugar and oil until oil begins to sizzle. Cover and shake until popcorn stops popping, 3-4 minutes.
2. Transfer to a large bowl. Drizzle with butter. Add salt; toss to coat.
1 CUP 91 cal., 6g fat (1g sat. fat), 5mg chol., 114mg sod., 11g carb. (4g sugars, 1g fiber), 1g pro.

SIMPLE GUACAMOLE

Because avocados can brown quickly, it's best to make this guacamole just before serving. If you do have to make it a little in advance, place the avocado pit in the guacamole until serving.
—*Heidi Main, Anchorage, AK*

TAKES: 10 min. • **MAKES:** 1½ cups

- 2   medium ripe avocados
- 1   Tbsp. lemon juice
- ¼   cup chunky salsa
- ⅛   to ¼ tsp. salt

Peel and chop avocados; place in a small bowl. Sprinkle with lemon juice. Add salsa and salt; mash coarsely with a fork. Refrigerate until serving.

2 TBSP. 53 cal., 5g fat (1g sat. fat), 0 chol., 51mg sod., 3g carb. (0 sugars, 2g fiber), 1g pro.

KIDS' FAVORITE PUMPKIN SEEDS

My kids love these pumpkin seeds and want them every fall. A little bit of pulp in the mix really adds to the flavor, so don't rinse the seeds.
—*Gwyn Reiber, Spokane, WA*

PREP: 5 min.
BAKE: 45 min. + cooling
MAKES: 2 cups

- 2   cups fresh pumpkin seeds
- ¼   cup butter, melted
- ½   tsp. garlic salt
- ¼   tsp. cayenne pepper
- ¼   tsp. Worcestershire sauce

In a small bowl, combine all ingredients; transfer to an ungreased 15x10x1-in. baking pan. Bake at 250° for 45-50 minutes or until lightly browned and dry, stirring occasionally. Cool completely. Store in an airtight container.

¼ CUP 122 cal., 9g fat (4g sat. fat), 15mg chol., 158mg sod., 9g carb. (0 sugars, 1g fiber), 3g pro.

REFRESHING RASPBERRY ICED TEA

This recipe makes two gallons, so it's a sensible thirst-quenching choice for a springtime party when you have a medium-size crowd. It freezes well, making it a timesaver for party prep.
—*Arlana Hendricks, Manchester, TN*

PREP/TOTAL: 20 min.
MAKES: 16 servings

- 6 cups water
- 1¾ cups sugar
- 8 tea bags
- ¾ cup frozen apple-raspberry juice concentrate
- 8 cups cold water
  Ice cubes
  Fresh raspberries, optional

In a large saucepan, bring 6 cups water and sugar to a boil; remove from heat. Add tea bags; steep, covered, 3-5 minutes according to taste. Discard tea bags. Add juice concentrate; stir in cold water. Serve over ice, with raspberries if desired.

1 CUP 108 cal., 0 fat (0 sat. fat), 0 chol., 7mg sod., 28g carb. (27g sugars, 0 fiber), 0 pro.

DID YOU KNOW?

Classic Southern sweet tea is made in large batches, with the sugar dissolved into the tea as part of the brewing process. If you're serving guests with differing tastes for sweetness, you can dial back the sugar in this recipe and sweeten individual glasses using simple syrup.

REFRESHING RASPBERRY ICED TEA

CREAMY VEGAN
CAULIFLOWER SOUP
PAGE 80

SOUPS & SANDWICHES

CREAMY VEGAN CAULIFLOWER SOUP

1. Onion
2. Cauliflower
3. Potato
4. Coconut Milk

Plus: Olive Oil, Salt, Pepper, optional toppings

PEPPERED PORK PITAS

POTATO CHOWDER

One of the ladies in our church quilting group brought this savory potato soup to a meeting, and everyone loved how the cream cheese and bacon made it so rich. It's easy to assemble in the morning so it can simmer on its own all day.
—*Anna Mayer, Fort Branch, IN*

PREP: 15 min.
COOK: 8 hours
MAKES: 12 servings (3 qt.)

- 8 cups diced potatoes
- 3 cans (14½ oz. each) chicken broth
- 1 can (10¾ oz.) condensed cream of chicken soup, undiluted
- ⅓ cup chopped onion
- ¼ tsp. pepper
- 1 pkg. (8 oz.) cream cheese, cubed and softened
- ½ lb. sliced bacon, cooked and crumbled, optional
  Minced chives, optional

1. In a 5-qt. slow cooker, combine potatoes, broth, soup, onion and pepper. Cover and cook on low for 8-10 hours or until potatoes are tender.
2. Add cream cheese; stir until blended. Garnish with bacon and chives if desired.

1 CUP 179 cal., 9g fat (5g sat. fat), 25mg chol., 690mg sod., 21g carb. (2g sugars, 2g fiber), 4g pro.

PEPPERED PORK PITAS

Believe it: Cracked black pepper is all it takes to give my pork pitas some pop. With these, any weeknight meal is awesome. I like to fill them with caramelized onions and garlic mayo.
—*Katherine White, Henderson, NV*

TAKES: 20 min.
MAKES: 4 servings

- 1 lb. boneless pork loin chops, cut into thin strips
- 1 Tbsp. olive oil
- 2 tsp. coarsely ground pepper
- 2 garlic cloves, minced
- 1 jar (12 oz.) roasted sweet red peppers, drained and julienned
- 4 whole pita breads, warmed
  Optional: Garlic mayonnaise and torn leaf lettuce

In a small bowl, combine pork, oil, pepper and garlic; toss to coat. Place a large skillet over medium-high heat. Add pork mixture; cook and stir until no longer pink. Stir in red peppers; heat through. Serve on pita breads. Top with mayonnaise and lettuce if desired.
1 SANDWICH 380 cal., 11g fat (3g sat. fat), 55mg chol., 665mg sod., 37g carb. (4g sugars, 2g fiber), 27g pro.
DIABETIC EXCHANGES 3 lean meat, 2 starch, 1 fat.

★ ★ ★ ★ ★ **READER REVIEW**

"Simple and delicious! I also made a cucumber sauce for it—this will become one of my family's staple meals."
—THANKSGRANDMA, TASTEOFHOME.COM

POTATO CHOWDER

BROCCOLI-CHEDDAR BEEF ROLLS

BROCCOLI-CHEDDAR BEEF ROLLS

My grandma's recipe for beef rolls is easy to change up. Load them with ham, veggies, or even olives, as you like!
—*Kent Call, Riverside, UT*

TAKES: 30 min.
MAKES: 6 servings

- ½ lb. lean ground beef (90% lean)
- 2 cups chopped fresh broccoli
- 1 small onion, chopped
- ½ tsp. salt
- ¼ tsp. pepper
- 6 hard rolls
- 2 cups shredded cheddar cheese, divided

1. Preheat to 325°. In a large skillet, cook beef with broccoli and onion over medium heat until beef is no longer pink, 4-6 minutes. Crumble beef and stir in salt and pepper.
2. Cut one-third off the top of each roll; discard or save for another use. Hollow out bottoms, leaving ½-in.-thick shells; place on a baking sheet.
3. Tear bread removed from centers into ½-in. pieces and place in a bowl. Stir 1½ cups cheese into beef mixture. Spoon into bread shells. Sprinkle with remaining ½ cup cheese. Bake until heated through and cheese is melted, 10-15 minutes.

1 STUFFED ROLL 394 cal., 18g fat (9g sat. fat), 61mg chol., 783mg sod., 34g carb. (2g sugars, 2g fiber), 23g pro.

GREEK TOMATO SOUP
WITH ORZO

❄ GREEK TOMATO SOUP WITH ORZO

My recipe for *manestra*, which means orzo in Greek, is effortless and very easy to make. You need only a few steps to transform simple ingredients into a creamy one-pot wonder.
—*Kiki Vagianos, Melrose, MA*

- -

PREP: 10 min. • **COOK:** 25 min.
MAKES: 4 servings

- 2 Tbsp. olive oil
- 1 medium onion, chopped
- 1¼ cups uncooked whole wheat orzo pasta

- 2 cans (14½ oz. each) whole tomatoes, undrained, coarsely chopped
- 3 cups reduced-sodium chicken broth
- 2 tsp. dried oregano
- ¼ tsp. salt
- ¼ tsp. pepper
    Optional: Crumbled feta cheese and minced fresh basil

1. In a large saucepan, heat oil over medium heat; saute onion until tender, 3-5 minutes. Add orzo; cook and stir until lightly toasted.

2. Stir in tomatoes, broth and seasonings; bring to a boil. Reduce heat; simmer, covered, until orzo is tender, 15-20 minutes, stirring occasionally. If desired, top with feta and basil.

FREEZE OPTION Freeze cooled soup in freezer containers. To use, partially thaw in refrigerator overnight. Heat through in a saucepan, stirring occasionally; add broth or water if necessary.

1 CUP 299 cal., 8g fat (1g sat. fat), 0 chol., 882mg sod., 47g carb. (7g sugars, 12g fiber), 11g pro.

LOW-FAT
BROCCOLI SOUP

LOW-FAT BROCCOLI SOUP

This delicious soup is a great way to serve up nutritious vegetables. It has a wonderful, fresh flavor.
—Kay Fairley, Charleston, IL

TAKES: 30 min.
MAKES: 4 servings

- 2 cups chopped fresh or frozen broccoli
- ½ cup chopped onion
- 1 can (14½ oz.) reduced-sodium chicken broth
- 2 Tbsp. cornstarch
- 1 can (12 oz.) fat-free evaporated milk
  Optional: Olive oil, cracked black pepper

1. In a large saucepan, combine broccoli, onion and broth; simmer 10-15 minutes or until vegetables are tender. Puree half the mixture in a blender; return to saucepan.
2. In a small bowl, combine cornstarch and 3 Tbsp. milk until smooth. Gradually add remaining milk. Stir into broccoli mixture. Bring to a boil; cook and stir until thickened, 2 minutes. If desired, serve with a drizzle of olive oil and black pepper.

¾ CUP 120 cal., 0 fat (0 sat. fat), 4mg chol., 385mg sod., 20g carb. (13g sugars, 2g fiber), 10g pro.
DIABETIC EXCHANGES 1 vegetable, 1 fat-free milk.

MINI CHICKEN & BISCUIT SANDWICHES

My 11-year-old son invented these sliders at dinner one night when he set his chicken on a biscuit. The rest of us tried it his way, and now we enjoy these sandwiches all the time.
—*Jodie Kolsan, Palm Coast, FL*

TAKES: 30 min.
MAKES: 5 servings

1 tube (12 oz.) refrigerated buttermilk biscuits
5 boneless skinless chicken breasts (4 oz. each)
½ tsp. salt
½ tsp. dried thyme
¼ tsp. pepper
1 Tbsp. canola oil
1 Tbsp. butter
  Optional: Cranberry chutney, lettuce leaves, sliced tomato and red onion

1. Bake biscuits according to package directions. Meanwhile, cut chicken crosswise in half. Pound with a meat mallet to ¼-in. thickness. Sprinkle with salt, thyme and pepper.
2. In a large skillet, heat oil and butter over medium-high heat. Add chicken in batches; cook until a thermometer reads 165°, 2-3 minutes on each side. Split biscuits in half; top with chicken and add toppings as desired. Replace biscuit tops.

2 MINI SANDWICHES 367 cal., 16g fat (4g sat. fat), 69mg chol., 1029mg sod., 28g carb. (4g sugars, 0 fiber), 27g pro.

ATHENIAN CHICKEN GRILLED CHEESE Prepare chicken as directed. Mix 6 oz. diced fresh mozzarella, ½ cup crumbled feta, ½ cup grated Parmesan, ⅓ cup chopped fresh mint, 2 Tbsp. minced fresh oregano and 2 Tbsp. capers. Divide half the mixture among 4 slices Italian bread; layer each with chicken breast, remaining mixture and a bread slice. Toast sandwiches in olive oil in a large skillet.

DID YOU KNOW?

Sliders originally got their name because they were extremely greasy—back in the 1940s, U.S. Navy sailors coined the name because the miniature sandwiches would "slide right down" in a couple of bites. Modern sliders place more emphasis on health, and cut back on the grease!

MINI CHICKEN & BISCUIT SANDWICHES

SLOW-COOKED BEEF VEGETABLE SOUP

EASY BUTTERNUT SQUASH SOUP

When the weather turns cold, get cozy with a bowl of this butternut squash soup. The cream adds richness, but if you're looking to cut calories, it can be omitted.
—Taste of Home *Test Kitchen*

TAKES: 30 min.
MAKES: 9 servings (2¼ qt.)

- 1 Tbsp. olive oil
- 1 large onion, chopped
- 3 garlic cloves, minced
- 1 medium butternut squash (3 lbs.), peeled and cubed
- 4 cups vegetable broth
- ¾ tsp. salt
- ¼ tsp. pepper
- ½ cup heavy whipping cream
  Optional: Additional heavy whipping cream and crispy sage leaves

1. In a large saucepan, heat oil over medium heat. Add onion; cook and stir until tender. Add garlic; cook 1 minute longer.
2. Stir in squash, broth, salt and pepper; bring to a boil. Reduce heat; simmer, covered, until squash is tender, 10-15 minutes.
3. Puree soup using an immersion blender. Or cool slightly and puree soup in batches in a blender; return to pan.
4. Add cream; cook and stir until heated through. If desired, garnish with additional heavy whipping cream and crispy sage.
1 CUP 157 cal., 7g fat (4g sat. fat), 17mg chol., 483mg sod., 23g carb. (6g sugars, 6g fiber), 3g pro.

SLOW-COOKED BEEF VEGETABLE SOUP

Convenient frozen veggies and hash browns make this meaty soup a snap to make. Simply brown the ground beef, then stir everything together to simmer all day. It's wonderful served with bread and a salad.
—Carol Calhoun, Sioux Falls, SD

PREP: 10 min. • **COOK:** 8 hours
MAKES: 10 servings (2½ qt.)

- 1 lb. ground beef
- 1 can (46 oz.) tomato juice
- 1 pkg. (16 oz.) frozen mixed vegetables, thawed
- 2 cups frozen cubed hash brown potatoes, thawed
- 1 envelope onion soup mix

1. In a large skillet, cook beef over medium heat until no longer pink, 5-7 minutes, crumbling meat; drain. Transfer to a 5-qt. slow cooker. Stir in juice, vegetables, potatoes and soup mix.
2. Cook, covered, on low for 8-10 hours.
1 CUP 139 cal., 4g fat (2g sat. fat), 22mg chol., 766mg sod., 16g carb. (6g sugars, 3g fiber), 11g pro.

EASY BUTTERNUT
SQUASH SOUP

CHICKEN CORDON
BLEU STROMBOLI

CHICKEN CORDON BLEU STROMBOLI

If chicken cordon bleu and stromboli had a baby, this would be it. Serve with jarred Alfredo sauce, homemade Alfredo sauce or classic Mornay sauce on the side if desired.
—*Cyndy Gerken, Naples, FL*

TAKES: 30 min.
MAKES: 6 servings

- 1 tube (13.8 oz.) refrigerated pizza crust
- 4 thin slices deli ham
- 1½ cups shredded cooked chicken
- 6 slices Swiss cheese
- 1 Tbsp. butter, melted
  Roasted garlic Alfredo sauce, optional

1. Preheat oven to 400°. Unroll pizza dough onto a baking sheet. Layer with ham, chicken and cheese to within ½ in. of edges. Roll up jelly-roll style, starting with a long side; pinch seam to seal and tuck ends under. Brush with melted butter.
2. Bake until crust is dark golden brown, 18-22 minutes. Let stand 5 minutes before slicing. Serve with Alfredo sauce for dipping if desired.

1 PIECE 298 cal., 10g fat (4g sat. fat), 53mg chol., 580mg sod., 32g carb. (4g sugars, 1g fiber), 21g pro.

> **TEST KITCHEN TIP**
> Don't let the stromboli stand too long before slicing and eating, or the underside of the crust will get soft.

MUSHROOM
SWISS BURGERS

MUSHROOM SWISS BURGERS

These skillet burgers are perfect cold-weather fare. Heaped with mushrooms and flavorful Swiss cheese, they really deliver. This recipe is sure to be requested often by your family.
—*James Bowles, Ironton, OH*

TAKES: 30 min.
MAKES: 6 servings

- 1½ lbs. ground beef
- 1 lb. sliced fresh mushrooms
- 1 can (10½ oz.) condensed cream of mushroom soup, undiluted
- 1 cup water
- 6 slices Swiss cheese
- 6 hamburger buns, split

1. Shape beef into six ½-in.-thick patties. In a large nonstick skillet, cook burgers over medium heat until a thermometer reads 160°, 5-7 minutes on each side. Remove to paper towels to drain. Discard drippings, reserving 2 Tbsp. in pan. Add mushrooms; cook and stir until tender, 4-6 minutes.
2. Meanwhile, in a microwave-safe bowl, combine soup and water. Cover and microwave on high until heated through, 2-3 minutes.
3. Return patties to skillet. Add soup mixture. Bring to a boil. Reduce heat; simmer, uncovered, 3 minutes. Top each patty with a slice of cheese. Remove from heat; cover and let stand until cheese is melted. Serve on buns topped with mushrooms.

1 BURGER 426 cal., 21g fat (8g sat. fat), 82mg chol., 665mg sod., 29g carb. (5g sugars, 2g fiber), 30g pro.

CREAMY VEGAN CAULIFLOWER SOUP

EASY SLOPPY JOES

Five ingredients are all you need for these hearty sandwiches, which are great for family gatherings. Onion soup mix and sweet pickle relish add zesty flavor without much effort.
—*Marge Napalo, Brunswick, OH*

- -

TAKES: 30 min.
MAKES: 14 servings

3 lbs. ground beef
3 cups ketchup
⅔ cup sweet pickle relish
1 envelope onion soup mix
14 hamburger buns, split

In a Dutch oven, cook beef over medium heat until no longer pink, 6-8 minutes, crumbling meat; drain. Stir in ketchup, relish and soup mix; heat through. Serve immediately on buns.

FREEZE OPTION Store cooled beef mixture in an airtight freezer container. Freeze up to 3 months. To use, thaw overnight in the refrigerator; place in a saucepan and heat through. Serve on buns.

½ CUP 344 cal., 11g fat (4g sat. fat), 48mg chol., 1193mg sod., 40g carb. (18g sugars, 1g fiber), 21g pro.

CREAMY VEGAN CAULIFLOWER SOUP

You will love this cozy, lightened-up version of cauliflower soup. What's our secret ingredient? Coconut milk! Once it is mixed in with the vegetables and broth, the result is a delicious, silky-smooth soup that's completely dairy free.
—*Jenna Urben, McKinney, TX*

- -

PREP: 15 min. • **COOK:** 30 min.
MAKES: 7 servings (1¾ qt.)

1 Tbsp. olive oil
1 small onion, chopped
1 medium head cauliflower, broken into florets (about 6 cups)
1 small potato, peeled and cubed
2 cans (14½ oz. each) vegetable broth
1 can (13.66 oz.) coconut milk
¾ tsp. salt
¼ tsp. pepper
   Optional: Nutritional yeast, chopped green onions and fresh herbs

1. In a large saucepan, heat oil over medium heat. Add onion; cook and stir until softened, 2-3 minutes. Stir in cauliflower, potato and broth; bring to a boil. Reduce heat; simmer, covered, about 20 minutes.

2. Remove from heat. Stir in coconut milk, salt and pepper; cool slightly. Puree in batches in a blender or food processor until smooth. If desired, top with nutritional yeast, green onions and fresh herbs.

FREEZE OPTION Before adding toppings, cool soup. Freeze soup in freezer containers. To use, thaw in refrigerator overnight. Heat through in a saucepan, stirring occasionally. Re-blend with blender or immersion blender if coconut milk does not melt fully. Sprinkle with toppings.

1 CUP 158 cal., 11g fat (9g sat. fat), 0 chol., 566mg sod., 12g carb. (4g sugars, 2g fiber), 3g pro.

ROASTED TOMATO SOUP WITH FRESH BASIL

Roasting brings out the tomatoes' rich, sweet flavor in this soup. It has a slightly chunky texture that indicates it's fresh and homemade. Fresh summertime basil is the classic companion.
—*Marie Forte, Raritan, NJ*

PREP: 20 min.
BAKE: 25 min.
MAKES: 6 servings (1½ qt.)

- 3½ lbs. tomatoes (about 11 medium), halved
- 1 small onion, quartered
- 2 garlic cloves, peeled and halved
- 2 Tbsp. olive oil
- 2 Tbsp. fresh thyme leaves
- 1 tsp. salt
- ¼ tsp. pepper
- 12 fresh basil leaves
  Optional: Salad croutons and thinly sliced fresh basil

1. Preheat oven to 400°. Place tomatoes, onion and garlic in a greased 15x10x1-in. baking pan; drizzle with oil. Sprinkle with thyme, salt and pepper; toss to coat. Roast for 25-30 minutes or until tender, stirring once. Cool slightly.
2. Working in batches, process tomato mixture and basil leaves in a blender until smooth. Transfer to a large saucepan; heat through. If desired, top with croutons and fresh basil.

1 CUP 107 cal., 5g fat (1g sat. fat), 0 chol., 411mg sod., 15g carb. (9g sugars, 4g fiber), 3g pro. **DIABETIC EXCHANGES** 1 starch, 1 fat.

ROASTED TOMATO SOUP WITH FRESH BASIL

HAM & JACK PUDGY PIE

Pepper jack cheese spices up these warm, melty sandwiches.
—*Terri McKitrick, Delafield, WI*

TAKES: 10 min.
MAKES: 1 serving

- 2 slices sourdough bread
- 2 Tbsp. diced fully cooked ham
- 2 Tbsp. canned sliced mushrooms
- 3 Tbsp. shredded pepper jack cheese
- 1 Tbsp. salsa

1. Place 1 slice bread in a greased sandwich iron. Top with ham, mushrooms, cheese, salsa and remaining bread slice. Close iron.
2. Cook over a hot campfire until golden brown and cheese is melted, 3-6 minutes, turning occasionally.
1 SANDWICH 268 cal., 9g fat (4g sat. fat), 33mg chol., 823mg sod., 32g carb. (4g sugars, 2g fiber), 15g pro.
DIABETIC EXCHANGES 2 starch, 2 medium-fat meat.

DID YOU KNOW?

Pudgy pies are an open-air classic—sandwiches cooked in a double-sided iron over a campfire. Depending on where you live, they're also called campfire pies, mountain pies, hobo pies or camping sandwiches. You don't have to wait for a trip to the woods to make this sandwich, though— you can cook it on the stovetop as you would a grilled cheese.

TURKEY & APRICOT WRAPS

For these wraps, I combined the traditional Southern appetizer of jam and cream cheese with the turkey, apple and Brie sandwiches we ate at my bridal luncheon. I like to sneak fresh spinach into recipes because it has such a mild flavor.
—*Kim Beavers, North Augusta, SC*

TAKES: 15 min.
MAKES: 4 servings

- ½ cup reduced-fat cream cheese
- 3 Tbsp. apricot preserves
- 4 whole wheat tortillas (8 in.), room temperature
- ½ lb. sliced reduced-sodium deli turkey
- 2 cups fresh arugula or baby spinach

In a small bowl, mix cream cheese and preserves. Spread about 2 Tbsp. over each tortilla to within ½ in. of edges. Layer with turkey and arugula. Roll up tightly. Serve immediately, or cover and refrigerate until serving.
1 WRAP 312 cal., 10g fat (4g sat. fat), 41mg chol., 655mg sod., 33g carb. (8g sugars, 2g fiber), 20g pro.
DIABETIC EXCHANGES 2 starch, 2 lean meat, 1 fat.

TURKEY & APRICOT WRAPS

WEEKNIGHT CHICKEN MOZZARELLA SANDWICHES

WEEKNIGHT CHICKEN MOZZARELLA SANDWICHES

My husband is a big garlic fan, so we use garlic bread crumbs and garlic sauce for our baked chicken sandwiches. They are so comforting on a chilly day.
—*Bridget Snyder, Syracuse, NY*

TAKES: 30 min.
MAKES: 4 servings

- 4 boneless skinless chicken breast halves (6 oz. each)
- 1 cup garlic bread crumbs
- 1 cup garlic and herb pasta sauce
- 1 cup shredded part-skim mozzarella cheese
  Grated Parmesan cheese, optional
- 4 kaiser rolls, split

1. Preheat oven to 400°. Pound chicken with a meat mallet to ½-in. thickness. Place bread crumbs in a shallow bowl. Add chicken, a few pieces at a time, and turn to coat. Transfer to a greased 15x10x1-in. baking pan.

2. Bake, uncovered, until no longer pink, 15-20 minutes. Spoon pasta sauce over chicken. Top with mozzarella cheese and, if desired, Parmesan cheese. Bake until cheese is melted, 2-3 minutes longer. Serve on rolls.

1 SANDWICH 509 cal., 13g fat (5g sat. fat), 112mg chol., 1125mg sod., 46g carb. (5g sugars, 3g fiber), 50g pro.

PEANUT BUTTER, HONEY & PEAR OPEN-FACED SANDWICHES

SLOW-COOKER MEATBALL SANDWICHES

Our approach to meatball sandwiches is simple: Cook the meatballs low and slow, load them into hoagie buns, and top them with provolone and pepperoncini.
—*Stacie Nicholls, Spring Creek, NV*

PREP: 5 min. • **COOK:** 3 hours
MAKES: 8 servings

- 2 pkg. (12 oz. each) frozen fully cooked Italian meatballs, thawed
- 2 jars (24 oz. each) marinara sauce
- 8 hoagie buns, split
- 8 slices provolone cheese
  Sliced pepperoncini, optional

1. Place meatballs and sauce in a 3- or 4-qt. slow cooker. Cook, covered, on low 3-4 hours or until meatballs are heated through.
2. On each bun bottom, layer cheese, meatballs and, if desired, pepperoncini; replace tops.

1 SANDWICH 526 cal., 20g fat (7g sat. fat), 93mg chol., 1674mg sod., 55g carb. (15g sugars, 4g fiber), 32g pro.

TEST KITCHEN TIP
For an extra layer of flavor, toast the buns and drizzle them with olive oil (either plain or flavored) before loading in the fillings.

PEANUT BUTTER, HONEY & PEAR OPEN-FACED SANDWICHES

I work a 12-hour night shift at a hospital, and when I come home in the morning, I don't want to cook a big breakfast. I love these sandwiches because they're versatile; sometimes I use apples instead of pears and different cheeses, such as Brie or grated Parmesan.
—*L.J. Washington, Carpinteria, CA*

TAKES: 10 min.
MAKES: 4 servings

- ¼ cup chunky peanut butter
- 4 slices honey whole wheat bread, toasted
- 1 medium pear, thinly sliced
- ¼ tsp. salt
- 4 tsp. honey
- ½ cup shredded cheddar cheese

Spread peanut butter over toast. Top with pear, salt, honey and cheese. Place on a microwave-safe plate; microwave on high 20-25 seconds or until cheese is melted.

1 OPEN-FACED SANDWICH 268 cal., 14g fat (4g sat. fat), 14mg chol., 446mg sod., 28g carb. (13g sugars, 4g fiber), 11g pro.

SLOW-COOKER MEATBALL
SANDWICHES

ITALIAN GRILLED CHEESE SANDWICHES

I made up this recipe for the students in the foods and nutrition class I teach. The kids like it so much that they often go home and fix it for their families.
—*Beth Hiott, York, SC*

TAKES: 25 min.
MAKES: 4 servings

- 8 slices Italian bread
- 4 Tbsp. prepared pesto
- 4 slices provolone cheese
- 4 slices part-skim mozzarella cheese
- 5 tsp. olive oil
  Marinara sauce, warmed, optional

1. Spread 4 bread slices with pesto. Layer with cheeses; top with remaining bread. Brush outsides of sandwiches with oil.
2. Using a large cast-iron skillet or electric griddle, toast sandwiches over medium heat until cheese is melted, 3-4 minutes on each side. If desired, serve with marinara.

1 SANDWICH 445 cal., 27g fat (10g sat. fat), 35mg chol., 759mg sod., 32g carb. (1g sugars, 2g fiber), 20g pro.

ITALIAN GRILLED CHEESE SANDWICHES

BACON-POTATO CORN CHOWDER

TORTELLINI PRIMAVERA SOUP

Years ago, I found the idea for tortellini with peas and carrots in a magazine. I added my own touch to it.
—*Kari George, Ellicott City, MD*

- -

TAKES: 25 min.
MAKES: 4 servings

2   cartons (32 oz. each) reduced-sodium chicken broth
1   pkg. (10 oz.) julienned carrots
1   pkg. (9 oz.) refrigerated cheese tortellini
1   cup frozen peas (about 4 oz.)
¼   tsp. pepper
    Thinly sliced fresh basil leaves

In a large saucepan, bring broth to a boil. Add carrots, tortellini, peas and pepper; return to a boil. Cook, uncovered, 7-9 minutes or until pasta is tender. Top individual servings with basil.

FREEZE OPTION Freeze cooled soup in freezer containers. To use, partially thaw in refrigerator overnight. Heat through in a saucepan, stirring occasionally.

2¼ CUPS 282 cal., 6g fat (3g sat. fat), 28mg chol., 1461mg sod., 43g carb. (9g sugars, 5g fiber), 17g pro.

BACON-POTATO CORN CHOWDER

I was raised on a farm, and a warm soup with homey ingredients, like this one, was always a treat after a chilly day outside. My hearty chowder nourishes the family.
—*Katie Lillo, Big Lake, MN*

- -

TAKES: 30 min.
MAKES: 6 servings

½   lb. bacon strips, chopped
¼   cup chopped onion
1½   lbs. Yukon Gold potatoes (about 5 medium), peeled and cubed
1   can (14¾ oz.) cream-style corn
1   can (12 oz.) evaporated milk
¼   tsp. salt
¼   tsp. pepper

1. In a large skillet, cook bacon over medium heat until crisp, stirring occasionally. Remove with a slotted spoon; drain on paper towels. Discard drippings, reserving 1½ tsp. in pan. Add onion to drippings; cook and stir over medium-high heat until tender.
2. Meanwhile, place potatoes in a large saucepan; add water to cover. Bring to a boil over high heat. Reduce heat to medium; cook, uncovered, 10-15 minutes or until tender. Drain, reserving 1 cup potato water.
3. Add corn, milk, salt, pepper, potatoes and reserved potato water to saucepan; heat through. Stir in bacon and onion.

1 CUP 335 cal., 13g fat (6g sat. fat), 37mg chol., 592mg sod., 44g carb. (10g sugars, 3g fiber), 12g pro.

TROPICAL
BEEF WRAP

TROPICAL BEEF WRAP

For my finicky little ones, I create fast, tasty recipes like this tropical sandwich wrap. You can even use up leftover roast beef in a pinch.
—Amy Tong, Anaheim, CA

TAKES: 15 min.
MAKES: 4 servings

- 1 carton (8 oz.) spreadable pineapple cream cheese
- 4 flour tortillas (10 in.)
- 4 cups fresh baby spinach (about 4 oz.)
- ¾ lb. thinly sliced deli roast beef
- 1 medium mango, peeled and sliced

Spread cream cheese over tortillas to within 1 in. of edges. Layer with spinach, roast beef and mango. Roll up tightly and serve.
1 WRAP 522 cal., 20g fat (10g sat. fat), 100mg chol., 1211mg sod., 58g carb. (21g sugars, 4g fiber), 26g pro.

★ ★ ★ ★ ★ **READER REVIEW**
"Tasty recipe! I used diced canned mango and mixed it with the homemade pineapple cream cheese. It turned out very well!"
—SCOLSON132, TASTEOFHOME.COM

WHITE BEAN & CHICKEN CHILI

WHITE BEAN & CHICKEN CHILI

To create this yummy white chili, I adapted three different recipes. It's mild, so everyone can dig in. It's won ribbons in several recipe contests!
—Julie White, Yacolt, WA

TAKES: 20 min.
MAKES: 6 servings

- 3 cans (15 oz. each) cannellini beans, undrained
- 1 can (4 oz.) chopped green chiles
- 3 tsp. chicken bouillon granules
- 3 tsp. ground cumin
- 2 cups water
- 3 cups cubed cooked chicken or turkey
  Minced fresh cilantro, optional

1. In a large saucepan, combine beans, green chiles, bouillon, cumin and water; bring to a boil. Reduce heat; simmer, uncovered, 2-3 minutes to allow flavors to blend, stirring occasionally.
2. Stir in chicken; heat through. If desired, sprinkle with cilantro.
FREEZE OPTION Freeze cooled chili in freezer containers. To use, partially thaw in refrigerator overnight. Heat through in a saucepan, stirring occasionally and adding water if necessary.
1 CUP 323 cal., 6g fat (1g sat. fat), 63mg chol., 1113mg sod., 34g carb. (3g sugars, 10g fiber), 34g pro.

SPICY POTATO SOUP

CHEESY WILD RICE SOUP

We often eat easy-to-make soups when there's not a lot of time to cook. I replaced the wild rice in the original recipe with a boxed rice mix. This creamy concoction is now a family favorite.
—*Lisa Hofer, Hitchcock, SD*

TAKES: 30 min.
MAKES: 8 servings (2qt.)

- 1   pkg. (6.2 oz.) fast-cooking long grain and wild rice mix
- 4   cups 2% milk
- 1   can (10¾ oz.) condensed cream of potato soup, undiluted
- 8   oz. Velveeta, cubed
- ½   lb. bacon strips, cooked and crumbled
      Optional: Minced chives and oyster crackers

In a large saucepan, prepare rice mix according to package directions. Add milk, soup and cheese. Cook and stir until cheese is melted. Garnish with bacon and, if desired, minced fresh chives and oyster crackers.
1 CUP 464 cal., 29g fat (14g sat. fat), 70mg chol., 1492mg sod., 29g carb. (9g sugars, 1g fiber), 21g pro.

SPICY POTATO SOUP

My sister-in-law, who is from Mexico, passed along this wonderful recipe. Since she prefers her foods much spicier than we do, I reduced the amount of pepper sauce, but you can add more if you prefer a bigger kick.
—*Audrey Wall, Industry, PA*

PREP: 20 min. • **COOK:** 70 min.
MAKES: 8 servings (2 qt.)

- 1   lb. ground beef
- 4   cups cubed peeled potatoes (½-in. cubes)
- 1   small onion, chopped
- 3   cans (8 oz. each) tomato sauce
- 4   cups water
- 2   tsp. salt
- 1½ tsp. pepper
- ½   to 1 tsp. hot pepper sauce

In a Dutch oven, brown beef over medium heat until no longer pink; drain. Add potatoes, onion and tomato sauce. Stir in water, salt, pepper and hot pepper sauce; bring to a boil. Reduce heat and simmer for 1 hour or until potatoes are tender and soup has thickened.
1 CUP 159 cal., 5g fat (2g sat. fat), 28mg chol., 764mg sod., 16g carb. (2g sugars, 2g fiber), 12g pro.

CHEESY WILD RICE SOUP

PEPPERONI ROLL-UPS

PEPPERONI ROLL-UPS

Here is a fast recipe that always goes over well at my house. Each bite has gooey melted cheese and real pizza flavor. Try serving them with pizza sauce for dipping.
—*Debra Purcell, Safford, AZ*

TAKES: 20 min.
MAKES: 4 servings

- 1 tube (8 oz.) refrigerated crescent rolls
- 16 slices pepperoni, cut into quarters
- 2 pieces string cheese (1 oz. each), cut into quarters
- ¾ tsp. Italian seasoning, divided
- ¼ tsp. garlic salt

1. Unroll crescent dough; separate into 8 triangles. Place 8 pepperoni pieces on each. Place a piece of cheese on short side of each triangle; sprinkle with ½ tsp. Italian seasoning. Roll up each, starting with short side; pinch seams to seal. Sprinkle with garlic salt and remaining ¼ tsp. Italian seasoning.

2. Place 2 in. apart on a greased baking sheet. Bake at 375° for 10-12 minutes or until golden brown. Serve warm.

2 ROLL-UPS 282 cal., 17g fat (5g sat. fat), 12mg chol., 766mg sod., 22g carb. (4g sugars, 0 fiber), 7g pro.

TEST KITCHEN TIP
Leftovers should be stored in the refrigerator, where they will last about a week. Wrap your leftover rolls in foil and pop into the oven at 375° to reheat. Unwrap for the last few minutes to crisp up the pastry again.

VEGAN CARROT SOUP

Yukon Gold potatoes—instead of cream—make this smooth carrot soup vegan and add a mild sweetness. If you don't have Yukon Golds on hand, russet potatoes will work too.
—Taste of Home *Test Kitchen*

TAKES: 30 min.
MAKES: 6 servings

- 1 medium onion, chopped
- 2 celery ribs, chopped
- 1 Tbsp. canola oil
- 4 cups vegetable broth
- 1 lb. carrots, sliced
- 2 large Yukon Gold potatoes, peeled and cubed
- 1 tsp. salt
- ¼ tsp. pepper
  Fresh cilantro leaves, optional

1. In a large saucepan, saute onion and celery in oil until tender. Add broth, carrots and potatoes; bring to a boil. Reduce heat; cover and simmer for 15-20 minutes or until vegetables are tender. Remove from heat; cool slightly.

2. Transfer to a blender; cover and process until smooth. Return to pan; stir in salt and pepper. Heat through. If desired, sprinkle with cilantro.

1 CUP 176 cal., 3g fat (0 sat. fat), 0 chol., 710mg sod., 35g carb. (7g sugars, 4g fiber), 4g pro.
DIABETIC EXCHANGES 2 starch, ½ fat.

VEGAN
CARROT SOUP

TURKEY-CRANBERRY BAGELS

Take care of that leftover turkey in a way your family loves. It's good with all sorts of cranberry sauces and chutneys, so have fun playing around.
—Taste of Home *Test Kitchen*

TAKES: 10 min.
MAKES: 4 servings

- 4 plain bagels, split and toasted
- 8 oz. thinly sliced cooked turkey
- 8 slices provolone cheese
- ½ cup whole-berry cranberry sauce

Preheat broiler. Place bagel halves on a baking sheet; layer with turkey and cheese. Broil 4-6 in. from heat until cheese is melted, 1-2 minutes. Top with cranberry sauce.

2 BAGEL HALVES 469 cal., 16g fat (8g sat. fat), 73mg chol., 645mg sod., 49g carb. (12g sugars, 2g fiber), 34g pro.

TEST KITCHEN TIP

This is a perfect way to use up Thanksgiving leftovers, but you can make these bagels any time of the year. If you haven't cooked a turkey, you can make them with sliced deli turkey and a jarred sauce or chutney.

TURKEY-CRANBERRY BAGELS

DILLY BEEF SANDWICHES

My younger sister shared this recipe with me. It puts a twist on the traditional barbecue sandwich and is a proven crowd-pleaser. Plus, it's incredibly convenient to make in the slow cooker.
—*Donna Blankenheim, Madison, WI*

PREP: 15 min.
COOK: 8 hours + cooling
MAKES: 12 servings

1   boneless beef chuck roast (3 to 4 lbs.)
1   jar (16 oz.) whole dill pickles, undrained
½   cup chili sauce
2   garlic cloves, minced
12   hamburger buns, split
Giardiniera, optional

1. Cut roast in half and place in a 5-qt. slow cooker. Add pickles with juice, chili sauce and garlic. Cover and cook on low 8-9 hours or until beef is tender.

2. Discard pickles. Remove roast. When cool enough to handle, shred meat. Return to slow cooker and heat through. Using a slotted spoon, fill each bun with about ½ cup of meat mixture. Top with giardiniera if desired.

1 SANDWICH 332 cal., 13g fat (5g sat. fat), 74mg chol., 863mg sod., 25g carb. (5g sugars, 1g fiber), 27g pro.

SLOW-COOKED POT ROAST SLIDERS

SLOW-COOKED POT ROAST SLIDERS

This recipe reminds me of my mother's famous pot roast. Best of all, these are so simple to make. I love that I can enjoy the flavors of Mom's roast with the delicious portability of a slider.
—*Lauren Drafke, Cape Coral, FL*

- -

PREP: 20 min. • **COOK:** 5 hours
MAKES: 2 dozen

- 1 boneless beef chuck roast (3 lbs.)
- 1½ cups water
- 1 envelope (1 oz.) onion soup mix
- 1 envelope (1 oz.) au jus gravy mix
- 2 pkg. (12 oz. each) Hawaiian sweet rolls, halved
- 12 slices Swiss cheese (¾ oz. each), cut in half
  Optional: Horseradish sauce, sliced tomato and baby arugula

1. Place roast in a 4-qt. slow cooker. In a small bowl, whisk together water and soup and gravy mixes. Pour mixture over roast. Cook, covered, on low until tender, 5-6 hours.
2. Remove from cooker. Cool slightly; shred meat with 2 forks.
3. Preheat broiler. Place halved rolls on a baking sheet. On each bottom half, place a cheese piece. Broil buns 4-6 in. from heat until cheese is melted and rolls start to brown, 1-2 minutes. Remove from broiler.
4. Using tongs, place meat mixture on roll bottoms. Layer with horseradish sauce, tomato and baby arugula if desired. Replace roll tops.
2 SLIDERS 487 cal., 22g fat (11g sat. fat), 124mg chol., 721mg sod., 36g carb. (12g sugars, 2g fiber), 36g pro.

TEST KITCHEN TIP
Try these sandwiches with a more flavorful cheese such as aged Swiss or white cheddar.

CHORIZO & CHICKPEA SOUP

Chorizo sausage adds its own spice to the broth of this soup, creating delicious flavor with no need for more seasonings. And while it's cooking, the whole house smells divine!
—*Jaclyn McKewan, Lancaster, NY*

PREP: 15 min. • **COOK:** 8¼ hours
MAKES: 6 servings

- 3 cups water
- 2 celery ribs, chopped
- 2 fully cooked Spanish chorizo links (3 oz. each), cut into ½-in. pieces
- ½ cup dried chickpeas or garbanzo beans
- 1 can (14½ oz.) petite diced tomatoes, undrained
- ½ cup ditalini or other small pasta
- ½ tsp. salt

1. Place water, celery, chorizo and chickpeas in a 4- or 5-qt. slow cooker. Cook, covered, on low until beans are tender, 8-10 hours.
2. Stir in tomatoes, pasta and salt; cook, covered, on high until pasta is tender, 15-20 minutes longer.
FREEZE OPTION Freeze cooled soup in freezer containers. To use, partially thaw in refrigerator overnight. Heat through in a saucepan, stirring occasionally; add broth or water if necessary.
1 CUP 180 cal., 8g fat (3g sat. fat), 18mg chol., 569mg sod., 23g carb. (3g sugars, 6g fiber), 9g pro.
DIABETIC EXCHANGES 1½ starch, 1 high-fat meat.

CHORIZO & CHICKPEA SOUP

BAKED BEAN CHILI

HAM & BRIE MELTS

Deli ham and apricot preserves pair up with melty special-occasion cheese in these crispy sandwiches that remind me of baked Brie.
—Bonnie Bahler, Ellington, CT

- -

TAKES: 20 min.
MAKES: 4 servings

- 8 slices multigrain bread
- ¼ cup apricot preserves
- ½ lb. sliced deli ham
- 1 round (8 oz.) Brie cheese, rind removed, sliced
- 3 Tbsp. butter, softened

1. Spread 4 bread slices with half the preserves. Layer with ham and cheese. Spread remaining bread with remaining preserves; place over cheese, preserves side down. Spread outsides of sandwiches with butter.
2. In a large cast-iron or other heavy skillet, toast sandwiches over medium heat until golden brown and cheese is melted, 2-3 minutes on each side.
1 SANDWICH 500 cal., 27g fat (16g sat. fat), 104mg chol., 1208mg sod., 39g carb. (14g sugars, 3g fiber), 27g pro.

BAKED BEAN CHILI

Who says a good chili has to simmer all day? This zippy chili—with a touch of sweetness—can be made on the spur of the moment. It's an excellent standby for unexpected guests. Served with bread and a salad. It's a hearty dinner everyone raves about.
—Nancy Wall, Bakersfield, CA

- -

TAKES: 30 min.
MAKES: 24 servings (6 qt.)

- 2 lbs. ground beef
- 3 cans (28 oz. each) baked beans
- 1 can (46 oz.) tomato juice
- 1 can (11½ oz.) V8 juice
- 1 envelope chili seasoning
  Optional: Sour cream, shredded cheddar cheese and sliced jalapenos

In a Dutch oven, cook beef over medium heat until no longer pink; drain. Stir in remaining ingredients. Bring to a boil. Reduce heat; simmer, uncovered, for 10 minutes. If desired, serve with sour cream, cheese and jalapenos.
NOTE Wear disposable gloves when cutting hot peppers; the oils can burn skin. Avoid touching your face.
1 CUP 189 cal., 6g fat (2g sat. fat), 30mg chol., 721mg sod., 23g carb. (2g sugars, 6g fiber), 13g pro.

REUBEN CALZONES

REUBEN CALZONES

I love a Reuben sandwich, so I tried the fillings in a pizza pocket instead of on rye bread. This hand-held dinner is a big winner at our house.
—*Nickie Frye, Evansville, IN*

TAKES: 30 min.
MAKES: 4 servings

- 1 tube (13.8 oz.) refrigerated pizza crust
- 4 slices Swiss cheese
- 1 cup sauerkraut, rinsed and well drained
- ½ lb. sliced cooked corned beef Thousand Island salad dressing

1. Preheat oven to 400°. On a lightly floured surface, unroll pizza crust dough and pat into a 12-in. square. Cut into 4 squares. Layer a fourth of cheese, sauerkraut and corned beef diagonally over half of each square to within ½ in. of edges. Fold one corner over filling to opposite corner, forming a triangle; press edges with a fork to seal. Place on greased baking sheets.
2. Bake 15-18 minutes or until golden brown. Serve with salad dressing on the side for dipping.
1 CALZONE 430 cal., 17g fat (6g sat. fat), 66mg chol., 1607mg sod., 49g carb. (7g sugars, 2g fiber), 21g pro.

SAUSAGE & SPINACH CALZONES
Substitute mozzarella for the Swiss cheese. Cook and drain ½ lb. bulk Italian sausage; add 3 cups fresh baby spinach and cook until wilted. Stir in ½ cup part-skim ricotta cheese and ¼ tsp. each salt and pepper. Proceed as directed. Serve with marinara sauce if desired.
ZESTY CALZONES Substitute mozzarella for the Swiss cheese. Layer each calzone with 2 thin slices each of deli ham and hard salami; sprinkle each with 1 Tbsp. each of chopped onion, green pepper and tomato. Proceed as directed. Omit salad dressing.

PAN–FRIED SALMON
PAGE 110

MAIN COURSES

PAN-FRIED SALMON

1. Salmon Fillets
2. Kosher Salt
3. Ground Pepper

Plus: Olive Oil

BEAN BURRITOS

BEAN BURRITOS

I always have the ingredients for this cheesy burrito recipe on hand. Cooking the rice and shredding the cheese the night before saves precious minutes at dinnertime.
—*Beth Osborne Skinner, Bristol, TN*

TAKES: 30 min.
MAKES: 6 servings

- 1 can (16 oz.) vegetarian refried beans
- 1 cup salsa
- 1 cup cooked long grain rice
- 2 cups shredded cheddar cheese, divided
- 12 flour tortillas (6 in.)

Optional: Shredded lettuce, sliced olives, halved grape tomatoes and sliced avocado

1. Preheat oven to 375°. In a large bowl, combine beans, salsa, rice and 1 cup cheese. Spoon about ⅓ cup mixture off-center on each tortilla. Fold sides and ends over filling and roll up.
2. Arrange burritos in a greased 13x9-in. baking dish. Sprinkle with remaining 1 cup cheese. Cover and bake until heated through, 20-25 minutes. Add toppings as desired.

2 BURRITOS 216 cal., 9g fat (4g sat. fat), 23mg chol., 544mg sod., 24g carb. (1g sugars, 3g fiber), 9g pro.
DIABETIC EXCHANGES 1½ starch, 1 lean meat, 1 fat.

ASPARAGUS NICOISE SALAD

I've used my Nicoise as an appetizer or a main-dish salad, and it's a winner every time I put it on the table. Here's to a colorful, make-ahead salad!
—*Jan Meyer, St. Paul, MN*

TAKES: 20 min.
MAKES: 4 servings

- 1 lb. small red potatoes (about 10), halved
- 1 lb. fresh asparagus, trimmed and halved crosswise
- 3 pouches (2½ oz. each) albacore white tuna in water
- ½ cup pitted Greek olives, halved, optional
- ½ cup zesty Italian salad dressing

1. Place potatoes in a large saucepan; cover with 2 in. water. Bring to a boil. Reduce heat; cook, uncovered, until tender, 10-12 minutes, adding asparagus during the last 2-4 minutes of cooking. Drain potatoes and asparagus; immediately drop into ice water.
2. To serve, drain potatoes and asparagus; pat dry and divide among 4 plates. Add tuna and, if desired, olives. Drizzle with dressing.

1 SERVING 233 cal., 8g fat (0 sat. fat), 22mg chol., 583mg sod., 23g carb. (4g sugars, 3g fiber), 16g pro.
DIABETIC EXCHANGES 2 lean meat, 1½ starch, 1½ fat, 1 vegetable.

ASPARAGUS
NICOISE SALAD

RED PEPPER & PARMESAN TILAPIA

My husband and I are always looking for light fish recipes because of their health benefits. This one's a hit with him, and we've served it at dinner parties too. It's become a staple!
—Michelle Martin, Durham, NC

TAKES: 20 min.
MAKES: 4 servings

- 1 large egg, lightly beaten
- ½ cup grated Parmesan cheese
- 1 tsp. Italian seasoning
- ½ to 1 tsp. crushed red pepper flakes
- ½ tsp. pepper
- 4 tilapia fillets (6 oz. each)

1. Preheat oven to 425°. Place egg in a shallow bowl. In another shallow bowl, combine cheese, Italian seasoning, pepper flakes and pepper. Dip fillets in egg and then in cheese mixture.

2. Place fillets in a 15x10x1-in. baking pan coated with cooking spray. Bake for 10-15 minutes or until fish just begins to flake easily with a fork.

1 FILLET 179 cal., 4g fat (2g sat. fat), 89mg chol., 191mg sod., 1g carb. (0 sugars, 0 fiber), 35g pro.
DIABETIC EXCHANGES 5 very lean meat, ½ fat.

RED PEPPER &
PARMESAN TILAPIA

BEST EVER
LAMB CHOPS

BEST EVER LAMB CHOPS

My mom just loved a good lamb chop, and this easy recipe was her favorite way to have them. I've also grilled these chops with great results.
—*Kim Mundy, Visalia, CA*

PREP: 10 min. + chilling
BROIL: 10 min.
MAKES: 4 servings

- 1 tsp. each dried basil, marjoram and thyme
- ½ tsp. salt
- 8 lamb loin chops (3 oz. each)
  Mint jelly, optional

1. Combine herbs and salt; rub over lamb chops. Cover and refrigerate for 1 hour.

2. Broil 4-6 in. from heat until meat reaches desired doneness, 5-8 minutes on each side (for medium-rare, a thermometer should read 135°; medium, 140°; medium-well, 145°). Serve with mint jelly if desired.

2 LAMB CHOPS 157 cal., 7g fat (2g sat. fat), 68mg chol., 355mg sod., 0 carb. (0 sugars, 0 fiber), 22g pro.
DIABETIC EXCHANGES 3 lean meat, ½ fat.

HONEY GLAZED LAMB CHOPS
Omit step 1, herbs and salt. In a saucepan over medium-low heat, combine ⅓ cup each honey and prepared mustard and ⅛ tsp. each onion salt and pepper until honey is melted, 2-3 minutes. Brush over both sides of lamb. Proceed as directed in step 2.

TEST KITCHEN TIP

Lamb chops, like pork chops and beef steaks, can be cooked many different ways. This recipe uses broiling, but pan-searing makes great chops, as does grilling. Braising or slow-cooking is a good option, especially for shoulder chops, because the fat will slowly break down and tenderize the meat.

CACIO E PEPE

This classic pasta dish (literally, "cheese and pepper") depends on quality ingredients to really shine. Make sure your cheese is finely grated—it's best to buy a block and grate it yourself—and add it gradually in order to prevent clumping.

—*Lindsay Mattison, Hillsboro, OR*

TAKES: 20 min.
MAKES: 4 servings

- 6 cups water
- 1½ Tbsp. kosher salt
- 8 oz. uncooked long pasta, such as spaghetti, linguine or fettuccine
- ¼ cup butter, cubed, divided
- 1 tsp. freshly ground black pepper
- ¼ cup finely shredded Parmesan cheese, Grana Padano or Pecorino Romano

1. In a large saucepan, bring water and salt to a boil. Add pasta; cook according to package directions for al dente.
2. Meanwhile, in a large skillet, melt 2 Tbsp. butter. Add pepper; cook and stir for 1 minute. Drain pasta, reserving ¾ cup pasta water. Add ½ cup pasta water to skillet; bring to a simmer. Add cooked pasta; toss to combine. Remove skillet from heat.
3. Add cheese and remaining 2 Tbsp. butter, stirring constantly until cheese is fully melted. Add additional pasta water if sauce appears too dry. Season with additional salt and pepper to taste. If desired, sprinkle with additional cheese.
1 CUP 334 cal., 14g fat (8g sat. fat), 34mg chol., 180mg sod., 43g carb. (2g sugars, 2g fiber), 9g pro.

BASIL PORK CHOPS

BASIL PORK CHOPS

These tender, glazed chops get a kick from basil, chili powder and a little brown sugar. Serve with your favorite roasted veggies and you've got a super comforting meal bursting with flavor.

—*Lisa Gilliland, Fort Collins, CO*

TAKES: 25 min.
MAKES: 4 servings

- ¼ cup packed brown sugar
- 1½ tsp. dried basil
- ½ tsp. salt
- ½ tsp. chili powder
- 2 Tbsp. canola oil, divided
- 4 boneless pork loin chops (½ in. thick and 4 oz. each)

1. Mix first 4 ingredients; gradually stir in 1 Tbsp. oil (mixture will be crumbly). Rub over both sides of pork chops.
2. In a large skillet, heat remaining 1 Tbsp. oil over medium heat; cook chops for 4-6 minutes per side or until a thermometer reads 145°. Let stand 5 minutes before serving.
1 PORK CHOP 152 cal., 8g fat (1g sat. fat), 14mg chol., 312mg sod., 14g carb. (13g sugars, 0 fiber), 6g pro.

BACON-WRAPPED CHICKEN

Tender chicken becomes extra-special when smothered in a creamy filling and wrapped with bacon strips. It's an easy entree that tastes as good as it looks.
—*MarlaKaye Skinner, Tucson, AZ*

PREP: 25 min. • **BAKE:** 35 min.
MAKES: 6 servings

- 6 boneless skinless chicken breast halves (6 oz. each)
- 1 carton (8 oz.) spreadable chive and onion cream cheese
- 1 Tbsp. butter
- ½ tsp. salt
- 6 bacon strips

1. Preheat oven to 400°. Flatten chicken to ½-in. thickness. Spread 3 Tbsp. cream cheese over each. Dot with butter and sprinkle with salt; roll up. Wrap each with a bacon strip, securing with toothpicks if necessary.

2. Place seam side down in a greased 13x9-in. baking pan. Bake, uncovered, 35-40 minutes or until a thermometer reads 165°. Broil 6 in. from heat for 5 minutes or until bacon is crisp. Remove toothpicks before serving.

1 CHICKEN BREAST HALF 414 cal., 26g fat (12g sat. fat), 142mg chol., 631mg sod., 3g carb. (2g sugars, 0 fiber), 40g pro.

BACON-WRAPPED STUFFED CHICKEN TIPS

What kind of bacon should I use for this recipe? Thin-cut bacon is best for bacon-wrapped recipes—it wraps around the chicken more easily and also cooks more evenly. Thick-cut bacon will work in a pinch, but it won't get as crispy, so you'll miss out on that deliciously crisp outer layer.

What else can I use for filling? If you don't have cream cheese on hand, try using other soft cheeses like goat cheese. Other types of cheese such as mozzarella, feta or cheddar work well as a stuffing too. You can also customize the stuffing by adding herbs or vegetables like spinach or pickled jalapenos.

Why is my chicken still pink after cooking? The chicken may remain slightly pink when it is wrapped in bacon. The nitrates in the bacon could tinge the chicken pink, or the chicken can have a pink hue from a pigment in the meat called myoglobin. As long as the meat (and the stuffing) reach an internal temperature of 165°, it's safe to eat.

How can I make this in advance? A couple of ways. You can prepare each component and flatten the chicken beforehand so it's ready to wrap on the night you cook it. Alternatively, you can stuff and wrap the chicken, then store it in the refrigerator for up to 2 days before cooking it.

BACON-WRAPPED CHICKEN

APRICOT HAM STEAK

APRICOT HAM STEAK

Ham is a versatile main menu item that's a standby with all country cooks. One of the best and easiest ways to serve ham slices is topped with a slightly sweet glaze, like this apricot version.
—Scott Woodward, Shullsburg, WI

TAKES: 10 min.
MAKES: 4 servings

- 2 Tbsp. butter, divided
- 4 fully cooked boneless ham steaks (5 oz. each)
- ½ cup apricot preserves
- 1 Tbsp. cider vinegar
- ¼ tsp. ground ginger
    Dash salt

1. In a large skillet, heat 1 Tbsp. butter over medium heat. Cook ham on both sides until lightly browned and heated through. Remove from pan; keep warm.
2. Add remaining 1 Tbsp. butter and remaining ingredients to pan; cook and stir over medium heat until blended and heated through. Serve over ham.
1 HAM STEAK 299 cal., 11g fat (5g sat. fat), 88mg chol., 1899mg sod., 26g carb. (17g sugars, 0 fiber), 26g pro.
GRILLED APRICOT HAM STEAKS
Melt 1 Tbsp. butter and brush over ham steaks. Grill, covered, over medium heat until lightly browned, 3-5 minutes on each side. Prepare sauce and serve as directed.

CHICKEN & ASIAN SLAW

CHICKEN & ASIAN SLAW

My family goes back to this one-bowl meal again and again. The zing comes from our favorite sesame ginger dressing.
—Melissa Jelinek, Apple Valley, MN

TAKES: 20 min.
MAKES: 4 servings

- 2 cups cubed fresh pineapple
- 2 cups sliced bok choy
- 2 cups shredded red cabbage
- ⅓ cup plus ¼ cup sesame ginger salad dressing, divided
- 4 boneless skinless chicken breast halves (4 oz. each)

1. Preheat broiler. In a large bowl, combine pineapple, bok choy, cabbage and ⅓ cup salad dressing; toss to coat.
2. Place chicken in a 15x10x1-in. baking pan. Brush both sides with remaining ¼ cup salad dressing. Broil 3-4 in. from heat for 4-5 minutes on each side or until a thermometer reads 165°.
3. Divide slaw among 4 bowls. Slice chicken; arrange over slaw. Serve immediately.
1 SERVING 302 cal., 13g fat (3g sat. fat), 63mg chol., 433mg sod., 21g carb. (16g sugars, 2g fiber), 24g pro. **DIABETIC EXCHANGES** 3 lean meat, 1½ fat, 1 starch, 1 vegetable, ½ fruit.

PAN-FRIED SALMON

PAN-FRIED SALMON

Easy, fast and flavorful, this pan-fried salmon is the perfect first step. Pair the fillet with side dishes for a simple, elegant meal, or use it as part of a salad bowl. Any way you use it, it's delicious!
—Taste of Home *Test Kitchen*

TAKES: 15 min.
MAKES: 4 servings

- 4 salmon fillets (6 oz. each)
- ½ tsp. kosher salt
- ¼ tsp. ground pepper
- 2 Tbsp. olive oil

Sprinkle salmon with salt and pepper. Heat oil in a large skillet over medium-high heat; add salmon skin side up and cook 4 minutes. Turn fish and cook until fish flakes easily with a fork, 3-4 minutes longer.

1 FILLET 325 cal., 22g fat (4g sat. fat), 85mg chol., 325mg sod., 0 carb. (0 sugars, 0 fiber), 29g pro. **DIABETIC EXCHANGES** 4 lean meat, 1½ fat.

ONE-POT MAC & CHEESE

This one-pot mac and cheese is a family favorite, and my 3-year-old is always thrilled to see it coming to the dinner table. We love to add sliced smoked sausage to this creamy mac recipe!
—Ashley Lecker, *Green Bay, WI*

PREP: 5 min. • **COOK:** 30 min.
MAKES: 10 servings

- 3½ cups whole milk
- 3 cups water
- 1 pkg. (16 oz.) elbow macaroni
- 4 oz. Velveeta, cubed
- 2 cups shredded sharp cheddar cheese
- ½ tsp. salt
- ½ tsp. coarsely ground pepper

1. In a Dutch oven, combine milk, water and macaroni; bring to a boil over medium heat. Reduce heat and simmer 12-15 minutes or until macaroni is tender and almost all cooking liquid has been absorbed, stirring frequently.
2. Reduce heat to low; stir in cheeses until melted. Season with salt and pepper.

1 CUP 344 cal., 14g fat (8g sat. fat), 42mg chol., 450mg sod., 39g carb. (6g sugars, 2g fiber), 16g pro.

SAVORY ROASTED CHICKEN

When you want an impressive centerpiece for Sunday dinner or a special-occasion meal, you can't go wrong with this golden chicken. The moist, tender meat is enhanced with hints of orange, savory and thyme.
—Taste of Home *Test Kitchen*

- -

PREP: 10 min.
BAKE: 1½ hours + standing
MAKES: 10 servings

1   roasting chicken (6 to 7 lbs.)
1   tsp. onion salt
½   tsp. dried thyme
½   tsp. dried savory
¼   tsp. grated orange zest
¼   tsp. pepper
1   tsp. canola oil

1. Preheat oven to 375°. Place chicken on a rack in a shallow roasting pan. Carefully loosen skin above breast meat. Combine onion salt, thyme, savory, orange zest and pepper; rub half herb mixture under loosened skin. Rub chicken skin with oil; sprinkle with remaining herb mixture.
2. Bake for 1½-2 hours or until a thermometer inserted in thickest part of thigh reads 170°-175°. Let stand for 10-15 minutes. Remove skin before carving. Skim fat and thicken pan juices for gravy if desired.

4 OZ. COOKED CHICKEN 197 cal., 8g fat (2g sat. fat), 86mg chol., 267mg sod., 0 carb. (0 sugars, 0 fiber), 29g pro. **DIABETIC EXCHANGES** 4 lean meat.

HEARTY BEANS & RICE

Filling and fast, this dish has become a favorite in my family. It could be served as a side or a main dish.
—*Barbara Musgrove, Fort Atkinson, WI*

- -

PREP: 10 min. • **COOK:** 25 min.
MAKES: 5 servings

1   lb. lean ground beef (90% lean)
1   can (15 oz.) black beans, rinsed and drained
1   can (14½ oz.) diced tomatoes with mild green chiles, undrained
1⅓   cups frozen corn, thawed
1   cup water
¼   tsp. salt
1½   cups instant brown rice

In a large saucepan, cook beef over medium heat until no longer pink, breaking into crumbles; drain. Stir in beans, tomatoes, corn, water and salt. Bring to a boil. Stir in rice; return to a boil. Reduce heat; cover and simmer for 5 minutes. Remove from heat; let stand, covered, 5 minutes.

1¼ CUPS 376 cal., 9g fat (3g sat. fat), 56mg chol., 647mg sod., 47g carb. (6g sugars, 7g fiber), 26g pro. **DIABETIC EXCHANGES** 3 starch, 3 lean meat, 1 vegetable.

SAVORY ROASTED CHICKEN

LEMON RICOTTA PASTA

This pasta is a perfect weeknight dinner, especially during the spring and summer months because of the bright lemon flavor. It also tastes great topped with a sprinkle of crushed red pepper and basil.
—Taste of Home *Test Kitchen*

- - - - - - - - - - - - - - - - - - - -

TAKES: 20 min.
MAKES: 6 servings

- 12 oz. uncooked spaghetti
- 1 cup whole-milk ricotta cheese
- ¼ cup grated Parmesan cheese
- 1 Tbsp. olive oil
- 2 tsp. grated lemon zest
- ½ tsp. salt
- ¼ tsp. pepper
  Chopped fresh parsley

1. Cook spaghetti according to package directions.
2. In a small bowl, whisk ricotta, Parmesan, oil, lemon zest, salt and pepper. Drain spaghetti, reserving ½ cup cooking liquid. Whisk reserved ½ cup cooking liquid into ricotta mixture.
3. Return drained pasta to pan. Add ricotta mixture and toss to coat. Cook, stirring, over low heat or until heated through. Sprinkle with parsley and additional lemon zest.
1 CUP 305 cal., 8g fat (4g sat. fat), 20mg chol., 310mg sod., 45g carb. (4g sugars, 2g fiber), 13g pro.

SAUSAGE POTATO SKILLET

While I was growing up, I often went home for lunch with my Italian girlfriend. Lunch was always the same—sausage, fried potatoes, green peppers and onions—but I could never get enough of my favorite meal.
—*Amelia Bordas, Springfield, VA*

- - - - - - - - - - - - - - - - - - - -

TAKES: 30 min.
MAKES: 2 servings

- 2 fresh Italian sausage links
- 1 Tbsp. canola oil
- 1 small onion, sliced
- ¼ cup each sliced green and sweet red pepper
- 2 small potatoes, sliced
  Salt and pepper to taste

In a large skillet, brown sausage in oil until a thermometer reads 160°. Add onion and peppers; saute until vegetables are tender. Add potatoes and 2 cups water; bring to a boil. Reduce heat; cover and simmer for 15 minutes or until potatoes are tender. Drain; add salt and pepper.
1 SERVING 416 cal., 22g fat (6g sat. fat), 45mg chol., 544mg sod., 40g carb. (6g sugars, 4g fiber), 15g pro.

SAUSAGE POTATO SKILLET

TACO PUFFS

TACO PUFFS

I got this recipe from a friend years ago and still make these cheesy sandwiches regularly. I serve them for dinner along with a steaming bowl of soup or a fresh green salad. Any leftovers taste even better the next day for lunch.
—*Jan Schmid, Hibbing, MN*

TAKES: 30 min.
MAKES: 8 servings

1 lb. ground beef
½ cup chopped onion
1 envelope taco seasoning
2 tubes (16.3 oz. each) large refrigerated flaky biscuits
2 cups shredded cheddar cheese

1. Preheat oven to 400°. In a large skillet, cook beef and onion over medium heat until meat is no longer pink, 5-7 minutes, breaking into crumbles; drain. Add taco seasoning and prepare according to package directions. Cool slightly.
2. Flatten half the biscuits into 4-in. circles; arrange on greased 15x10x1-in. baking pans. Spoon ¼ cup meat mixture onto each circle; sprinkle each with ¼ cup cheese. Flatten remaining biscuits; place over filling and pinch edges to seal tightly.
3. Bake until crust is golden brown, 12-15 minutes.
FREEZE OPTION Freeze cooled pastries in an airtight container. To use, microwave pastry on high on a microwave-safe plate until heated through.
1 TACO PUFF 574 cal., 28g fat (13g sat. fat), 63mg chol., 1538mg sod., 55g carb. (9g sugars, 2g fiber), 23g pro.

FRENCH ONION
MEAT LOAF

FRENCH ONION MEAT LOAF

As a teacher and farm wife, I'm always looking for quick and easy menu ideas, especially during planting and harvesting seasons. I keep the ingredients on hand for this simple-to-prepare meat loaf.
—*Jan Peters, Chandler, MN*

- -

PREP: 20 min.
BAKE: 1 hour + standing
MAKES: 8 servings

- 3 eggs
- 1 can (10½ oz.) condensed French onion soup, undiluted
- 1 pkg. (6 oz.) beef-flavored stuffing mix, crushed
- 2 lbs. lean ground beef
  Beef gravy, optional

1. Preheat oven to 350°. In a large bowl, combine eggs, soup and stuffing crumbs; mix well. Crumble beef over mixture and mix lightly but thoroughly. Shape into a loaf in a greased 13x9-in. baking pan.
2. Bake, uncovered, for 1 hour or until meat is no longer pink and a thermometer reads 160°. Let stand 10 minutes before slicing. If desired, serve with gravy.
1 SERVING 304 cal., 12g fat (4g sat. fat), 150mg chol., 749mg sod., 18g carb. (4g sugars, 1g fiber), 27g pro.

TEST KITCHEN TIP
If cooking for two, shape the meat mixture into two smaller loaves instead of one large one. Bake for about 45 minutes or until a meat thermometer reads 160°. Enjoy one loaf and freeze the other to reheat another night.

RAVIOLI LASAGNA

RAVIOLI LASAGNA

When you first taste this dish, you'll think it's a from-scratch recipe—but it starts with frozen ravioli!
—*Patricia Smith, Asheboro, NC*

- -

PREP: 25 min. • **BAKE:** 40 min.
MAKES: 8 servings

- 1 lb. ground beef
- 1 jar (28 oz.) spaghetti sauce
- 1 pkg. (25 oz.) frozen sausage or cheese ravioli
- 1½ cups shredded part-skim mozzarella cheese
  Minced fresh basil, optional

1. In a large skillet, cook and crumble beef over medium heat until no longer pink, 5-7 minutes; drain. In a greased 2½-qt. baking dish, layer a third of spaghetti sauce, half the ravioli and beef, and ½ cup cheese; repeat layers. Top with remaining sauce and cheese.
2. Cover and bake at 400° for 40-45 minutes or until heated through. If desired, sprinkle with basil.
1 CUP 438 cal., 18g fat (7g sat. fat), 77mg chol., 1178mg sod., 42g carb. (7g sugars, 5g fiber), 26g pro.
ULTIMATE CHEESE RAVIOLI Replace beef with 2 cups (16 oz.) small-curd 4% cottage cheese; use cheese ravioli. Increase mozzarella to 4 cups (16 oz.). Assemble and bake as directed, layering 2 cups mozzarella each time. Sprinkle ¼ cup grated Parmesan over top. Bake as directed, uncovering during last 10 minutes.

PESTO RAVIOLI

PESTO RAVIOLI

This easy dinner comes together in minutes with just a few ingredients. Instead of plum tomatoes, you could use whole grape tomatoes or drained diced tomatoes. If you'd like a bit of extra flavor and crunch, top with toasted pine nuts or walnuts.
—Taste of Home *Test Kitchen*

TAKES: 20 min.
MAKES: 4 servings

- 1 pkg. (20 oz.) refrigerated cheese ravioli
- 1 Tbsp. olive oil
- 3 cups fresh baby spinach
- ½ cup prepared pesto
- 3 plum tomatoes, chopped
   Optional: Shredded Parmesan cheese and crushed red pepper

1. Cook ravioli according to package directions; drain.
2. Meanwhile, in a large skillet, heat oil over medium-high heat; add spinach. Cook and stir until wilted, 3-5 minutes.
3. Add ravioli and pesto, stirring gently to coat. Stir in tomatoes. If desired, top with Parmesan and red pepper.

ABOUT 6 RAVIOLI 609 cal., 32g fat (8g sat. fat), 77mg chol., 1166mg sod., 62g carb. (4g sugars, 6g fiber), 21g pro.

PESTO RAVIOLI TIPS

Which pesto should I use?
We tested this recipe with prepared basil pesto, but you could try parsley pesto or nut-free pesto too.

What else can I add?
Sauteed shrimp, grilled chicken, roasted asparagus or steamed green beans. For a richer dish, stir heavy cream before serving.

How long will it last? Store leftovers in the refrigerator for 2 to 3 days. Reheat gently on the stovetop or in short intervals in the microwave.

ASIAN SALMON TACOS

This Asian/Mexican fusion dish is ready in minutes—perfect when time is tight! If the salmon begins to stick, add 2-3 tablespoons of water and continue cooking.
—*Marisa Raponi, Vaughan, ON*

TAKES: 20 min.
MAKES: 4 servings

- 1 lb. salmon fillet, skin removed, cut into 1-in. cubes
- 2 Tbsp. hoisin sauce
- 1 Tbsp. olive oil
  Shredded lettuce
- 8 corn tortillas (6 in.), warmed
- 1½ tsp. black sesame seeds
  Mango salsa, optional

1. Toss salmon with hoisin sauce. In a large nonstick skillet, heat oil over medium-high heat. Cook salmon for 3-5 minutes or until it begins to flake easily with a fork, turning gently to brown all sides.
2. Serve salmon and lettuce in tortillas; sprinkle with sesame seeds. If desired, top with salsa.

2 TACOS 335 cal., 16g fat (3g sat. fat), 57mg chol., 208mg sod., 25g carb. (3g sugars, 3g fiber), 22g pro.
DIABETIC EXCHANGES 3 lean meat, 2 starch, 1 fat.

FRIED PORK CHOPS

The subtle flavor of sage and a crunchy panko coating add zest to weeknight pork chops. You can apply this same breading technique to boneless chops or pork medallions too.
—*Lauren Habermehl, Pewaukee, WI*

PREP: 20 min. + resting
COOK: 10 min. • **MAKES:** 4 servings

- 4 bone-in pork loin chops (1-in. thick)
- 1 tsp. rubbed sage
- ¾ tsp. salt, divided
- ¾ tsp. pepper, divided
- ⅓ cup all-purpose flour
- 1 large egg, room temperature, beaten
- 1½ cups panko bread crumbs
- ¼ cup canola oil

1. Remove pork chops from refrigerator and let rest at room temperature for 15-30 minutes. Mix sage, ½ tsp. salt and ½ tsp. pepper; rub onto both sides of pork chops.
2. In a shallow bowl, mix flour and remaining ¼ tsp. salt and ¼ tsp. pepper. Place egg in a separate shallow bowl. Place bread crumbs on a large sheet of parchment. Pat chops dry with a paper towel. Dip chops in flour mixture to coat both sides; shake off excess. Dip in egg, then in crumbs, patting to help coating adhere.
3. In a large cast-iron skillet, heat oil over medium heat. Add pork chops; cook 4-5 minutes on each side or until a thermometer reads 145°. Remove pork chops to a clean serving platter and cover loosely with foil. Let rest at least 5 minutes before serving.

1 PORK CHOP 569 cal., 34g fat (8g sat. fat), 158mg chol., 590mg sod., 21g carb. (1g sugars, 1g fiber), 41g pro.

ASIAN SALMON TACOS

PARMESAN
BAKED COD

PARMESAN BAKED COD

This is a goof-proof way to keep oven-baked cod moist and flavorful. My mom shared this recipe with me years ago and I've loved it ever since.
—Mary Jo Hoppe, Pewaukee, WI

TAKES: 25 min.
MAKES: 4 servings

- 4 cod fillets (4 oz. each)
- ⅔ cup mayonnaise
- 4 green onions, chopped
- ¼ cup grated Parmesan cheese
- 1 tsp. Worcestershire sauce

1. Preheat oven to 400°. Place cod in an 8-in. square baking dish coated with cooking spray. Mix remaining ingredients; spread over fillets.
2. Bake, uncovered, until fish just begins to flake easily with a fork, 15-20 minutes.

1 FILLET 247 cal., 15g fat (2g sat. fat), 57mg chol., 500mg sod., 7g carb. (2g sugars, 0 fiber), 20g pro.
DIABETIC EXCHANGES 3 lean meat, 3 fat.

DID YOU KNOW?

Worcestershire sauce is made of soy sauce, vinegar, garlic, onions, tamarind, molasses and various seasonings. White wine Worcestershire sauce, which is pale in color, is also commercially available, although less common.

MAPLE MUSTARD CHICKEN

MAPLE MUSTARD CHICKEN

My husband loves this chicken dish. It calls for only five ingredients, and we try to have them all on hand for a delicious and cozy dinner anytime.
—Jennifer Seidel, Midland, MI

PREP: 5 min. • **COOK:** 3 hours
MAKES: 6 servings

- 6 boneless skinless chicken breast halves (6 oz. each)
- ½ cup maple syrup
- ⅓ cup stone-ground mustard
- 2 Tbsp. quick-cooking tapioca
  Hot cooked brown rice

Place chicken in a 3-qt. slow cooker. In a small bowl, combine syrup, mustard and tapioca; pour over chicken. Cover and cook on low for 3-4 hours or until tender. Serve with rice.

FREEZE OPTION Cool chicken in sauce. Freeze in airtight freezer containers. To use, partially thaw in refrigerator overnight. Heat through slowly in a covered skillet until a thermometer inserted in chicken reads 165°, stirring occasionally; add broth or water if necessary.

1 CHICKEN BREAST HALF 289 cal., 4g fat (1g sat. fat), 94mg chol., 296mg sod., 24g carb. (17g sugars, 2g fiber), 35g pro.

**EASY CHICKEN PESTO
STUFFED PEPPERS**

EASY CHICKEN PESTO STUFFED PEPPERS

On busy weeknights, I don't want to spend more than 30 minutes preparing dinner, nor do I want to wash a towering pile of dishes. This recipe delivers on both counts without having to sacrifice flavor!
—Olivia Cruz, Greenville, SC

- -

TAKES: 25 min.
MAKES: 4 servings

4 medium sweet yellow
  or orange peppers
1½ cups shredded rotisserie
  chicken
1½ cups cooked brown rice
1 cup prepared pesto
½ cup shredded Havarti cheese
  Fresh basil leaves, optional

1. Preheat broiler. Cut peppers lengthwise in half; remove stems and seeds. Place peppers on a baking sheet, skin side up. Broil 4 in. from heat until skins blister, about 5 minutes. Reduce oven temperature to 350°.
2. Meanwhile, in a large bowl, combine chicken, rice and pesto. When peppers are cool enough to handle, fill with chicken mixture; return to baking sheet. Bake until heated through, about 5 minutes. Sprinkle with cheese; bake until cheese is melted, 3-5 minutes longer. If desired, sprinkle with basil before serving.
2 STUFFED PEPPER HALVES
521 cal., 31g fat (7g sat. fat), 62mg chol., 865mg sod., 33g carb. (7g sugars, 5g fiber), 25g pro.

SAUSAGE SPINACH SALAD

SAUSAGE SPINACH SALAD

Want a fast way to turn a salad into a hearty meal? Add sausage. The mustard dressing also goes well with smoked salmon or chicken.
—*Deborah Williams*, *Peoria, AZ*

TAKES: 20 min.
MAKES: 2 servings

- 4 tsp. olive oil, divided
- 2 fully cooked Italian chicken sausage links (3 oz. each), cut into ¼-in. slices
- ½ medium onion, halved and sliced
- 4 cups fresh baby spinach
- 1½ tsp. balsamic vinegar
- 1 tsp. stone-ground mustard

1. In a large nonstick skillet, heat 1 tsp. oil over medium heat. Add sausage and onion; cook and stir until sausage is lightly browned and onion is crisp-tender.

2. Place spinach in a large bowl. In a small bowl, whisk vinegar, mustard and remaining oil. Drizzle over spinach; toss to coat. Add sausage mixture; serve immediately.

2½ CUPS 244 cal., 16g fat (3g sat. fat), 65mg chol., 581mg sod., 8g carb. (3g sugars, 2g fiber), 17g pro.
DIABETIC EXCHANGES 2 vegetable, 2 lean meat, 2 fat.

★ ★ ★ ★ ★ **READER REVIEW**
"When I made this, instead of serving it as a salad, I added the spinach to the skillet when the sausage and onion were just about fully cooked. I continued sauteing until the spinach cooked down ... it was delicious!"
—MURPHYNJ, TASTEOFHOME.COM

GARLIC HERBED BEEF TENDERLOIN

PARMESAN PORK MEDALLIONS

I was so happy to find this recipe. I have served it countless times for family and friends. It takes very little prep time and adapts easily to serve any number.
—*Angela Ciocca, Saltsburg, PA*

TAKES: 20 min.
MAKES: 2 servings

- ½ lb. pork tenderloin
- 2 Tbsp. seasoned bread crumbs
- 1 Tbsp. grated Parmesan cheese
- ¼ tsp. salt
  Dash pepper
- 2 tsp. canola oil
- ¼ cup sliced onion
- 1 garlic clove, minced

1. Cut pork into 4 slices; flatten to ¼-in. thickness. In a large shallow dish, combine bread crumbs, cheese, salt and pepper. Add pork, 1 slice at a time, and turn to coat.
2. In a large skillet over medium heat, cook pork in oil until meat is no longer pink, 2-3 minutes on each side. Remove and keep warm.
3. Add onion to pan; cook and stir until tender. Add garlic, cook 1 minute longer. Serve with pork.
3 OZ. COOKED PORK 220 cal., 9g fat (2g sat. fat), 65mg chol., 487mg sod., 8g carb. (1g sugars, 1g fiber), 25g pro. **DIABETIC EXCHANGES** 3 lean meat, 1 fat, ½ starch.

GARLIC HERBED BEEF TENDERLOIN

You don't need much seasoning to add flavor to this tender beef roast. The mild blend of rosemary, basil and garlic does the trick.
—*Ruth Andrewson, Leavenworth, WA*

PREP: 5 min.
BAKE: 40 min. + standing
MAKES: 12 servings

- 1 beef tenderloin roast (3 lbs.)
- 2 tsp. olive oil
- 2 garlic cloves, minced
- 1 tsp. salt
- 1 tsp. pepper
- 1 tsp. dried basil
- ¾ tsp. dried rosemary, crushed

1. Tie tenderloin at 2-in. intervals with a kitchen string. Combine oil and garlic; brush over meat. Combine salt, pepper, basil and rosemary; sprinkle evenly over meat. Place on a rack in a shallow roasting pan.
2. Bake, uncovered, at 425° until meat reaches desired doneness (for medium-rare, a thermometer should read 135°; medium, 140°; medium-well, 145°), 40-50 minutes. Let stand for 10 minutes before slicing.
3 OZ. COOKED BEEF 198 cal., 10g fat (4g sat. fat), 78mg chol., 249mg sod., 1g carb. (0 sugars, 0 fiber), 25g pro. **DIABETIC EXCHANGES** 3 lean meat.

PARMESAN PORK
MEDALLIONS

GNOCCHI CHICKEN SKILLET

Potato gnocchi are little dumplings made from a dough of potatoes, flour and sometimes eggs. Look for gnocchi in the pasta, ethnic or frozen section of your grocery store.
—Taste of Home *Test Kitchen*

TAKES: 20 min.
MAKES: 4 servings

- 1   pkg. (16 oz.) potato gnocchi
- 1   lb. ground chicken
- ½   cup chopped onion
- 2   Tbsp. olive oil
- 1   jar (26 oz.) spaghetti sauce
- ¼   tsp. salt
- ¼   to ½ tsp. dried oregano
     Shredded Parmesan cheese, optional

1. Cook gnocchi according to package directions. Meanwhile, in a large cast-iron or other heavy skillet, cook chicken and onion in oil over medium heat until chicken is no longer pink; drain if necessary. Stir in spaghetti sauce, salt and oregano; cook until heated through, 5-10 minutes.
2. Drain gnocchi; gently stir into skillet. If desired, sprinkle with Parmesan cheese.

1½ CUPS 598 cal., 24g fat (6g sat. fat), 88mg chol., 1632mg sod., 66g carb. (19g sugars, 6g fiber), 30g pro.

WEEKDAY BEEF STEW

WEEKDAY BEEF STEW

Beef stew capped with flaky puff pastry adds hearty comfort to the weeknight menu. Make a salad and call your crowd to the table.
—*Daniel Anderson, Kenosha, WI*

TAKES: 30 min.
MAKES: 4 servings

- 1   sheet frozen puff pastry, thawed
- 1   pkg. (15 oz.) refrigerated beef roast au jus
- 2   cans (14½ oz. each) diced tomatoes, undrained
- 1   pkg. (16 oz.) frozen vegetables for stew
- ¾   tsp. pepper
- 2   Tbsp. cornstarch
- 1¼ cups water

1. Preheat oven to 400°. Unfold puff pastry. Using a 4-in. round cookie cutter, cut out 4 circles. Place 2 in. apart on a greased baking sheet. Bake until golden brown, 14-16 minutes.
2. Meanwhile, shred beef with 2 forks; transfer to a large saucepan. Add tomatoes, vegetables and pepper; bring to a boil. In a small bowl, mix cornstarch and water until smooth; stir into beef mixture. Return to a boil, stirring constantly. Cook and stir until thickened, 1-2 minutes.
3. Ladle stew into 4 bowls; top each serving with a pastry round.
1½ CUPS WITH 1 PASTRY ROUND 604 cal., 25g fat (8g sat. fat), 73mg chol., 960mg sod., 65g carb. (10g sugars, 9g fiber), 32g pro.

MUSHROOM PORK TENDERLOIN

This juicy pork tenderloin in a savory gravy is the best you'll ever taste. Prepared with canned soups, it couldn't be easier.
—*Donna Hughes, Rochester, NH*

PREP: 5 min. • **COOK:** 4 hours
MAKES: 6 servings

- 2 pork tenderloins (1 lb. each)
- 1 can (10¾ oz.) condensed cream of mushroom soup, undiluted
- 1 can (10¾ oz.) condensed golden mushroom soup, undiluted
- 1 can (10½ oz.) condensed French onion soup, undiluted
  Hot mashed potatoes, optional

Place pork in a 3-qt. slow cooker. In a bowl, combine soups; stir until smooth. Pour over pork. Cook, covered, on low until pork is tender, 4-5 hours. If desired, serve with mashed potatoes.

4 OZ. COOKED PORK WITH ⅔ CUP SAUCE 269 cal., 10g fat (3g sat. fat), 89mg chol., 951mg sod., 10g carb. (2g sugars, 2g fiber), 32g pro.

MUSHROOM PORK TENDERLOIN

SIMPLE SHRIMP SCAMPI

This is an extremely easy recipe designed to impress your guests. It can serve as an appetizer for a large feast, or a main course for a light meal.
—*Lisa Boehm, Deepwater, MO*

TAKES: 10 min.
MAKES: 6 servings

- ¾ cup butter, cubed
- 2 lbs. uncooked shrimp (31-40 per lb.), peeled and deveined
- 5 tsp. lemon-pepper seasoning
- 2 tsp. garlic powder
  Optional: Lemon wedges and minced parsley

In a large skillet over medium heat, melt butter. Add shrimp, lemon pepper and garlic powder; cook and stir until shrimp turn pink, 5-8 minutes. Transfer to serving dishes. If desired, serve with lemon wedges and parsley.

ABOUT 12 SHRIMP 335 cal., 25g fat (15g sat. fat), 245mg chol., 629mg sod., 2g carb. (0 sugars, 0 fiber), 25g pro.

TEST KITCHEN TIP

You can make this recipe a little more traditional by deglazing the pan with ⅓ cup dry white wine (think pinot grigio or sauvignon blanc) or chicken broth and fresh lemon juice after you remove the shrimp. Simmer until slightly reduced and pour over the shrimp. And don't forget to pass the freshly grated Parm!

CHICKEN WITH ROSEMARY
BUTTER SAUCE

CHICKEN WITH ROSEMARY BUTTER SAUCE

It takes only a few ingredients to make a rich and creamy sauce with a mellow wine flavor. You can substitute your favorite fresh herb for the rosemary if you prefer.
—*Connie McDowell, Greenwood, DE*

- -

TAKES: 25 min.
MAKES: 4 servings

- 4 boneless skinless chicken breast halves (6 oz. each)
- 4 Tbsp. butter, divided
- ½ cup white wine or chicken broth
- ½ cup heavy whipping cream
- 1 Tbsp. minced fresh rosemary

1. In a large skillet over medium heat, cook chicken in 1 Tbsp. butter for 4-5 minutes on each side or until a thermometer reads 165°. Remove and keep warm.
2. Add wine to pan; cook over medium-low heat, stirring to loosen browned bits from pan. Add cream and bring to a boil. Reduce heat; cook and stir until slightly thickened. Stir in rosemary and remaining 3 Tbsp. butter until blended. Serve sauce with chicken.
1 CHICKEN BREAST HALF 411 cal., 26g fat (15g sat. fat), 158mg chol., 183mg sod., 2g carb. (1g sugars, 0 fiber), 35g pro.

TORTELLINI WITH SAUSAGE & MASCARPONE

TORTELLINI WITH SAUSAGE & MASCARPONE

When I crave Italian comfort food on a busy night and don't have a lot of time to cook, this dish comes to the rescue. It's yummy and you can have it on the table in less time than it takes to get takeout.
—*Gerry Vance, Millbrae, CA*

- -

TAKES: 20 min.
MAKES: 6 servings

- 1 pkg. (20 oz.) refrigerated cheese tortellini
- 8 oz. bulk Italian sausage
- 1 jar (24 oz.) pasta sauce with mushrooms
- ½ cup shredded Parmesan cheese
- 1 carton (8 oz.) mascarpone cheese
  Crushed red pepper flakes, optional

1. Prepare tortellini according to package directions. Meanwhile, in a large cast-iron or other heavy skillet, cook sausage over medium heat until no longer pink, 6-8 minutes, breaking into crumbles; drain. Stir in pasta sauce; heat through.
2. Drain tortellini, reserving 1 cup cooking water. Add tortellini to sauce with enough reserved cooking water to reach desired consistency; toss to coat. Stir in Parmesan cheese; dollop with mascarpone cheese. If desired, sprinkle with red pepper flakes.
1 CUP 637 cal., 37g fat (17g sat. fat), 113mg chol., 1040mg sod., 57g carb. (11g sugars, 4g fiber), 24g pro.

GRILLED STEAK BRUSCHETTA SALAD FOR 2

Fire up the grill for this tasty salad. The meat will be done in a snap, leaving you more time to enjoy the summer evening.
—*Devon Delaney, Westport, CT*

- -

TAKES: 25 min.
MAKES: 2 servings

- ½ lb. beef tenderloin steaks (1 in. thick)
- ¼ tsp. salt
- ⅛ tsp. pepper
- 2 slices Italian bread (½ in. thick)
- 1 cup fresh arugula or fresh baby spinach
- ⅓ cup jarred or prepared bruschetta topping
- ⅓ cup blue cheese salad dressing

1. Sprinkle steaks with salt and pepper. Grill, covered, over medium heat until meat reaches desired doneness (for medium-rare, a thermometer should read 135°; medium, 140°; medium-well, 145°), 6-8 minutes on each side. Let stand for 5 minutes.

2. Grill bread, covered, until toasted, 1-2 minutes on each side; place on salad plates.

3. Thinly slice steak; arrange over toast. Top with arugula and bruschetta topping. Drizzle with dressing.

NOTE Look for bruschetta topping in the pasta aisle of your grocer's deli case.

1 SERVING 460 cal., 31g fat (7g sat. fat), 57mg chol., 1183mg sod., 17g carb. (3g sugars, 1g fiber), 28g pro.

WEEKNIGHT RAVIOLI LASAGNA

My husband and I love lasagna, but it's time-consuming to build and we always end up with too much. Using frozen ravioli fixes the problem!
—*Pamela Nicholson, Festus, MO*

- -

PREP: 15 min. • **BAKE:** 45 min.
MAKES: 6 servings

 1 jar (24 oz.) pasta sauce
 1 pkg. (25 oz.) frozen meat
    or cheese ravioli
 3 cups fresh baby spinach
 1½ cups shredded part-skim
    mozzarella cheese

1. Preheat oven to 350°. In a small saucepan, heat sauce 5-7 minutes over medium heat or just until simmering, stirring occasionally.
2. Spread ½ cup sauce into a greased 11x7-in. baking dish. Layer with half the ravioli, 1½ cups spinach, ½ cup cheese and half the remaining sauce; repeat layers. Sprinkle with remaining ½ cup cheese.
3. Bake, uncovered, until edges are bubbly and cheese is melted, 45-50 minutes. Let stand for 5 minutes before serving.
1 CUP 344 cal., 10g fat (5g sat. fat), 26mg chol., 850mg sod., 45g carb. (10g sugars, 5g fiber), 17g pro.
DIABETIC EXCHANGES 3 starch, 2 medium-fat meat.

WEEKNIGHT RAVIOLI LASAGNA

MANGO & GRILLED CHICKEN SALAD

We live in the hot South, and this awesome fruity chicken salad is a weeknight standout. I buy salad greens and add veggies for color and crunch.

—Sheryl Little, Cabot, AR

- -

TAKES: 25 min.
MAKES: 4 servings

  1 lb. chicken tenderloins
  ½ tsp. salt
  ¼ tsp. pepper
SALAD
  6 cups torn mixed salad greens
  ¼ cup raspberry or balsamic vinaigrette
  1 medium mango, peeled and cubed
  1 cup fresh sugar snap peas, halved lengthwise

1. Toss chicken with salt and pepper. On a lightly oiled rack, grill chicken, covered, over medium heat or broil 4 in. from heat on each side until no longer pink, 3-4 minutes. Cut chicken into 1-in. pieces.

2. Divide greens among 4 plates; drizzle with vinaigrette. Top with chicken, mango and peas; serve immediately.

1 SERVING 210 cal., 2g fat (0 sat. fat), 56mg chol., 447mg sod., 22g carb. (16g sugars, 4g fiber), 30g pro.
DIABETIC EXCHANGES 3 lean meat, 2 vegetable, ½ starch, ½ fat.

MANGO & GRILLED CHICKEN SALAD

CRISPY BAKED
CHICKEN THIGHS

BEEF IN MUSHROOM GRAVY

This is one of the best and easiest meals I've ever made. It has only four ingredients, and they all go into the pot at once. The meat is nicely seasoned and makes its own gravy. It tastes wonderful over mashed potatoes.
—*Margery Bryan, Moses Lake, WA*

PREP: 10 min. • **COOK:** 7 hours
MAKES: 6 servings

- 2½ lbs. beef top round steak
- 1 to 2 envelopes onion soup mix
- 1 can (10¾ oz.) condensed cream of mushroom soup, undiluted
- ½ cup water
  Mashed potatoes, optional

Cut steak into 6 serving pieces; place in a 3-qt. slow cooker. Combine soup mix, soup and water; pour over beef. Cook, covered, on low for 7-8 hours or until meat is tender. If desired, serve with mashed potatoes.
FREEZE OPTION Place beef in freezer containers; top with gravy. Cool and freeze. To use, partially thaw in refrigerator overnight. Heat through in a covered saucepan, stirring occasionally; add water if necessary.
1 SERVING 241 cal., 7g fat (2g sat. fat), 87mg chol., 810mg sod., 7g carb. (1g sugars, 1g fiber), 35g pro.

CRISPY BAKED CHICKEN THIGHS

Easy and economical, this meal is one your whole family will enjoy. To save even more time, add potatoes or other vegetables to the pan to roast along with the chicken.
—*Michelle Miller, Bend, OR*

PREP: 10 min. • **BAKE:** 25 min.
MAKES: 6 servings

- 6 bone-in chicken thighs (about 2¼ lbs.)
- 2 Tbsp. olive oil
- 2 tsp. garlic powder
- 2 tsp. minced fresh thyme or ¾ tsp. dried thyme
- 1 tsp. sea salt
- 1 tsp. paprika
- 1 tsp. pepper

1. Preheat oven to 425°. Pat chicken dry with paper towels. Place chicken in 15x10x1-in. baking pan; drizzle with oil. Combine remaining ingredients; rub over chicken.
2. Bake, uncovered, 25-30 minutes or until a thermometer reads 170°-175°. Sprinkle with additional fresh thyme, if desired.
1 CHICKEN THIGH 269 cal., 19g fat (5g sat. fat), 81mg chol., 389mg sod., 1g carb. (0 sugars, 0 fiber), 23g pro.

CABBAGE & NOODLES, PAGE 153

SIDES, SALADS & BREADS

CABBAGE & NOODLES

1. Butter
2. Cabbage
3. Egg Noodles

Plus: Pepper, Salt

LEMON-SCENTED BROCCOLINI

CHEESY SAUSAGE POTATOES

For a satisfying brunch, try these tender potato slices with lots of sausage and cheese. Everyone loves them, and the pan always empties.
—*Linda Hill, Marseilles, IL*

TAKES: 25 min.
MAKES: 10 servings

- 3 lbs. potatoes, peeled and cut into ¼-in. slices
- 1 lb. bulk pork sausage
- 1 medium onion, chopped
- ¼ cup butter, melted
- 2 cups shredded cheddar cheese

1. Place the potatoes in a large saucepan and cover with water. Bring to a boil. Reduce the heat; simmer, uncovered, until tender, 8-10 minutes. Meanwhile, crumble sausage into a large skillet; add onion. Cook over medium heat until the meat is no longer pink; drain if necessary.
2. Drain potatoes; arrange in an ungreased 13x9-in. baking dish. Drizzle with melted butter. Add the sausage mixture; stir gently. Sprinkle with cheddar cheese.
3. Bake, uncovered, at 350° until cheese is melted, 5-7 minutes.
¾ CUP 252 cal., 13g fat (8g sat. fat), 37mg chol., 220mg sod., 26g carb. (2g sugars, 3g fiber), 9g pro.

LEMON-SCENTED BROCCOLINI

Even the most finicky eaters will eagerly eat this vegetable seasoned with lemon pepper, lemon zest and lemon juice. If you prefer, use broccoli instead.
—*Kim Champion, Phoenix, AZ*

TAKES: 30 min.
MAKES: 12 servings

- 2½ lbs. Broccolini or broccoli spears
- 6 Tbsp. butter
- 1 Tbsp. plus 1½ tsp. lemon juice
- 1 Tbsp. lemon-pepper seasoning
- 1 tsp. grated lemon zest
- ¼ tsp. salt

1. In a large saucepan, bring 4 cups water to a boil. Add the Broccolini; cook, uncovered, until just tender, 5-7 minutes. Drain and immediately place Broccolini in ice water. Drain and pat dry.
2. In a large skillet, melt butter. Stir in the lemon juice, lemon pepper, lemon zest and salt. Add the broccolini; toss until heated through.
1 SERVING 90 cal., 6g fat (4g sat. fat), 15mg chol., 232mg sod., 7g carb. (2g sugars, 1g fiber), 3g pro.
DIABETIC EXCHANGES 1 vegetable, 1 fat.

ZESTY BROCCOLINI Cook the Broccolini as directed. Saute 3 minced garlic cloves and 1 tsp. grated fresh ginger in ¼ cup olive oil for 1 minute. Add the Broccolini and ¼ tsp. crushed pepper flakes; saute for 1-2 minutes or until heated through.

CHEESY SAUSAGE POTATOES

MINTY WATERMELON-
CUCUMBER SALAD

MINTY WATERMELON-CUCUMBER SALAD

Capturing the fantastic flavors of summer, this refreshing, beautiful salad will be the talk of any picnic or potluck.
—Roblynn Hunnisett, Guelph, ON

TAKES: 20 min.
MAKES: 16 servings

- 8 cups cubed seedless watermelon
- 2 English cucumbers, halved lengthwise and sliced
- 6 green onions, chopped
- ¼ cup minced fresh mint
- ¼ cup balsamic vinegar
- ¼ cup olive oil
- ½ tsp. salt
- ½ tsp. pepper

In a large bowl, combine the watermelon, cucumbers, green onions and mint. In a small bowl, whisk the remaining ingredients. Pour over salad and toss to coat. Serve immediately, or refrigerate, covered, for up to 2 hours before serving if desired.

¾ CUP 60 cal., 3g fat (0 sat. fat), 0 chol., 78mg sod., 9g carb. (8g sugars, 1g fiber), 1g pro. **DIABETIC EXCHANGES** ½ fruit, ½ fat.

★ ★ ★ ★ ★ **READER REVIEW**

"Very easy and quite tasty. I used white balsamic vinegar to keep the colors vibrant. I halved the recipe with excellent results."

—BARBARA942, TASTEOFHOME.COM

WHOLE WHEAT
REFRIGERATOR ROLLS

WHOLE WHEAT REFRIGERATOR ROLLS

I like to prepare the dough for these rolls in advance and let it rise in the refrigerator. The recipe is easy and versatile.
—*Sharon Mensing, Greenfield, IA*

PREP: 20 min. + rising
BAKE: 10 min. • **MAKES:** 2 dozen

- 2 pkg. (¼ oz. each) active dry yeast
- 2 cups warm water (110° to 115°)
- ½ cup sugar
- 1 large egg, room temperature
- ¼ cup canola oil
- 2 tsp. salt
- 4½ to 5 cups all-purpose flour
- 2 cups whole wheat flour

1. In a large bowl, dissolve yeast in warm water. Add sugar, egg, oil, salt and 3 cups all-purpose flour. Beat on medium speed for 3 minutes. Stir in whole wheat flour and enough of remaining all-purpose flour to make a soft dough.

2. Turn onto a lightly floured surface. Knead until smooth and elastic, 6-8 minutes. Place in a greased bowl, turning once to grease top. Cover and let rise until doubled or cover and refrigerate overnight.

3. Punch down dough; divide into 24 portions. Divide and shape each portion into 3 balls. Place 3 balls in each of the 24 greased muffin cups. Cover and let rise until doubled, about 1 hour for dough prepared the same day or 1-2 hours for refrigerated dough.

4. Bake at 375° until crust is light golden brown, 10-12 minutes. Serve warm.

NOTE If desired, dough may be kept up to 4 days in the refrigerator. Punch down daily.

1 ROLL 159 cal., 3g fat (0 sat. fat), 9mg chol., 200mg sod., 29g carb. (5g sugars, 2g fiber), 4g pro.

ROASTED
BEET WEDGES

ROASTED BEET WEDGES

This recipe makes ordinary beets taste tender and delicious with just a few sweet and good-for-you ingredients. For a milder flavor, try using fresh thyme instead of fresh rosemary.
—Wendy Stenman, Germantown, WI

PREP: 15 min. • **BAKE:** 1 hour
MAKES: 4 servings

- 1 lb. fresh beets (about 3 medium), peeled
- 4 tsp. olive oil
- ½ tsp. kosher salt
- 3 to 5 fresh rosemary sprigs

1. Preheat oven to 400°. Cut each beet into 6 wedges; place in a shallow dish. Add olive oil and salt; toss gently to coat.
2. Cut a piece of heavy-duty foil about 12 in. long; place in a 15x10x1-in. baking pan. Arrange beets on foil; top with rosemary. Fold foil around beets; seal tightly.
3. Bake until tender, about 1 hour. Open foil carefully to allow steam to escape. Discard rosemary sprigs.
3 BEET WEDGES 92 cal., 5g fat (1g sat. fat), 0 chol., 328mg sod., 12g carb. (9g sugars, 3g fiber), 2g pro.
DIABETIC EXCHANGES 1 vegetable, 1 fat.

ROASTED BEETS TIPS

Can I make these ahead of time? You may make these beets a day before and either reheat them in a microwave or serve them cold—they are wonderful tossed in salads with a bit of creamy goat cheese!

Do I have to peel the beets? You don't have to peel beets before you roast them. However, if you decide to leave the skin on, make sure you scrub them extra well to get rid of any residual dirt.

HOMEMADE FRY BREAD

Crispy, doughy and totally delicious, this fry bread is fantastic with nearly any sweet or savory toppings you can think of. We love it with a little butter, a drizzle of honey and a squeeze of lemon.
—*Thelma Tyler, Dragoon, AZ*

PREP: 20 min. + standing
COOK: 15 min. • **MAKES:** 12 servings

- 2   cups all-purpose flour
- ½   cup nonfat dry milk powder
- 3   tsp. baking powder
- ½   tsp. salt
- 4½ tsp. shortening
- ⅔   to ¾ cup water
     Oil for deep-fat frying
     Optional: Butter, honey and fresh lemon juice

1. Combine flour, milk powder, baking powder and salt; cut in shortening until crumbly. Add water gradually, mixing to form a firm ball. Divide dough; shape into 12 balls. Let stand, covered, for 10 minutes. Roll each ball into a 6-in. circle. With a sharp knife, cut a ½-in.-diameter hole in the center of each.
2. In a large cast-iron skillet, heat oil over medium-high heat. Fry dough circles, 1 at a time, until puffed and golden, about 1 minute on each side. Drain on paper towels. Serve warm, with butter, honey and fresh lemon juice if desired.
1 PIECE 124 cal., 5g fat (1g sat. fat), 1mg chol., 234mg sod., 17g carb. (2g sugars, 1g fiber), 3g pro.

CARROT FRITTERS

Crispy and mild flavored, this fun finger food always gets snatched up quickly. If there are any leftovers, they reheat well for a snack the next day.
—*Susan Witt, Fairbury, NE*

TAKES: 30 min.
MAKES: 20 fritters

- 1   cup all-purpose flour
- 1   tsp. salt
- 1   tsp. baking powder
- 2   large eggs, room temperature
- ½   cup 2% milk
- 1   tsp. canola oil
- 3   cups shredded carrots
     Canola oil for frying
     Optional: Fresh chervil or chopped parsley, and ranch salad dressing or sour cream

1. In a large bowl, combine the flour, salt and baking powder. Whisk the eggs, milk and oil; stir into the dry ingredients just until moistened. Fold in carrots.
2. In a large cast-iron or other heavy skillet, heat ¼ in. oil over medium heat. Working in batches, drop batter by 2 tablespoonfuls into the hot oil. Press lightly to flatten. Fry until golden brown, 1-2 minutes on each side, carefully turning once.
3. Drain fritters on paper towels. If desired, top with chervil or chopped parsley and serve with ranch dressing or sour cream.
2 FRITTERS 204 cal., 15g fat (2g sat. fat), 38mg chol., 326mg sod., 13g carb. (2g sugars, 1g fiber), 3g pro.

HOMEMADE FRY BREAD

BOK CHOY TOSS

BOK CHOY TOSS

Chop some fresh veggies, add a gingery bottled dressing and savor this unique salad that's big on flavor and crunch.
—*Andrew McDowell, Lake Villa, IL*

- -

TAKES: 20 min.
MAKES: 10 servings

- 1   head bok choy, thinly sliced
- 3   medium tomatoes, seeded and chopped
- 1   yellow summer squash, quartered and sliced
- ¼   cup orange ginger vinaigrette
- 2   Tbsp. sesame seeds, toasted

In a large bowl, combine the bok choy, tomatoes and squash. Drizzle with dressing and toss to coat. Sprinkle with sesame seeds. Serve immediately.
¾ CUP 47 cal., 2g fat (0 sat. fat), 0 chol., 135mg sod., 6g carb. (4g sugars, 2g fiber), 2g pro. **DIABETIC EXCHANGES** 1 vegetable.

SEA SALT STICKS

When my daughter was in school, her class had a recipe exchange— the kids all brought something to eat to share with the class and included the recipe. She raved about these breadsticks and wanted to make them for the family. These sticks go well with spaghetti. You can even add 2 tablespoons poppy seeds to the flour before mixing.
—*Marina Castle Kelley, Canyon Country, CA*

- -

PREP: 45 min. + rising
BAKE: 20 min.
MAKES: 20 servings

- 1   Tbsp. sugar
- 1   pkg. (¼ oz.) quick-rise yeast
- 1   tsp. sea salt

SEA SALT STICKS

- 3¼ to 3¾ cups all-purpose flour
- 1¼ cups water
- ¼   cup olive oil

TOPPING

- 1   large egg white
- 1   Tbsp. water
      Coarse sea salt

1. Preheat oven to 325°. In a large bowl, mix sugar, yeast, salt and 2 cups flour. In a small saucepan, heat water and oil to 120°-130°; stir into dry ingredients. Stir in enough remaining flour to form a soft dough (dough will be sticky).
2. Turn out onto a floured surface; knead until smooth and elastic, 6-8 minutes. Place in a greased bowl, turning once to grease the top. Cover and let rest 10 minutes.

3. Divide dough into 20 portions. On a lightly floured surface, roll each portion into a 14-in. rope. Place ropes 1 in. apart on greased baking sheets. Cover and let rise in a warm place until almost doubled, 15-20 minutes.
4. Whisk egg white with water; brush over tops of dough. Sprinkle with coarse sea salt. Bake until light brown, 20-25 minutes. Remove from pans to wire racks. Serve warm.
1 BREADSTICK 102 cal., 3g fat (0 sat. fat), 0 chol., 97mg sod., 16g carb. (1g sugars, 1g fiber), 2g pro.

HONEY GARLIC GREEN BEANS

Green beans are wonderful, but they can seem ordinary on their own. Just a couple of extra ingredients give them a sweet and salty attitude.
—*Shannon Dobos, Calgary, AB*

TAKES: 20 min.
MAKES: 8 servings

- 4 Tbsp. honey
- 2 Tbsp. reduced-sodium soy sauce
- 4 garlic cloves, minced
- ¼ tsp. salt
- ¼ tsp. crushed red pepper flakes
- 2 lbs. fresh green beans, trimmed

1. In a bowl, whisk together first 5 ingredients; set aside. In a 6-qt. stockpot, bring 10 cups water to a boil. Add beans in batches; cook, uncovered, just until crisp-tender, 2-3 minutes. Remove beans and immediately drop into ice water. Drain and pat dry.
2. Coat stockpot with cooking spray. Add beans; cook, stirring constantly, over high heat until slightly blistered, 2-3 minutes.
3. Add sauce; continue stirring until beans are coated and the sauce starts to evaporate slightly, 2-3 minutes. Remove from heat.
¾ CUP 72 cal., 0 fat (0 sat. fat), 0 chol., 225mg sod., 18g carb. (12g sugars, 4g fiber), 2g pro. **DIABETIC EXCHANGES** 1 vegetable, ½ starch.

AIR-FRYER PARMESAN BREADED SQUASH

These baked squash slices are beautifully crisp. You don't have to turn the pieces, but keep an eye on them to make sure they don't burn.
—*Debi Mitchell, Flower Mound, TX*

PREP: 15 min.
COOK: 10 min./batch
MAKES: 4 servings

- 4 cups thinly sliced yellow summer squash (3 medium)
- 3 Tbsp. olive oil
- ½ tsp. salt
- ½ tsp. pepper
- ⅛ tsp. cayenne pepper
- ¾ cup panko bread crumbs
- ¾ cup grated Parmesan cheese

1. Preheat air fryer to 350°. Place the squash in a large bowl. Add oil and seasonings; toss to coat.
2. In a shallow bowl, mix the bread crumbs and cheese. Dip squash in crumb mixture to coat both sides, patting to help coating adhere.
3. In batches, arrange squash in a single layer on tray in air-fryer basket. Cook until the squash is tender and coating is golden brown, about 10 minutes.
½ CUP 203 cal., 14g fat (3g sat. fat), 11mg chol., 554mg sod., 13g carb. (4g sugars, 2g fiber), 6g pro. **DIABETIC EXCHANGES** 3 fat, 1 vegetable, ½ starch.

AIR-FRYER PARMESAN BREADED SQUASH

SMASHED
POTATOES

SKILLET CORNBREAD

This skillet bread looks like a puffy pancake but has the easy-to-cut texture of conventional cornbread. It complements everything from chicken to chili.
—*Kathy Teela, Tucson, AZ*

TAKES: 15 min.
MAKES: 8 servings

- ¼ cup all-purpose flour
- ¼ cup cornmeal
- ½ tsp. baking powder
- ¼ tsp. salt
- 1 large egg
- ¼ cup 2% milk
- 4 tsp. canola oil, divided

1. In a small bowl, combine the flour, cornmeal, baking powder and salt. In another small bowl, whisk the egg, milk and 3 tsp. oil; stir into the dry ingredients just until moistened.
2. Heat remaining 1 tsp. oil in a heavy 8-in. skillet over low heat. Pour batter into the hot skillet; cover and cook for 4-5 minutes. Turn and cook 4 minutes longer or until golden brown.
1 PIECE 66 cal., 3g fat (1g sat. fat), 24mg chol., 117mg sod., 7g carb. (0 sugars, 0 fiber), 2g pro.

TEST KITCHEN TIPS
This recipe works best when baked in a cast-iron skillet on the stovetop. If you don't have cast iron, use your favorite large frying pan.

You can add spicy flavor to cornbread by adding diced jalapenos to the batter and a sprinkling of red pepper flakes or herbs. Cornbread is a wonderful canvas for experimentation.

SMASHED POTATOES

I wouldn't dream of making my favorite steak without making these potatoes, too—they're perfect together!
—*Jennifer Shaw, Dorchester, MA*

TAKES: 25 min.
MAKES: 4 servings

- 2 lbs. medium red potatoes (about 7), quartered
- 2 Tbsp. butter
- ¼ cup sour cream
- ¼ cup 2% milk
- ¼ tsp. salt
- ¼ tsp. pepper
  Pinch ground nutmeg

1. Place potatoes and water to cover in a large saucepan; bring to a boil. Reduce heat; cook, uncovered, until tender, 10-15 minutes.
2. Drain; return to pan. Mash potatoes to desired consistency; stir in remaining ingredients.
1 CUP 254 cal., 10g fat (6g sat. fat), 20mg chol., 219mg sod., 38g carb. (4g sugars, 4g fiber), 5g pro.

POTATO KUGEL

The secret to keeping potatoes their whitest is to shred them alternatively with onions in your food processor or box grater.
—*Ellen Ruzinsky,*
Yorktown Heights, NY

PREP: 20 min. • **BAKE:** 40 min.
MAKES: 12 servings

- 2 large eggs
- ¼ cup matzo meal
- 2 tsp. kosher salt
  Dash pepper
- 6 large potatoes (about 4¾ lbs.), peeled
- 1 large onion, cut into 6 wedges
- ¼ cup canola oil

1. Preheat oven to 375°. In a large bowl, whisk eggs, matzo meal, salt and pepper.
2. In a food processor fitted with the grating attachment, alternately grate potatoes and onion. Add to egg mixture; toss to coat. In a small saucepan, heat oil over medium heat until warmed. Stir into potato mixture. Transfer to a greased 13x9-in. baking dish. Bake 40-50 minutes or until golden brown.
1 SERVING 210 cal., 6g fat (1g sat. fat), 35mg chol., 515mg sod., 36g carb. (3g sugars, 3g fiber), 5g pro.

TEST KITCHEN TIP
Russet potatoes are the best choice for potato kugel as they best withstand the baking time. Red and gold potatoes are softer and will become very creamy in this recipe without achieving the desirable crispy top.

QUINOA WITH
PEAS & ONION

QUINOA WITH PEAS & ONION

Even picky eaters will love this protein-packed dish. If you have freshly shelled peas on hand, substitute them for the frozen.
—*Lori Panarella, Phoenixville, PA*

PREP: 30 min. • **COOK:** 15 min.
MAKES: 6 servings

- 2 cups water
- 1 cup quinoa, rinsed
- 1 small onion, chopped
- 1 Tbsp. olive oil
- 1½ cups frozen peas
- ½ tsp. salt
- ¼ tsp. pepper
- 2 Tbsp. chopped walnuts

1. In a large saucepan, bring water to a boil. Add quinoa. Reduce heat; cover and simmer until water is absorbed, 12-15 minutes. Remove from the heat; fluff with a fork.
2. Meanwhile, in a large cast-iron or other heavy skillet, saute onion in oil until tender, 2-3 minutes. Add the peas; cook and stir until heated through. Stir in the cooked quinoa, salt and pepper. Sprinkle with walnuts.
⅔ CUP 174 cal., 6g fat (1g sat. fat), 0 chol., 244mg sod., 26g carb. (2g sugars, 4g fiber), 6g pro. **DIABETIC EXCHANGES** 1½ starch, 1 fat.
HOT & ZESTY QUINOA Omit peas, salt, pepper and walnuts. Prepare quinoa as directed. Saute onion in oil until tender. Add 3 minced garlic cloves; cook 1 minute. Add 2 cans (10 oz. each) tomatoes with green chilies. Bring to a boil over medium heat. Reduce heat; simmer, uncovered, 10 minutes. Stir in quinoa and ¼ cup chopped marinated quartered artichoke hearts; heat through. Sprinkle with 2 Tbsp. grated Parmesan cheese.

OLD-FASHIONED BROWN BREAD

This chewy bread boasts a slightly sweet flavor that will transport you back to the old days.
—*Patricia Donnelly,*
Kings Landing, NB

- -

PREP: 20 min. + rising
BAKE: 35 min. + cooling
MAKES: 2 loaves (16 pieces each)

2⅓ cups boiling water
1 cup old-fashioned oats
½ cup butter, cubed
⅓ cup molasses
5½ to 6½ cups all-purpose flour
5 tsp. active dry yeast
2 tsp. salt

1. In a large bowl, pour boiling water over oats. Stir in butter and molasses. Let stand until mixture cools to 110°-115°; stir occasionally.
2. In a second bowl, combine 3½ cups flour, yeast and salt. Beat in oat mixture until blended. Stir in enough remaining flour to form a soft dough.
3. Turn the dough onto a floured surface; knead until smooth and elastic, about 6-8 minutes. Place in a greased bowl, turning once to grease the top. Cover and let rise in a warm place until doubled, about 1 hour.
4. Punch dough down. Turn onto a lightly floured surface; divide in half. Shape into loaves. Place in 2 greased 9x5-in. loaf pans. Cover and let rise until doubled, about 30 minutes. Preheat oven to 375°.
5. Bake 35-40 minutes or until golden brown. Remove from pans to wire racks to cool.
1 PIECE 124 cal., 3g fat (2g sat. fat), 8mg chol., 170mg sod., 21g carb. (2g sugars, 1g fiber), 3g pro.

OLD-FASHIONED BROWN BREAD

CAPRESE SALAD

GARLIC KNOTTED ROLLS

Using frozen yeast dough is an easy way to make homemade rolls. The cute knots add a special touch to any menu.
—*Kathy Harding, Richmond, MO*

- -

PREP: 15 min. + rising
BAKE: 15 min. • **MAKES:** 10 rolls

- 1 loaf (1 lb.) frozen bread dough, thawed
- 1½ tsp. dried minced onion
- 3 Tbsp. butter
- 4 garlic cloves, minced
- ⅛ tsp. salt
- 1 large egg, beaten
  Poppy seeds, optional

1. Pat out the dough on a work surface; sprinkle with minced onion and knead until combined. Divide dough in half. Shape each half into 5 balls. To form knots, roll each ball into a 10-in. rope; tie into a knot. Tuck ends under. Place rolls 2 in. apart on a greased baking sheet.
2. In a small skillet, melt butter over medium heat. Add garlic and salt; cook and stir for 1-2 minutes. Brush over rolls. Cover and let rise until doubled, about 30 minutes. Preheat oven to 375°.
3. Brush the roll tops with egg, sprinkle with poppy seeds if desired. Bake rolls until golden brown, 15-20 minutes.
1 ROLL 168 cal., 6g fat (2g sat. fat), 30mg chol., 315mg sod., 22g carb. (2g sugars, 2g fiber), 5g pro.

CAPRESE SALAD

My husband and I love Caprese salad, but not the high prices we have to pay for it in restaurants. So we created our own version which tastes incredibly close, if not better, than any restaurant version we've tried.
—*Melissa Pearson, Sandy, UT*

- -

TAKES: 15 min.
MAKES: 4 servings

- 4 medium tomatoes, sliced
- ½ lb. fresh mozzarella cheese, sliced
- ¼ cup fresh basil leaves

BALSAMIC VINAIGRETTE
- 2 Tbsp. olive oil
- 2 Tbsp. balsamic vinegar
- 1 tsp. ground mustard
- ⅛ tsp. salt
- ⅛ tsp. pepper

Arrange tomatoes, cheese and basil on a serving platter. Whisk vinaigrette ingredients; drizzle over salad. If desired, sprinkle with additional salt and pepper.
1 SERVING 256 cal., 19g fat (9g sat. fat), 45mg chol., 161mg sod., 8g carb. (6g sugars, 2g fiber), 11g pro.

GARLIC
KNOTTED ROLLS

SWEET CANDIED
CARROTS

SWEET CANDIED CARROTS

These tender, vibrant carrots have a buttery glaze and a mild sweetness. It's a simple dish but it sure makes carrots seem special!
—P. Lauren Fay-Neri, Syracuse, NY

TAKES: 30 min.
MAKES: 8 servings

- 2 lbs. carrots, sliced
- ¼ cup butter
- ¼ cup packed brown sugar
- ¼ tsp. salt
- ⅛ tsp. white pepper
   Minced fresh parsley,
   optional

1. Place the carrots in a large saucepan; add 1 in. water. Bring to a boil. Reduce heat; cover and simmer for 8-10 minutes or until crisp-tender. Drain and set aside.
2. In the same pan, combine the butter, brown sugar, salt and pepper; cook and stir until butter is melted. Return carrots to the pan; cook and stir over medium heat for 5 minutes or until glazed. If desired, sprinkle with parsley.
½ CUP 125 cal., 6g fat (4g sat. fat), 15mg chol., 174mg sod., 18g carb. (14g sugars, 3g fiber), 1g pro.

SWEET CANDIED CARROTS TIPS

How should I store candied carrots? Like other carrot dishes, these last 3-5 days when stored in the fridge in an airtight container.

Can I make this dish ahead of time? You can precook the carrots, then add the brown sugar candy coating before serving.

How else can I cook candied carrots? You can cook the carrots in a slow or pressure cooker and then glaze them on the stovetop.

CHEESY ZUCCHINI CASSEROLE

Tender zucchini gets pleasant flavor from a cheesy sauce and cracker-crumb topping in this fast-to-fix side dish.
—*Kathi Grenier, Auburn, ME*

TAKES: 30 min.
MAKES: 6 servings

2½ lbs. zucchini, cubed
1 cup diced Velveeta
2 Tbsp. butter
½ tsp. salt
⅛ tsp. pepper
⅓ cup crushed saltines (about 10 crackers)

1. Preheat the oven to 400°. Place zucchini in a saucepan and cover with water; cook over medium heat until tender, about 8 minutes. Drain well. Add Velveeta, butter, salt and pepper; stir until the cheese is melted.
2. Transfer mixture to a greased shallow 1½-qt. baking dish. Sprinkle with cracker crumbs. Bake, uncovered, until lightly browned, 10-15 minutes.

1 CUP 136 cal., 9g fat (5g sat. fat), 22mg chol., 508mg sod., 9g carb. (5g sugars, 2g fiber), 6g pro.

CRISPY BAKED ONION RINGS

These crispy, lightly browned rings are a healthy alternative to the deep-fried version. Thyme and paprika enhance flavor of the tender onions.
—*Della Stamp, Long Beach, CA*

PREP: 15 min. + soaking
BAKE: 20 min. • **MAKES:** 4 servings

1 lb. sweet onions
3 large egg whites
1 cup dry bread crumbs
2 tsp. dried thyme
1 tsp. salt
1 tsp. paprika
¼ tsp. pepper

1. Cut onions into ½-in. slices; separate into rings and place in a bowl. Cover with ice water; soak for 30 minutes. Drain.
2. In a small bowl, beat the egg whites until foamy. In a shallow dish, combine the bread crumbs, thyme, salt, paprika and pepper. Dip a third of the onions into the egg whites and then add rings, a few at a time, to the crumb mixture; turn to coat. Place the rings on a baking sheet coated with cooking spray.
3. Repeat with remaining onions and crumb mixture. Bake at 400° for 20 minutes or until lightly browned and crisp.

1 SERVING 159 cal., 2g fat (0 sat. fat), 0 chol., 838mg sod., 29g carb. (8g sugars, 3g fiber), 7g pro.

CHEESY ZUCCHINI CASSEROLE

LEEK POTATO PANCAKES

LEEK POTATO PANCAKES

I received this recipe from my great-grandmother. She brought it over from England, where her family enjoyed leeks immensely during the fall and winter.
—*Suzanne Kesel, Cohocton, NY*

- -

PREP: 30 min. + chilling
COOK: 5 min./batch
MAKES: 6 servings

- ½ lb. russet potatoes, peeled and quartered (about 1 large)
- 2 lbs. medium leeks (white portion only), thinly sliced
- 4 large eggs, lightly beaten
- ½ cup dry bread crumbs
- ⅓ cup grated Parmesan cheese
- 1 tsp. salt
- ¼ tsp. pepper
- ¼ cup canola oil, divided
  Optional: Sour cream, apple sauce and chopped chives

1. Place the potato quarters in a large saucepan and cover with water. Bring to a boil. Reduce heat; cover and cook for 15-20 minutes or until tender, adding the leeks during the last 3 minutes. Drain.
2. Transfer potatoes and leeks to a large bowl; mash with the eggs, bread crumbs, cheese, salt and pepper. Cover and refrigerate for 1 hour.
3. Heat 1 Tbsp. oil in a large cast-iron or other heavy skillet over medium heat. Drop batter by ¼ cupfuls into oil. Fry in batches until golden brown on both sides, using remaining oil as needed.
4. Drain the pancakes on paper towels. If desired, serve with sour cream, apple sauce and top with chopped chives.
2 PANCAKES 340 cal., 18g fat (4g sat. fat), 131mg chol., 623mg sod., 37g carb. (7g sugars, 4g fiber), 10g pro.

CREAMY POLENTA

CREAMY POLENTA

Serve this hearty side with roasted chicken or grilled pork instead of potatoes or rice. Dress up the polenta by topping with sauteed mushrooms, onions and spinach.
—Taste of Home *Test Kitchen*

- -

TAKES: 25 min.
MAKES: 4 servings

- 4 cups water
- ¾ tsp. salt
- 1 cup yellow cornmeal
- 2 Tbsp. butter
- ½ cup grated Parmesan cheese, optional

1. In a large heavy saucepan, bring water and salt to a boil.
2. Reduce heat to a gentle boil; slowly whisk in cornmeal. Cook and stir with a wooden spoon for 15-20 minutes or until polenta is thickened and pulls away cleanly from the side of the pan. Stir in butter until melted. If desired, stir in Parmesan cheese.

1 CUP 196 cal., 6g fat (4g sat. fat), 15mg chol., 491mg sod., 31g carb. (1g sugars, 2g fiber), 3g pro.
DIABETIC EXCHANGES 2 starch, 1½ fat.

TRADITIONAL PITA BREAD

My husband taught me how to make this pita bread when we were first dating. He always has his eye out for good recipes!
—Lynne Hartke, Chandler, AZ

- -

PREP: 20 min. + rising
BAKE: 5 min.
MAKES: 6 pita breads

- 1 pkg. (¼ oz.) active dry yeast
- 1¼ cups warm water (110° to 115°)
- 2 tsp. salt
- 3 to 3½ cups all-purpose flour

1. In a large bowl, dissolve yeast in warm water. Stir in salt and enough flour to form a soft dough. Turn onto a floured surface; knead until smooth and elastic, 6-8 minutes. Do not let rise.
2. Divide dough into 6 pieces; knead each piece for 1 minute, then roll into a 5-in. circle. Cover and let rise in a warm place until doubled, about 45 minutes. Preheat oven to 500°.
3. Place upside down on greased baking sheets. Bake until puffed and lightly browned, 5-10 minutes. Remove from pans to wire racks to cool.

1 PITA BREAD 231 cal., 1g fat (0 sat. fat), 0 chol., 789mg sod., 48g carb. (0 sugars, 2g fiber), 7g pro.

HOMEMADE PITA BREAD TIPS

Why is my pita bread not puffing up? Homemade pita bread depends on super high heat to activate steam in the dough. Allow for plenty of time to preheat your oven, and use an oven thermometer to make sure the oven has heated to the right temperature before you put your bread in.

How do you make pockets in pita bread? The pockets in pita bread occur when the water in the dough quickly turns to steam, forcing the bread to expand. To help encourage these pockets, roll the dough thinly so the heat can hit the center of the dough quickly and force the rise. After rolling out your pitas, be careful not to tear the dough, which could keep it from fully expanding. Finally, keep your pitas from drying out by wrapping them in a clean kitchen towel after you take them out of the oven.

What goes well with pita bread? Pita bread, with its unique pocket, makes fabulous sandwiches. It's also wonderful paired with hummus or vegetable dips, or baked into pita chips as appetizers or snacks. You can spice up your pita bread by adding a little bit of za'atar or garam masala when you stir in the salt and flour.

GREAT
GARLIC BREAD

GREAT GARLIC BREAD

This tasty garlic bread topped with cheese adds wow to any pasta dish.
—Taste of Home *Test Kitchen*

- -

TAKES: 15 min.
MAKES: 8 servings

- ½ cup butter, melted
- ¼ cup grated Romano cheese
- 4 garlic cloves, minced
- 1 loaf (1 lb.) French bread, halved lengthwise
- 2 Tbsp. minced fresh parsley

1. Preheat the oven to 350°. In a small bowl, mix butter, cheese and garlic; brush over cut sides of bread. Place on a baking sheet, cut sides up. Sprinkle with minced parsley.
2. Bake 7-9 minutes or until light golden brown. Cut into pieces; serve warm.
1 PIECE 283 cal., 14g fat (8g sat. fat), 34mg chol., 457mg sod., 33g carb. (1g sugars, 1g fiber), 8g pro.

★ ★ ★ ★ ★ **READER REVIEW**

"This is the recipe I've been using for years. It is a simple garlic bread that is always a hit."
—RANDCBRUNS, TASTEOFHOME.COM

CABBAGE & NOODLES

CABBAGE & NOODLES

The contrast between the mild, tender noodles and the subtle tang of just-softened cabbage makes this deceptively simple side dish a winner.
—Jeanie Castor, Decatur, IL

- -

TAKES: 30 min.
MAKES: 6 servings

- 3 Tbsp. butter
- ½ medium head cabbage, thinly sliced
- 2 cups uncooked wide egg noodles
- ½ tsp. salt
- ⅛ tsp. pepper

1. In a large skillet, melt the butter over medium heat. Add cabbage; cover and cook on low until tender, about 20 minutes, stirring occasionally.
2. Meanwhile, cook egg noodles according to package directions; drain. Stir into skillet. Add salt and pepper; heat through.
¾ CUP 70 cal., 6g fat (4g sat. fat), 15mg chol., 158mg sod., 4g carb. (2g sugars, 2g fiber), 1g pro.
DIABETIC EXCHANGES 1 vegetable, 1 fat.

AIR-FRYER SWEET POTATO FRIES

AIR-FRYER SWEET POTATO FRIES

I can never get enough of sweet potato fries! Even though my grocery store sells them in the frozen foods section, I still love to pull sweet potatoes out of my garden and slice them up fresh!
—*Amber Massey, Argyle, TX*

TAKES: 20 min.
MAKES: 4 servings

- 2 large sweet potatoes, cut into thin strips
- 2 Tbsp. canola oil
- 1 tsp. garlic powder
- 1 tsp. paprika
- 1 tsp. kosher salt
- ¼ tsp. cayenne pepper

Preheat air fryer to 400°. Combine all ingredients; toss to coat. Place strips on greased tray in air-fryer basket. Cook until lightly browned, 10-12 minutes, stirring once. Serve immediately.

1 SERVING 243 cal., 7g fat (1g sat. fat), 0 chol., 498mg sod., 43g carb. (17g sugars, 5g fiber), 3g pro.

AIR-FRYER SWEET POTATO FRIES TIPS

What if I don't have an air fryer? You can also make these in an oven—prepare as directed, then spread in a single layer on 2 baking sheets. Bake at 425° until crisp, 35-40 minutes.

What goes well with these fries? The classic burger and fries combo is terrific, but don't forget other pub fare such as fried fish. For healthier options, pair sweet potato fries with grilled chicken or seafood and sheet pan suppers.

CHEESY GRITS

BIBB LETTUCE WITH ROASTED RED ONIONS

Forget boring tossed salads! This side will have your guests asking for the recipe. Top with bacon, or substitute feta for the Gorgonzola for a change of taste.
—*Josh Carter, Birmingham, AL*

PREP: 25 min. • **BAKE:** 20 min.
MAKES: 8 servings

- 2 medium red onions, cut into ¼-in. wedges
- 1 Tbsp. olive oil
- ⅛ tsp. salt
- ⅛ tsp. pepper
- 1⅓ cups balsamic vinegar
- 6 Tbsp. orange juice
- 4 heads Boston or Bibb lettuce, halved lengthwise
- ½ cup crumbled Gorgonzola cheese
  Toasted chopped walnuts, optional

1. Preheat oven to 400°. Place onions on a foil-lined baking sheet. Drizzle with oil. Sprinkle with salt and pepper; toss to coat. Roast until tender, 20-25 minutes, stirring occasionally.
2. In a small saucepan, combine vinegar and juice. Bring to a boil; cook until reduced by half, 8-10 minutes.
3. Top lettuce halves with roasted onions. Drizzle with sauce and top with cheese. Sprinkle with additional black pepper and, if desired, chopped walnuts.
1 SERVING 101 cal., 4g fat (2g sat. fat), 6mg chol., 135mg sod., 15g carb. (13g sugars, 1g fiber), 2g pro.
DIABETIC EXCHANGES 2 vegetable, 1 fat.

CHEESY GRITS

As a comfy side dish, grits have terrific potential but sometimes need a flavor boost. For the add-ins, try red pepper flakes, fresh rosemary or crushed garlic.
—*Paula Hughes, Birmingham, AL*

TAKES: 25 min.
MAKES: 8 servings

- 2 cups 2% milk
- 1 cup chicken or vegetable broth
- 1 cup water
- 1 tsp. salt
- 1 cup uncooked old-fashioned grits
- 2 to 3 cups shredded sharp cheddar or Monterey Jack cheese
  Pepper and additional salt to taste

1. Combine the milk, broth and water in a large saucepan; bring to a boil. Add salt. Whisk in grits; reduce heat to low. Cook, stirring frequently, until creamy, 15-20 minutes.
2. Stir in cheese until melted. Season with the pepper and additional salt to taste.
½ CUP 225 cal., 11g fat (6g sat. fat), 34mg chol., 629mg sod., 20g carb. (3g sugars, 1g fiber), 10g pro.

SIMPLE ROAST BRUSSELS SPROUTS

Oven temps vary, so keep an eye on these Brussels sprouts to make sure they get crisp but don't burn. Feel free to toss in some fresh herbs for variety.
—*Karen Keefe, Phoenix, AZ*

PREP: 10 min. • **COOK:** 20 min.
MAKES: 6 servings

2 lbs. Brussels sprouts, halved
6 bacon strips, chopped
2 Tbsp. olive oil
½ tsp. kosher salt
½ tsp. pepper
2 Tbsp. balsamic glaze

Preheat oven to 450°. In a large bowl, toss Brussels sprouts, bacon, oil, salt and pepper. Transfer to a 15x10x1-in. baking sheet. Roast, stirring halfway through cooking, until sprouts are tender and lightly browned, 20-25 minutes. Drizzle with the balsamic glaze; serve warm.
¾ CUP 227 cal., 16g fat (4g sat. fat), 18mg chol., 381mg sod., 16g carb. (5g sugars, 5g fiber), 8g pro.

TEST KITCHEN TIP

Premade balsamic glaze is available in markets—it's usually shelved near the vinegars and salad dressings—but it's easy to make at home. To make your own balsamic glaze, also known as balsamic reduction, simmer balsamic vinegar over medium heat with either sugar or honey until it thickens.

TARRAGON ASPARAGUS SALAD

TARRAGON ASPARAGUS SALAD

I love asparagus, and I love it even more when drizzled with my light, lemony vinaigrette dressing with a touch of tarragon. It's perfect as a side for fresh spring meals.
—*Linda Lacek, Winter Park, FL*

PREP: 15 min. + chilling
COOK: 5 min. • **MAKES:** 4 servings

2 Tbsp. lemon juice
2 Tbsp. olive oil
1 tsp. minced fresh tarragon or ¼ tsp. dried tarragon
1 garlic clove, minced
½ tsp. Dijon mustard
¼ tsp. pepper
Dash salt
1 lb. fresh asparagus, cut into 2-in. pieces

1. Place the first 7 ingredients in a jar with a tight-fitting lid; shake well. Refrigerate at least 1 hour.
2. In a large skillet, bring ½ in. water to a boil. Add asparagus; cook, covered, until crisp-tender, 1-3 minutes. Remove asparagus and immediately drop into ice water. Drain and pat dry. Refrigerate, covered, until serving.
3. To serve, shake dressing again. Spoon over asparagus.
1 SERVING 77 cal., 7g fat (1g sat. fat), 0 chol., 387mg sod., 3g carb. (1g sugars, 1g fiber), 2g pro. **DIABETIC EXCHANGES** 1½ fat, 1 vegetable.

SIMPLE BISCUITS

It's so easy to whip up a batch of these biscuits to serve with breakfast or dinner. The dough is easy to work with, so there's no need for a rolling pin—just pat to the right thickness. The key is not to overwork the dough.
—Taste of Home *Test Kitchen*

- -

TAKES: 25 min.
MAKES: 15 biscuits

2 cups all-purpose flour
3 tsp. baking powder
1 tsp. salt
⅓ cup cold butter, cubed
⅔ cup 2% milk

1. Preheat the oven to 450°. In a large bowl, whisk flour, baking powder and salt. Cut in butter until mixture resembles coarse crumbs. Add milk; stir just until moistened.
2. Turn onto a lightly floured surface; knead gently 8-10 times. Pat dough to ½-in. thickness. Cut with a 2½-in. biscuit cutter.
3. Place biscuits 1 in. apart on an ungreased baking sheet. Bake until golden brown, 10-15 minutes. Serve warm.
1 BISCUIT 153 cal., 7g fat (4g sat. fat), 18mg chol., 437mg sod., 20g carb. (1g sugars, 1g fiber), 3g pro.

★ ★ ★ ★ ★ **READER REVIEW**

"I have used this recipe twice and my results have been excellent. Over 2 inches high, fluffy and yummy! Thank you for such an easy recipe!"
—DIANA4709, TASTEOFHOME.COM

SIMPLE BISCUITS

CREAMY
CAULIFLOWER RICE

CREAMY CAULIFLOWER RICE

What began as a quick-fix dish has become a staple in our house. It's an amazing way to add veggies to a meal, and it's a nice change from traditional cauliflower.
—Caresse Caton, Mobile, AL

- -

TAKES: 30 min.
MAKES: 10 servings

3 cups uncooked long grain rice
3 cups frozen cauliflower, thawed
6 cups reduced-sodium chicken broth
6 oz. cream cheese, cubed
¾ tsp. salt
¼ tsp. pepper

1. In a large saucepan, combine rice, cauliflower and broth; bring to a boil. Reduce heat; simmer, covered, 15-20 minutes or until the liquid is absorbed and rice is tender.

2. Remove from heat. Add cream cheese, salt and pepper; stir until melted.

¾ CUP 301 cal., 6g fat (4g sat. fat), 17mg chol., 584mg sod., 52g carb. (2g sugars, 2g fiber), 8g pro.

EASY POPOVERS

Popovers have a brown crisp exterior with an almost hollow interior. As they bake, the heat causes the liquid in the batter to turn to steam, making the batter pop up. After baking, prick the tops to let the steam escape.
—Lourdes Dewick, Fort Lauderdale, FL

PREP: 20 min. • **BAKE:** 45 min.
MAKES: 6 servings

1 Tbsp. shortening
2 large eggs, room temperature
1 cup whole milk
1 Tbsp. butter, melted
1 cup all-purpose flour
½ tsp. salt

1. Using ½ tsp. shortening for each cup, grease the bottoms and sides of six 6-oz. custard cups or the cups of a popover pan. If using custard cups, place on a 15x10x1-in. baking pan.

2. In a small bowl, beat eggs; blend in milk and butter. Beat in flour and salt until smooth (do not overbeat).

3. Fill cups half full. Bake at 450° for 15 minutes. Reduce heat to 350°; bake until very firm, about 30 minutes longer. Remove from oven and prick each popover to allow steam to escape. Serve immediately.

1 POPOVER 160 cal., 7g fat (3g sat. fat), 71mg chol., 253mg sod., 18g carb. (2g sugars, 1g fiber), 6g pro.

EASY POPOVERS

POPOVERS TIPS

Why didn't my popovers puff up? The secret to puffy popovers lies in the batter. It should be thin; take special care not to over-mix. A wet batter will steam up in the hot oven, causing a good rise in the dough. Make sure your oven is fully heated to 450°—the initial blast of hot air will jump-start the puffing. Lastly, make sure you keep your oven door closed during the entire baking process!

Can I use a muffin tin to make popovers? You can! They won't be quite as tall as popovers baked in a traditional popover pan, but they'll still bake up and taste just the same.

What can I serve with popovers? Popovers are delicious spread with butter and jam or drizzled with honey and served with tea as an afternoon snack. As part of a meal, popovers can be served with pretty much anything, but they are wonderful vehicles for soaking up rich gravy. Try them with beef stew, pot roast or roast beef.

GIANT SOFT PRETZELS

GIANT SOFT PRETZELS

My husband, friends and family love these soft chewy pretzels. Let your machine mix the dough, then all you have to do is shape and bake these fun snacks.
—*Sherry Peterson, Fort Collins, CO*

- -

PREP: 20 min. + rising
BAKE: 10 min. • **MAKES:** 8 pretzels

- 1   cup plus 2 Tbsp. water (70° to 80°), divided
- 3   cups all-purpose flour
- 3   Tbsp. brown sugar
- 1½ tsp. active dry yeast
- 2   qt. water
- ½   cup baking soda
    Coarse salt

1. In a bread machine pan, place 1 cup water and the next 3 ingredients in order suggested by the manufacturer. Select dough setting. Check dough after 5 minutes of mixing; add 1–2 Tbsp. water or flour if needed.
2. When the cycle is completed, turn dough onto a lightly floured surface. Divide dough into 8 balls. Roll each into a 20-in. rope; form into pretzel shape.
3. Preheat oven to 425°. In a large saucepan, bring 2 qt. water and the baking soda to a boil. Drop the pretzels into boiling water, 2 at a time; boil for 10-15 seconds. Remove with a slotted spoon; drain on paper towels.
4. Place pretzels on greased baking sheets. Bake until golden brown, 8-10 minutes. Spritz or lightly brush with the remaining 2 Tbsp. water. Sprinkle with salt.
1 PRETZEL 193 cal., 1g fat (0 sat. fat), 0 chol., 380mg sod., 41g carb. (5g sugars, 1g fiber), 5g pro.

BACON PEA SALAD

BACON PEA SALAD

My husband absolutely loves peas. My middle son isn't the biggest fan, but he loves bacon. So I decided to combine the two ingredients, and it was perfect! This salad is an awesome side dish, especially for barbecues.
—*Angela Lively, Conroe, TX*

- -

PREP: 10 min. + chilling
MAKES: 6 servings

- 4   cups frozen peas (about 16 oz.), thawed
- ½   cup shredded sharp cheddar cheese
- ½   cup ranch salad dressing
- ⅓   cup chopped red onion
- ¼   tsp. salt
- ¼   tsp. pepper
- 4   bacon strips, cooked and crumbled

Combine the first 6 ingredients; toss to coat. Refrigerate, covered, at least 30 minutes. Stir in bacon before serving.
¾ CUP 218 cal., 14g fat (4g sat. fat), 17mg chol., 547mg sod., 14g carb. (6g sugars, 4g fiber), 9g pro.

CUCUMBERS WITH DRESSING

AIR-FRYER FRENCH FRIES

These low-calorie french fries are perfect because I can whip them up at a moment's notice with ingredients I have on hand. They're so crispy, you won't miss the deep fryer!
—*Dawn Parker, Surrey, BC*

PREP: 10 min. + soaking
COOK: 30 min. • **MAKES:** 4 servings

3 medium potatoes, cut into ½-in. strips
2 Tbsp. coconut or avocado oil
½ tsp. garlic powder
¼ tsp. salt
¼ tsp. pepper
   Chopped fresh parsley, optional

1. Preheat the air fryer to 400°. Add potatoes to a large bowl; add enough ice water to cover. Soak for 15 minutes. Drain; place potatoes on towels and pat dry.
2. Combine the potatoes, oil, garlic powder, salt and pepper in a second large bowl; toss to coat. In batches, place potatoes in a single layer on greased tray in air-fryer basket. Cook until crisp and golden brown, 15-17 minutes, stirring and turning every 5-7 minutes. If desired, sprinkle with parsley.
¾ CUP 185 cal., 7g fat (6g sat. fat), 0 chol., 157mg sod., 28g carb. (1g sugars, 3g fiber), 3g pro. **DIABETIC EXCHANGES** 2 starch, 1½ fat.

CUCUMBERS WITH DRESSING

It wouldn't be summer if Mom didn't make lots of these creamy cucumbers. Just a few simple ingredients—mayonnaise, sugar, vinegar and salt—are all you need to dress them up.
—*Michelle Beran, Claflin, KS*

PREP: 10 min. + chilling
MAKES: 6 servings

1 cup mayonnaise
¼ cup sugar
¼ cup white vinegar
¼ tsp. salt
4 cups thinly sliced cucumbers

In a bowl, mix first 4 ingredients; toss with cucumbers. Refrigerate, covered, 2 hours.
¾ CUP 283 cal., 27g fat (4g sat. fat), 3mg chol., 286mg sod., 11g carb. (10g sugars, 0 fiber), 0 pro.

★ ★ ★ ★ ★ **READER REVIEW**

"The combo of mayonnaise, rice vinegar and sugar hits every taste bud. Warning: Hard not to eat it all in one sitting."
—REDAPPLE, TASTEOFHOME.COM

AIR-FRYER
FRENCH FRIES

LIME-CILANTRO SHRIMP
SKEWERS, PAGE 174

GRILLING

LIME-CILANTRO SHRIMP SKEWERS

1. Lime Juice
2. Cilantro
3. Soy Sauce
4. Shrimp

Plus: Olive Oil

GRILLED STEAK & MUSHROOM SALAD

GRILLED LEMON-GARLIC SALMON

Many fish for salmon here on the shore of Lake Michigan, so I've developed quite a few recipes for it, including this one. I love it, and so do my friends and family. When it's out of season, I look for wild-caught fresh Alaskan salmon at the grocery store.
—*Diane Nemitz, Ludington, MI*

TAKES: 30 min. + standing
MAKES: 4 servings

- 2 garlic cloves, minced
- 2 tsp. grated lemon zest
- ½ tsp. salt
- ½ tsp. minced fresh rosemary
- ½ tsp. pepper
- 4 salmon fillets (6 oz. each)

1. In a small bowl, mix the first 5 ingredients; rub over fillets. Let stand 15 minutes.
2. Place salmon on a lightly oiled grill rack, skin side up. Grill, covered, over medium heat or broil 4 in. from heat for 4 minutes. Turn; grill for 3-6 minutes longer or until fish just begins to flake easily with a fork.

1 SALMON FILLET 268 cal., 16g fat (3g sat. fat), 85mg chol., 381mg sod., 1g carb. (0 sugars, 0 fiber), 29g pro. **DIABETIC EXCHANGES** 5 lean meat.

GRILLED STEAK & MUSHROOM SALAD

My husband loves this salad, especially during summer. He says he feels as if he's eating a healthy salad and getting his steak too! I always serve it with some fresh homemade bread.
—*Julie Cashion, Sanford, FL*

TAKES: 30 min.
MAKES: 6 servings

- 6 Tbsp. olive oil, divided
- 2 Tbsp. Dijon mustard, divided
- ½ tsp. salt
- ¼ tsp. pepper
- 1 beef top sirloin steak (1½ lbs.)
- 1 lb. sliced fresh mushrooms
- ¼ cup red wine vinegar
- 1 medium bunch romaine, torn

1. In a small bowl, whisk 1 Tbsp. oil, 1 Tbsp. mustard, salt and pepper; set aside.
2. Grill steak, covered, over medium-high heat 4 minutes. Turn; spread with mustard mixture. Grill 4 minutes longer or until meat reaches desired doneness (for medium-rare, a thermometer should read 135°; medium, 140°; medium-well, 145°).
3. Meanwhile, in a large skillet, cook mushrooms in 1 Tbsp. oil until tender. Stir in vinegar and remaining oil and mustard.
4. Thinly slice steak across grain; add to mushroom mixture. Serve over romaine.

1 SERVING 299 cal., 20g fat (4g sat. fat), 63mg chol., 378mg sod., 6g carb. (1g sugars, 2g fiber), 25g pro.

GRILLED LEMON-GARLIC
SALMON

SUGAR COOKIE S'MORES

SUGAR COOKIE S'MORES

Change up traditional s'mores by using sugar cookies and candy bars in place of the traditional ingredients. This fun twist on the campfire classic will delight everyone!
—Taste of Home *Test Kitchen*

TAKES: 15 min.
MAKES: 4 servings

8   fun-size Milky Way candy bars
8   sugar cookies (3 in.)
4   large marshmallows

1. Place 2 candy bars on each of 4 cookies; place on grill rack. Grill, uncovered, over medium-high heat for 1-1½ minutes or until bottoms of cookies are browned.
2. Meanwhile, use a long-handled fork to toast marshmallows 6 in. from heat until golden brown, turning occasionally. Remove marshmallows from fork and place over candy bars; top with remaining cookies. Serve immediately.

1 SANDWICH COOKIE 271 cal., 10g fat (5g sat. fat), 13mg chol., 123mg sod., 43g carb. (31g sugars, 1g fiber), 3g pro.

SPINACH STEAK PINWHEELS

SPINACH STEAK PINWHEELS

Bacon and spinach bring plenty of flavor to these sirloin steak spirals. It's an easy dish to make and perfect for backyard grilling. I always get lots of compliments.
—Helen Vail, Glenside, PA

TAKES: 25 min.
MAKES: 6 servings

- 1½ lbs. beef top sirloin steak
- 8 bacon strips, cooked
- 1 pkg. (10 oz.) frozen chopped spinach, thawed and squeezed dry
- ¼ cup grated Parmesan cheese
- ½ tsp. salt
- ⅛ tsp. cayenne pepper

1. Lightly score steak by making shallow diagonal cuts into top of steak at 1-in. intervals; repeat cuts in opposite direction. Cover steak with plastic wrap; pound with a meat mallet to ½-in. thickness. Remove plastic.

2. Place bacon widthwise at center of steak. In a bowl, mix remaining ingredients; spoon over bacon. Starting at a short side, roll up steak jelly-roll style; secure with toothpicks. Cut into 6 slices.

3. Place on an oiled grill rack. Grill pinwheels, covered, over medium heat until beef reaches desired doneness (for medium-rare, a thermometer should read 135°; medium, 140°), 5-6 minutes on each side. Discard toothpicks before serving.

1 PINWHEEL 227 cal., 10g fat (4g sat. fat), 60mg chol., 536mg sod., 3g carb. (0 sugars, 1g fiber), 31g pro. **DIABETIC EXCHANGES** 4 lean meat, 1 fat.

BARBECUED RIBS WITH BEER

These ribs are so simple to make that you will want to make them often. They always are juicy and have a wonderful taste.
—*Catherine Santich, Alamo, CA*

- -

PREP: 2¼ hours • **GRILL:** 10 min.
MAKES: 3 servings

- 1 tsp. salt
- 1 tsp. Italian seasoning
- ½ tsp. pepper
- 1 rack pork spareribs (3 to 4 lbs.)
- 1 bottle (12 oz.) beer
- ⅔ cup barbecue sauce

1. Rub salt, Italian seasoning and pepper over ribs. Place ribs in a shallow roasting pan; add beer. Cover and bake at 325° until tender, about 2 hours.
2. Drain ribs. Spoon some of the sauce over ribs. Grill, covered, on a lightly oiled grill rack over medium heat until browned, 8-10 minutes, turning occasionally and basting with sauce.
1 SERVING 935 cal., 65g fat (24g sat. fat), 255mg chol., 1494mg sod., 12g carb. (11g sugars, 1g fiber), 63g pro.

BREAKFAST SKEWERS

These spicy-sweet kabobs are an unexpected offering for a brunch. They're a perfect companion to any kind of egg dish.
—*Bobi Raab, St. Paul, MN*

- -

TAKES: 20 min.
MAKES: 5 servings

- 1 pkg. (7 oz.) frozen fully cooked breakfast sausage links, thawed
- 1 can (20 oz.) pineapple chunks, drained
- 10 medium fresh mushrooms
- 2 Tbsp. butter, melted
   Maple syrup

1. Cut sausages in half; on 5 metal or soaked wooden skewers, alternately thread sausages, pineapple and mushrooms. Brush with butter and syrup.
2. Grill, uncovered, over medium heat, turning and basting with syrup, until sausages are lightly browned and fruit is heated through, about 8 minutes.
1 SKEWER 246 cal., 20g fat (8g sat. fat), 37mg chol., 431mg sod., 13g carb. (12g sugars, 1g fiber), 7g pro.

BREAKFAST SKEWERS

GRILLED CABBAGE

SMOKED DEVILED EGGS

Grilling deviled eggs gives them a distinctive, smoky flavor that will have everyone talking.
—*Catherine Woods, Lexington, MO*

PREP: 20 min.
GRILL: 10 min. + chilling
MAKES: 2 dozen

- ½ cup soaked hickory wood chips
- 12 hard-cooked large eggs, peeled
- ½ cup Miracle Whip
- 1 tsp. prepared mustard
- ¼ tsp. salt
- ⅛ tsp. pepper
- ⅛ tsp. paprika
  Minced fresh parsley, optional

1. Add wood chips to grill according to manufacturer's directions. Place eggs on grill rack. Grill, covered, over indirect medium heat until golden brown, 7-10 minutes. Cool slightly.
2. Cut eggs lengthwise in half. Remove yolks, reserving whites. In a small bowl, mash yolks. Stir in Miracle Whip, mustard, salt, pepper and paprika. Spoon or pipe mixture into egg whites. If desired, top with additional paprika and chopped parsley. Refrigerate, covered, until serving.

1 FILLED EGG HALF 52 cal., 4g fat (1g sat. fat), 94mg chol., 91mg sod., 1g carb. (1g sugars, 0 fiber), 3g pro.

GRILLED CABBAGE

I don't really like cabbage, but I tried this recipe and couldn't believe how good it was! We threw some burgers on the grill and our dinner was complete. I never thought I'd skip dessert because I was full from eating too much cabbage!
—*Elizabeth Wheeler, Thornville, OH*

TAKES: 30 min.
MAKES: 8 servings

- 1 medium head cabbage (about 1½ lbs.)
- ⅓ cup butter, softened
- ¼ cup chopped onion
- ½ tsp. garlic salt
- ¼ tsp. pepper

1. Cut cabbage into 8 wedges; place on a double thickness of heavy-duty foil (about 24x12 in.). Spread cut sides of cabbage with butter. Sprinkle with onion, garlic salt and pepper.
2. Fold foil around cabbage and seal tightly. Grill, covered, over medium heat until tender, about 20 minutes. Open foil carefully to allow steam to escape.

1 WEDGE 98 cal., 8g fat (5g sat. fat), 20mg chol., 188mg sod., 7g carb. (4g sugars, 3g fiber), 2g pro.
DIABETIC EXCHANGES 1½ fat, 1 vegetable.

GRILLED POTATOES

GRILLED POTATOES

Need a simple sidekick to serve with steaks or chops? Try these potatoes, which are bursting with fresh flavor. I make this recipe for picnics and potlucks. The potatoes turn out tender and well-seasoned. Plus, there's one less pot to wash!
—*Jena Coffey, Rock Hill, MO*

- -

PREP: 10 min. • **GRILL:** 30 min.
MAKES: 4 servings

- 1 Tbsp. olive oil
- 2 garlic cloves, minced
- ½ tsp. dried basil
- ¼ tsp. salt
- ⅛ tsp. pepper
- 3 medium baking potatoes, peeled and cut into 1-in. cubes

1. In a large bowl, combine oil, garlic, basil, salt and pepper. Add potatoes; toss to coat. Spoon mixture onto a greased double thickness of heavy-duty foil (about 18-in. square).
2. Fold foil around potato mixture and seal tightly. Grill, covered, over medium heat until potatoes are tender, turning once, 30-35 minutes. Open foil carefully to allow steam to escape.
¾ CUP 125 cal., 3g fat (1g sat. fat), 0 chol., 151mg sod., 22g carb. (2g sugars, 2g fiber), 2g pro. **DIABETIC EXCHANGES** 1½ starch, ½ fat.

TEST KITCHEN TIPS
The best potatoes to grill are Yukon Golds! In a pinch, sweet or Idaho potatoes could do the job too.

You can tell your potatoes are done if you can slide a fork or wooden skewer smoothly into the flesh.

GRILLED BROCCOLI

GRILLED BROCCOLI

I started using this recipe in 1987, when I began cooking light, and it's been a favorite side dish ever since. With its lemon and Parmesan flavors, it once took second place in a cooking contest.
—*Alice Nulle, Woodstock, IL*

- -

PREP: 5 min. + standing
GRILL: 20 min.
MAKES: 6 servings

- 6 cups fresh broccoli spears
- 2 Tbsp. plus 1½ tsp. lemon juice
- 2 Tbsp. olive oil
- ¼ tsp. salt
- ¼ tsp. pepper
- ¾ cup grated Parmesan cheese
  Optional: Grilled lemon slices and red pepper flakes

1. Place broccoli in a large bowl. Combine lemon juice, oil, salt and pepper; drizzle over broccoli and toss to coat. Let stand for 30 minutes.
2. Toss broccoli and then drain, discarding marinade. Place cheese in a small shallow bowl. Add broccoli, a few pieces at a time, tossing to coat.
3. Prepare grill for indirect heat using a drip pan. Place broccoli over drip pan on an oiled grill rack. Grill, covered, over indirect medium heat for 8-10 minutes on each side or until crisp-tender. If desired, garnish with grilled lemon slices and red pepper flakes.
1 CUP 107 cal., 8g fat (3g sat. fat), 8mg chol., 304mg sod., 5g carb. (2g sugars, 2g fiber), 6g pro. **DIABETIC EXCHANGES** 1½ fat, 1 vegetable.

LIME-CILANTRO SHRIMP SKEWERS

LIME-CILANTRO SHRIMP SKEWERS

A friend gave me this grill-friendly recipe. The combination of lime, cilantro and soy sauce gives these shrimp skewers a memorable taste reminiscent of tropical cuisine. To make it into a main dish, serve the skewers with rice or couscous.
—*Theresa Dibert, Cynthiana, KY*

PREP: 10 min. + marinating
GRILL: 10 min. • **MAKES:** 1 dozen

⅓ cup lime juice
3 Tbsp. minced fresh cilantro
2 Tbsp. soy sauce
3 garlic cloves, minced
2 tsp. olive oil
1¼ lbs. uncooked (26-30 per lb.), peeled and deveined
1 cup soaked mesquite wood chips, optional

1. In a large bowl, whisk lime juice, cilantro, soy sauce, garlic and oil until blended. Add shrimp; toss to coat. Refrigerate, covered, for 30 minutes.

2. If desired, add wood chips to grill according to manufacturer's directions. Drain shrimp, discarding marinade. Thread shrimp on 12 soaked wooden appetizer skewers.

3. Grill on an oiled rack, covered, over medium heat until shrimp turn pink, 3-4 minutes per side.

1 SKEWER 43 cal., 1g fat (0 sat. fat), 57mg chol., 94mg sod., 1g carb. (0 sugars, 0 fiber), 8g pro.

GRILLED STONE FRUITS WITH BALSAMIC SYRUP

Get ready to experience another side of stone fruits. Hot off the grill, this late-summer dessert practically melts in your mouth.
—*Sonya Labbe, West Hollywood, CA*

- -

TAKES: 20 min.
MAKES: 4 servings

- ½ cup balsamic vinegar
- 2 Tbsp. brown sugar
- 2 medium peaches, peeled and halved
- 2 medium nectarines, peeled and halved
- 2 medium plums, peeled and halved

1. In a small saucepan, combine vinegar and brown sugar. Bring to a boil; cook until liquid is reduced by half.

2. On a lightly oiled rack, grill peaches, nectarines and plums, covered, over medium heat or broil 4 in. from heat until tender, 3-4 minutes on each side.

3. Slice fruit; arrange on a serving plate. Drizzle with sauce.

1 SERVING 114 cal., 1g fat (0 sat. fat), 0 chol., 10mg sod., 28g carb. (24g sugars, 2g fiber), 2g pro. **DIABETIC EXCHANGES** 1 starch, 1 fruit.

GRILLED STONE FRUITS
WITH BALSAMIC SYRUP

CAMPFIRE
DESSERT CONES

CAMPFIRE DESSERT CONES

Kids love to make these! Set out the ingredients so they can mix and match their own creations.
—*Bonnie Hawkins, Elkhorn, WI*

TAKES: 20 min.
MAKES: 8 servings

- 8 ice cream sugar cones
- ½ cup milk chocolate M&M's
- ½ cup miniature marshmallows
- ½ cup salted peanuts
- ½ cup white baking chips

1. Prepare campfire or grill for medium heat. Fill cones with M&M's, marshmallows, peanuts and white chips. Fully wrap each cone with foil, sealing tightly.

2. Place packets over campfire or grill; cook until heated through, 7-10 minutes. Open foil carefully.
1 FILLED CONE 217 cal., 11g fat (5g sat. fat), 4mg chol., 78mg sod., 26g carb. (18g sugars, 1g fiber), 5g pro.

TEST KITCHEN TIP
Whether you eat the filling with a spoon before biting down on the cone or just dig right in to the whole thing, there's no wrong way to eat this fun treat. Use your favorite candies to fill the cones. We love the idea of miniature peanut butter cups.

GINGER POUND CAKE S'MORES

Kids love this knockoff of the classic campfire dessert, and adults do too. It's easy to prepare, and any kind of chocolate can be used. These can be made in batches in a cast-iron skillet as well.
—*Peter Halferty, Corpus Christi, TX*

TAKES: 20 min.
MAKES: 8 servings

- 8 large marshmallows
- 5 oz. bittersweet chocolate candy bars, broken into 8 pieces
- 8 tsp. crystallized ginger
- 16 slices pound cake (¼ in. thick)
- 3 Tbsp. butter, softened

1. Cut each marshmallow lengthwise into 4 slices. Place a chocolate piece, 4 marshmallow slices and 1 tsp. ginger on each of 8 cake slices; top with remaining cake. Spread outsides of cake slices with butter.
2. Grill, covered, over medium heat until toasted, 1-2 minutes on each side.
1 S'MORE 382 cal., 24g fat (13g sat. fat), 144mg chol., 272mg sod., 44g carb. (10g sugars, 2g fiber), 5g pro.

GINGER POUND CAKE
S'MORES

MAPLE-BALSAMIC SALMON

I have a few good recipes for family-favorite, heart-healthy salmon, but this one is always a hit. I serve it this way at least once a week!
—*David Krisko, Becker, MN*

TAKES: 20 min.
MAKES: 4 servings

- ¼ cup ruby red grapefruit juice
- 2 Tbsp. balsamic vinegar
- 2 Tbsp. maple syrup
- 2 garlic cloves, minced
- 2 tsp. olive oil
- 4 salmon fillets (4 oz. each)
- ¼ tsp. salt
- ¼ tsp. pepper
  Fresh thyme sprigs, optional

1. In a small saucepan, bring grapefruit juice, vinegar, syrup and garlic to a boil. Reduce heat; simmer, uncovered, for 5 minutes. Transfer 2 Tbsp. to a small bowl; add oil. Set remaining glaze aside.
2. Sprinkle salmon with salt and pepper; place skin side down on an oiled grill rack. Grill, covered, over medium heat or broil 4-6 in. from heat until fish flakes easily with a fork, 10-12 minutes, basting occasionally with maple oil mixture. Drizzle with reserved glaze. If desired, garnish with fresh thyme sprigs.
1 FILLET 266 cal., 15g fat (3g sat. fat), 67mg chol., 218mg sod., 10g carb. (9g sugars, 0 fiber), 23g pro.
DIABETIC EXCHANGES 3 lean meat, ½ starch, ½ fat.

GRILLED WAFFLE TREATS

I made these super sandwiches for family and friends for the first time on the Fourth of July. Everyone loved the generous portions and shared their memories of making and eating s'mores while camping.
—*Chris Seger, Lombard, IL*

TAKES: 15 min.
MAKES: 4 servings

- 8 frozen waffles
- 1 cup miniature marshmallows
- 1 cup semisweet chocolate chips

1. Place 1 waffle on a greased double thickness of heavy-duty foil (about 12-in. square). Sprinkle with ¼ cup each marshmallows and chocolate chips; top with another waffle. Fold foil around sandwich and seal tightly. Repeat 3 times.

2. Grill, covered, over medium heat for 8-10 minutes or until chocolate is melted, turning once. Open foil carefully to allow steam to escape.

1 TREAT 440 cal., 19g fat (9g sat. fat), 10mg chol., 457mg sod., 67g carb. (33g sugars, 4g fiber), 7g pro.

SIMPLE MARINATED GRILLED PORK CHOPS

This marinade is so simple that I use it on all kinds of meat. For a more robust flavor, let the meat marinate in the refrigerator overnight.
—*Lori Daniels, Beverly, WV*

PREP: 10 min. + marinating
GRILL: 10 min. • **MAKES:** 4 servings

- ½ cup packed brown sugar
- ½ cup soy sauce
- 2 garlic cloves, minced
- ¼ tsp. pepper
- 4 bone-in pork loin chops (1 in. thick and 8 oz. each)

1. In a bowl or shallow dish, combine brown sugar, soy sauce, garlic and pepper. Add pork chops and turn to coat. Cover and refrigerate 8 hours or overnight.

2. Drain pork chops, discarding marinade. Grill chops on greased grill rack, covered, over medium heat or broil 4-5 in. from heat for 4-5 minutes on each side or until meat reaches desired doneness (for medium-rare, a thermometer should read 145°; medium, 160°). Let meat stand for 5 minutes before serving.

1 CHOP 362 cal., 18g fat (7g sat. fat), 111mg chol., 695mg sod., 9g carb. (9g sugars, 0 fiber), 37g pro.

MARINATED GRILLED PORK CHOPS TIPS

How do I keep pork chops from drying out? Because pork chops are so quick-cooking, they can dry out super fast. Use an instant-read thermometer while grilling and keep an eye on it. When the internal temp is 145°, remove the pork chops from the grill and let them rest for a few minutes before serving.

Can pork marinate too long? Pork can get mushy if it spends too much time marinating in an acidic bath. If it contains an acid like soy sauce or lemon juice, let it marinate for no longer than 8 hours to prevent the surface of pork chops from breaking down too much.

SIMPLE MARINATED GRILLED PORK CHOPS

ARTICHOKE STEAK WRAPS

This simple, fast and flavorful dish is one the whole family loves. It's surprisingly easy to make, and you can broil the steak if you don't want to venture outside.
—*Greg Fontenot, The Woodlands, TX*

TAKES: 30 min.
MAKES: 6 servings

- 8 oz. frozen artichoke hearts (about 2 cups), thawed and chopped
- 2 medium tomatoes, chopped
- ¼ cup chopped fresh cilantro
- ¾ tsp. salt, divided
- 1 lb. beef flat iron or top sirloin steak (1¼ lbs.)
- ¼ tsp. pepper
- 6 whole wheat tortillas (8 in.), warmed

1. Toss artichoke hearts and tomatoes with cilantro and ¼ tsp. salt.
2. Sprinkle steak with pepper and remaining ½ tsp. salt. Grill, covered, over medium heat or broil 4 in. from heat until meat reaches desired doneness (for medium-rare, a thermometer should read 135°; medium, 140°), 5-6 minutes per side. Remove from heat; let stand for 5 minutes. Cut into thin slices. Serve steak and salsa in tortillas, folding bottoms and sides of tortillas to close.

1 WRAP 301 cal., 11g fat (4g sat. fat), 61mg chol., 506mg sod., 27g carb. (1g sugars, 5g fiber), 24g pro.
DIABETIC EXCHANGES 3 lean meat, 1½ starch.

ARTICHOKE STEAK WRAPS

GRILLED TERIYAKI CHICKEN

CAROLINA MARINATED PORK TENDERLOIN

Three bold ingredients will change your grilled pork tenderloin for life. This is exactly the kind of rich, savory, easy-to-prepare recipe I like to serve to company.
—*Sharisse Dunn, Rocky Point, NC*

PREP: 10 min. + marinating
GRILL: 20 min. • **MAKES:** 4 servings

¼ cup molasses
2 Tbsp. spicy brown mustard
1 Tbsp. cider vinegar
1 pork tenderloin (1 lb.)

1. In a bowl or shallow dish, combine molasses, mustard and vinegar. Add pork and turn to coat; refrigerate for 8 hours or overnight.
2. Drain and discard marinade. Grill pork, covered, on a lightly oiled rack over indirect medium-high heat for 20-27 minutes or until a thermometer reads 145°, turning occasionally. Let stand for 5 minutes before slicing.
3 OZ. COOKED PORK 160 cal., 4g fat (1g sat. fat), 63mg chol., 90mg sod., 7g carb. (5g sugars, 0 fiber), 22g pro. **DIABETIC EXCHANGES** 3 lean meat, ½ starch.

GRILLED TERIYAKI CHICKEN

This dish is so tasty that my husband insists it could be served in a restaurant.
—*Joan Hallford, North Richland Hills, TX*

PREP: 15 min. + marinating
GRILL: 15 min. • **MAKES:** 2 servings

⅓ cup water
¼ cup sherry or chicken broth
¼ cup reduced-sodium soy sauce
2 garlic cloves, minced
½ tsp. ground ginger
2 boneless skinless chicken breast halves (6 oz. each)

1. In a small saucepan, combine water, broth, soy sauce, garlic and ginger. Bring to a boil over medium heat; cook for 1 minute. Cool for 10 minutes. Pour into a shallow dish; add chicken and turn to coat. Cover and refrigerate for at least 2 hours.
2. Drain and discard marinade. Grill chicken, covered, over medium heat for 7-8 minutes on each side or until a thermometer reads 165°.
1 CHICKEN BREAST HALF 203 cal., 4g fat (1g sat. fat), 94mg chol., 417mg sod., 2g carb. (0 sugars, 0 fiber), 35g pro. **DIABETIC EXCHANGES** 5 very lean meat.

EASY GRILLED SQUASH

EASY GRILLED SQUASH

This is one of the best ways to prepare butternut squash and is great alongside grilled steak or chicken. As a bonus, butternut squash is full of vitamin A.
—*Esther Horst, Monterey, TN*

TAKES: 20 min.
MAKES: 4 servings

3 Tbsp. olive oil
2 garlic cloves, minced
¼ tsp. salt
¼ tsp. pepper
1 small butternut squash, peeled and cut lengthwise into ½-in. slices

1. In a small bowl, combine oil, garlic, salt and pepper. Brush over squash slices.

2. Grill squash, covered, over medium heat or broil 4 in. from heat for 4-5 minutes on each side or until tender.

2 PIECES 178 cal., 10g fat (1g sat. fat), 0 chol., 156mg sod., 23g carb. (5g sugars, 7g fiber), 2g pro.
DIABETIC EXCHANGES 1½ starch, 1½ fat.

CAKE & BERRY CAMPFIRE COBBLER

This warm cobbler is one of our favorite ways to end a day of fishing, hiking, swimming or rafting. It's yummy with ice cream—and so easy to make!
—*June Dress, Meridian, ID*

PREP: 10 min.
GRILL: 30 min.
MAKES: 12 servings

- 2 cans (21 oz. each) raspberry pie filling
- 1 pkg. yellow cake mix (regular size)
- 1¼ cups water
- ½ cup canola oil
  Vanilla ice cream, optional

1. Prepare grill or campfire for low heat, using 16-20 charcoal briquettes or large wood chips.
2. Line an ovenproof Dutch oven with heavy-duty aluminum foil; add pie filling. In a large bowl, combine cake mix, water and oil. Spread over pie filling.
3. Cover Dutch oven. When briquettes or wood chips are covered with white ash, place Dutch oven directly on top of 8-10 of them. Using long-handled tongs, place remaining briquettes on pot cover.
4. Cook until filling is bubbly and a toothpick inserted in topping comes out clean, 30-40 minutes. To check for doneness, use tongs to carefully lift cover. If desired, serve with ice cream.
1 SERVING 342 cal., 12g fat (2g sat. fat), 0 chol., 322mg sod., 57g carb. (34g sugars, 2g fiber), 1g pro.

DID YOU KNOW?

A cobbler is a baked dessert that has a fruit-based filling and is topped with a batter or some sort of dough. Common variations are made with peaches, berries or apples. This clever recipe uses a Dutch oven to bake the cobbler over an open grill or campfire—no household oven needed!

CAKE & BERRY CAMPFIRE COBBLER

GRILLED SIRLOIN KABOBS WITH PEACH SALSA

Having a new way to cook with salsa is just one of the perks of this quick and easy dish. Peaches three ways—fresh, as preserves and in salsa—star in these beef kabobs with a blend of hot and sweet flavors.
—*Beth Royals, Richmond, VA*

TAKES: 25 min.
MAKES: 6 servings

- 3 Tbsp. peach preserves
- 1 Tbsp. finely chopped seeded jalapeno pepper
- 1 beef top sirloin steak (1½ lbs.), cut into 1-in. cubes
- ½ tsp. salt
- ¼ tsp. pepper
- 3 medium peaches, each cut into 6 slices
- 1½ cups peach salsa

1. In a small bowl, mix preserves and jalapeno. Season beef with salt and pepper. Alternately thread beef cubes and peach slices onto 6 metal or soaked wooden skewers.
2. Place kabobs on greased grill rack. Grill kabobs, covered, over medium heat or broil 4 in. from heat for 6-8 minutes or until beef reaches desired doneness, turning occasionally.
3. Remove from grill; brush with preserves mixture. Serve with salsa.
NOTE Wear disposable gloves when cutting hot peppers; the oils can burn skin. Avoid touching your face.
1 KABOB WITH ¼ CUP SALSA 219 cal., 5g fat (2g sat. fat), 46mg chol., 427mg sod., 17g carb. (16g sugars, 3g fiber), 25g pro. **DIABETIC EXCHANGES** 3 lean meat, ½ starch, ½ fruit.

JALAPENO SWISS
BURGERS

JALAPENO SWISS BURGERS

Mexican culture greatly influences our regional cuisine, and we eat a lot of spicy foods. In this recipe, the mellow flavor of Swiss cheese cuts the heat of the jalapenos.
—*Jeanine Richardson, Floresville, TX*

TAKES: 30 min.
MAKES: 4 servings

- 2   lbs. ground beef
- 4   slices Swiss cheese
- 1   small onion, finely chopped
- 2   to 3 pickled jalapeno peppers, seeded and finely chopped
- 4   hamburger buns, split and toasted
     Optional: Lettuce leaves and ketchup

1. Shape beef into 8 thin patties. Top 4 patties with cheese, onion and jalapenos. Top with remaining patties; press edges firmly to seal.
2. Grill, covered, over medium heat or broil 4 in. from heat until a thermometer reads 160° and juices run clear, 8-9 minutes on each side. Serve on buns. If desired, serve with lettuce and ketchup.

NOTE Wear disposable gloves when cutting hot peppers; the oils can burn skin. Avoid touching your face.

1 BURGER 665 cal., 37g fat (16g sat. fat), 175mg chol., 423mg sod., 24g carb. (5g sugars, 2g fiber), 55g pro.

SPICY GRILLED EGGPLANT

SPICY GRILLED EGGPLANT

This grilled side goes well with pasta or meats also made on the grill. Thanks to the Cajun seasoning, it gets more attention than an ordinary veggie.
—*Greg Fontenot, The Woodlands, TX*

TAKES: 20 min.
MAKES: 8 servings

- 2   small eggplants, cut into ½-in. slices
- ¼   cup olive oil
- 2   Tbsp. lime juice
- 3   tsp. Cajun seasoning

1. Brush eggplant slices with oil. Drizzle with lime juice; sprinkle with Cajun seasoning. Let stand for 5 minutes.
2. Grill eggplant, covered, over medium heat or broil 4 in. from heat until tender, 4-5 minutes per side.

1 SERVING 88 cal., 7g fat (1g sat. fat), 0 chol., 152mg sod., 7g carb. (3g sugars, 4g fiber), 1g pro. **DIABETIC EXCHANGES** 1½ fat, 1 vegetable.

GRILLED
FRENCH ONIONS

GRILLED FRENCH ONIONS

This savory delicacy lets you enjoy all the flavors of French onion soup during summertime. Serve it with toast as another nod to a bowl of the beloved classic.
—*Krista Slack, Simi Valley, CA*

PREP: 10 min. • **GRILL:** 35 min.
MAKES: 2 servings

- 2 large sweet onions
- 1 to 2 tsp. beef bouillon granules
- ½ cup butter, softened
- 2 slices Swiss cheese
  Minced fresh thyme, optional

1. Prepare grill for indirect heat. Cut ¼ in. from top and bottom of each onion; peel. Core onions, leaving bottom fourth of onions intact. Place each onion on a double thickness of heavy-duty foil (about 12-in. square). Place bouillon in each onion; top with butter and seal tightly.
2. Grill, covered, over medium heat for 35-40 minutes or until onions are tender.
3. Carefully unwrap; top each onion with a cheese slice. If desired, top with fresh thyme. Serve immediately.

1 ONION 556 cal., 49g fat (31g sat. fat), 132mg chol., 807mg sod., 26g carb. (17g sugars, 3g fiber), 6g pro.

★ ★ ★ ★ ★ **READER REVIEW**

"This was a hit tonight, even with my 8-year-old. I served it with cheese toast instead of putting the cheese on the onion."

—STEPHANIE514, TASTEOFHOME.COM

CONTEST-WINNING GRILLED MUSHROOMS

Mushrooms cooked over hot coals always taste good, but this easy recipe makes them taste fantastic. As a mother of two, I love to cook entire meals on the grill. It's fun spending time outdoors with the kids.

—*Melanie Knoll, Marshalltown, IA*

TAKES: 15 min.
MAKES: 4 servings

- ½ lb. medium fresh mushrooms
- ¼ cup butter, melted
- ½ tsp. dill weed
- ½ tsp. garlic salt
  Grilled lemon wedges, optional

1. Thread mushrooms on 4 metal or soaked wooden skewers. Combine butter, dill and garlic salt; brush over mushrooms.
2. Grill, covered, over medium-high heat for 10-15 minutes or until tender, basting and turning every 5 minutes. Serve with grilled lemon wedges if desired.

1 SKEWER 77 cal., 8g fat (5g sat. fat), 20mg chol., 230mg sod., 2g carb. (1g sugars, 0 fiber), 1g pro.

CONTEST-WINNING GRILLED MUSHROOMS

BACON-WRAPPED STUFFED JALAPENOS

Sunday is grill-out day for my husband, and these zesty peppers are one of his specialties. We usually feature them at our annual Daytona 500 party. They disappear from the appetizer tray in no time.
—Therese Pollard, Hurst, TX

PREP: 1 hour • **GRILL:** 40 min.
MAKES: 2 dozen

- 24 medium jalapeno peppers
- 1 lb. uncooked chorizo or bulk spicy pork sausage
- 2 cups shredded cheddar cheese
- 12 bacon strips, cut in half

1. Make a lengthwise cut in each jalapeno, about ⅛ in. deep; remove seeds. Combine sausage and cheese; stuff into jalapenos. Wrap each with a piece of bacon; secure with toothpicks.
2. Grill, covered, over indirect medium heat for 35-40 minutes or until a thermometer reads 160°, turning once. Grill, covered, over direct heat for 1-2 minutes or until bacon is crisp.
NOTE Wear disposable gloves when cutting hot peppers; the oils can burn skin. Avoid touching your face.
1 STUFFED JALAPENO 132 cal., 10g fat (4g sat. fat), 30mg chol., 365mg sod., 1g carb. (1g sugars, 0 fiber), 8g pro.

🕒 FIRECRACKER SHRIMP

These delightful grilled shrimp are coated in a sweet and spicy glaze that comes together in moments for sizzling shrimp skewers.
—Mary Tallman, Arbor Vitae, WI

TAKES: 20 min.
MAKES: 2½ dozen

- ½ cup apricot preserves
- 1 tsp. canola oil
- 1 tsp. soy sauce
- ½ tsp. crushed red pepper flakes
- 1 lb. uncooked large shrimp, peeled and deveined

1. In a small bowl, combine preserves, oil, soy sauce and pepper flakes. Thread shrimp onto metal or soaked wooden skewers.
2. Grill, uncovered, over medium heat or broil 4 in. from heat until shrimp turn pink, 2-3 minutes on each side, basting frequently with apricot mixture.
1 SHRIMP 27 cal., 0 fat (0 sat. fat), 18mg chol., 30mg sod., 4g carb. (2g sugars, 0 fiber), 3g pro.

FIRECRACKER SHRIMP

BALSAMIC-GOAT CHEESE GRILLED PLUMS

GRILLED TILAPIA WITH MANGO

Here's a new twist on tilapia that I created for my wife. She enjoys the combination of mango with Parmesan. Somehow it tastes even better outside on the deck with a cold glass of iced tea!
—*Gregg May, Columbus, OH*

TAKES: 20 min.
MAKES: 4 servings

    4   tilapia fillets (6 oz. each)
    1   Tbsp. olive oil
    ½   tsp. salt
    ½   tsp. dill weed
    ¼   tsp. pepper
    1   Tbsp. grated
        Parmesan cheese
    1   medium lemon, sliced
    1   medium mango, peeled
        and thinly sliced

1. Brush fillets with oil; sprinkle with salt, dill and pepper.
2. Grill tilapia, covered, on a lightly oiled rack over medium heat for 5 minutes. Turn tilapia; top with cheese, lemon and mango. Grill 4-6 minutes longer or until fish flakes easily with a fork.
1 FILLET 213 cal., 5g fat (1g sat. fat), 84mg chol., 377mg sod., 10g carb. (8g sugars, 1g fiber), 32g pro.
DIABETIC EXCHANGES 5 lean meat, ½ fruit, ½ fat.

HEALTH TIP
Add mango to your regular fruit rotation to boost your intake of important nutrients like vitamins C and A, and potassium.

BALSAMIC-GOAT CHEESE GRILLED PLUMS

Make a bold statement with this simple yet elegant treat. Ripe plums are grilled and then dressed with a balsamic reduction and tangy goat cheese.
—*Ariana Abelow, Holliston, MA*

TAKES: 25 min.
MAKES: 8 servings

    1   cup balsamic vinegar
    2   tsp. grated lemon zest
    4   medium firm plums,
        halved and pitted
    ½   cup crumbled goat cheese

1. For glaze, in a small saucepan, combine vinegar and lemon zest; bring to a boil. Cook 10-12 minutes or until mixture is thickened and reduced to about ⅓ cup (do not overcook).
2. Grill plums, covered, over medium heat 2-3 minutes on each side or until tender. Drizzle with glaze; top with cheese.
1 PLUM HALF WITH 1 TBSP. CHEESE AND 2 TSP. GLAZE 58 cal., 2g fat (1g sat. fat), 9mg chol., 41mg sod., 9g carb. (8g sugars, 1g fiber), 2g pro.
DIABETIC EXCHANGES ½ starch, ½ fat.

GRILLED
BUTTERMILK CHICKEN

GRILLED BUTTERMILK CHICKEN

I created this recipe years ago after one of our farmers market customers, a chef, shared the idea of marinating chicken in buttermilk. It's easy to prepare and always turns out moist and delicious! I bruise the thyme sprigs by twisting them before adding them to the buttermilk mixture; this releases the oils in the leaves and flavors the chicken better.
—*Sue Gronholz, Beaver Dam, WI*

- -

PREP: 10 min. + marinating
GRILL: 10 min.
MAKES: 12 servings

- 1½ cups buttermilk
- 4 fresh thyme sprigs
- 4 garlic cloves, halved
- ½ tsp. salt
- 12 boneless skinless chicken breast halves (about 4½ lbs.)

1. Place buttermilk, thyme, garlic and salt in a large bowl or shallow dish. Add chicken and turn to coat. Refrigerate 8 hours or overnight, turning occasionally.
2. Drain chicken, discarding marinade. Grill, covered, over medium heat 5-7 minutes per side or until a thermometer reads 165°.
1 CHICKEN BREAST HALF 189 cal., 4g fat (1g sat. fat), 95mg chol., 168mg sod., 1g carb. (1g sugars, 0 fiber), 35g pro. **DIABETIC EXCHANGES** 5 lean meat.

GRILLED CORN IN HUSKS

GRILLED CORN IN HUSKS

Seasoned with butter, Parmesan cheese and parsley, grilled corn is especially good. Be sure to give the ears a long soak before putting them on the grill. Hot off the grate, the kernels are moist and tender with a wonderful, sweet flavor.
—*Nancy Zimmerman, Cape May Court House, NJ*

- -

PREP: 20 min. + soaking
GRILL: 20 min. • **MAKES:** 4 servings

- 4 large ears sweet corn in husks
- ¼ cup butter, softened
- 2 Tbsp. minced fresh parsley
- ¼ cup grated Parmesan cheese

1. Carefully peel back husks from corn to within 1 in. of bottom; remove silk. Soak in cold water for 20 minutes.
2. Drain corn; pat dry. Combine butter and parsley; spread over corn. Rewrap corn in husks and secure with string.
3. Grill corn, covered, over medium heat until tender, turning often, 20-25 minutes. Sprinkle with cheese.
1 EAR 196 cal., 9g fat (5g sat. fat), 24mg chol., 186mg sod., 28g carb. (9g sugars, 4g fiber), 8g pro. **DIABETIC EXCHANGES** 2 starch, 1 fat.

GRILLED GREEN BEANS

I cook almost everything outdoors, including green beans. I prepare this snappy side dish while the entree is cooking. The recipe has won over my picky eaters.
—*Carol Traupman-Carr, Breinigsville, PA*

PREP: 25 min. • **GRILL:** 10 min.
MAKES: 4 servings

- 1 lb. fresh green beans, trimmed
- 2 Tbsp. butter
- 1 small shallot, minced
- 1 garlic clove, minced
- ½ cup grated Parmesan cheese

1. In a 6-qt. stockpot, bring 4 qt. water to a boil. Add beans; cook, uncovered, just until crisp-tender, 2-3 minutes. Remove beans and immediately drop into ice water.
2. In a small skillet, melt butter over medium-high heat. Add shallot; cook and stir until lightly browned, 2-3 minutes. Add garlic; cook 30 seconds longer. Remove from heat. Drain beans and pat dry.
3. In a large bowl, combine beans, shallot mixture and cheese; toss to coat. Transfer to a piece of heavy-duty foil (about 18-in. square) coated with cooking spray. Fold foil around beans, sealing tightly.
4. Grill, covered, over medium heat or broil 4 in. from heat until cheese is melted, 7-9 minutes. Open foil carefully to allow steam to escape.
1 CUP 137 cal., 9g fat (5g sat. fat), 24mg chol., 234mg sod., 12g carb. (3g sugars, 4g fiber), 5g pro.
DIABETIC EXCHANGES 2 fat, 1 vegetable.

GRILLED NECTARINE & CHEESE CROSTINI

GRILLED NECTARINE & CHEESE CROSTINI

At our house, we love the summer tastes of sweet grilled nectarines and fresh basil over goat cheese. I can usually find all the ingredients at the farmers market.
—*Brandy Hollingshead, Grass Valley, CA*

TAKES: 25 min.
MAKES: 1 dozen

- ½ cup balsamic vinegar
- 1 Tbsp. olive oil
- 12 slices French bread baguette (¼ in. thick)
- 2 medium nectarines, halved
- ¼ cup fresh goat cheese, softened
- ¼ cup loosely packed basil leaves, thinly sliced

1. In a small saucepan, bring vinegar to a boil; cook for 10-15 minutes or until liquid is reduced to 3 Tbsp. Remove from heat.
2. Brush oil over both sides of baguette slices. Grill, uncovered, over medium heat until golden brown on both sides. Grill nectarines 45-60 seconds on each side or until tender and lightly browned. Cool slightly.
3. Spread goat cheese over toasts. Cut nectarines into thick slices; arrange over cheese. Drizzle with balsamic syrup; sprinkle with basil. Serve immediately.
1 APPETIZER 48 cal., 2g fat (1g sat. fat), 5mg chol., 55mg sod., 6g carb. (3g sugars, 0 fiber), 1g pro.
DIABETIC EXCHANGES ½ starch.

KENTUCKY GRILLED CHICKEN

This chicken is perfect for an outdoor summer meal, and my family thinks it's fantastic. It takes about an hour on the grill but is definitely worth the wait! I use a new paintbrush to mop on the basting sauce.
—*Jill Evely, Wilmore, KY*

PREP: 5 min. + marinating
GRILL: 40 min.
MAKES: 10 servings

 1 cup cider vinegar
½ cup canola oil
 5 tsp. Worcestershire sauce
 4 tsp. hot pepper sauce
 2 tsp. salt
10 bone-in chicken breast halves (10 oz. each)

1. In a shallow dish, combine vinegar, oil, Worcestershire sauce, pepper sauce and salt. Pour 1 cup marinade into a separate bowl; add chicken and turn to coat. Cover and refrigerate for at least 4 hours. Cover and refrigerate remaining marinade for basting.
2. Drain chicken, discarding marinade. Prepare grill for indirect heat, using a drip pan.

3. Place chicken breasts, bone side down, on oiled rack. Grill, covered, over indirect medium heat until a thermometer reads 170°, about 20 minutes on each side, basting occasionally with reserved marinade.

1 CHICKEN BREAST HALF 284 cal., 11g fat (2g sat. fat), 113mg chol., 406mg sod., 0 carb. (0 sugars, 0 fiber), 41g pro. **DIABETIC EXCHANGES** 6 lean meat, 2 fat.

KENTUCKY GRILLED CHICKEN TIPS

What other ingredients can I add to this Kentucky grilled chicken marinade? So many, so get creative! Your favorite spice blends, a squeeze of fresh citrus, chopped fresh herbs or even sliced onion and bell pepper for added flavor.

What kind of grill should I use for grilled chicken? It's really your preference—a charcoal or gas grill works fine, so just pay attention to doneness cues. If you're limited on outdoor space, try an electric countertop grill or a grill pan.

How do you store grilled chicken leftovers? Like most leftovers, this grilled chicken will last 3-4 days refrigerated in an airtight container. You can also freeze this recipe for up to 6 months and pull it out to use in a pinch.

KENTUCKY GRILLED CHICKEN

CHOCOLATE-COVERED
ESPRESSO BEANS, PAGE 218

COOKIES, BARS & CANDIES

CHOCOLATE-COVERED ESPRESSO BEANS

1. Chocolate Chips
2. Shortening
3. Espresso Beans

Plus: Baking Cocoa

BUTTERSCOTCH TOFFEE COOKIES

CANDIED CHERRIES

These sweet, sugary morsels can be used so many ways—as garnishes, in any recipe that calls for candied or glace fruit, or just as a standalone sweet treat!
—Taste of Home *Test Kitchen*

- -

PREP: 5 min.
COOK: 35 min. + cooling
MAKES: 1¼ cups

- 1 jar (16 oz.) maraschino cherries, undrained
- ¾ cup sugar

1. Drain cherries; reserve ⅓ cup juice. Place juice and sugar in a small heavy saucepan; stir gently to moisten all the sugar. Cook over medium-low heat, gently swirling pan occasionally, until sugar is dissolved.
2. Add cherries; bring to a boil. Reduce heat. Simmer, covered, until a candy thermometer reads 235° (soft-ball stage) and cherries are slightly wrinkled, 35-40 minutes, gently stirring every 10 minutes.
3. Remove from heat; uncover pan. Cool to room temperature. Using a slotted spoon, transfer cherries to a parchment-lined baking sheet. Store in an airtight container in the refrigerator for up to 6 months.
1 CANDIED CHERRY 33 cal., 0 fat (0 sat. fat), 0 chol., 0 sod., 9g carb. (9g sugars, 0 fiber), 0 pro.

BUTTERSCOTCH TOFFEE COOKIES

With its big butterscotch and chocolate flavor, my cookie stands out. I like to enjoy it with a glass of milk or a cup of coffee. It's my fallback recipe when I'm short on time and need something delicious fast.
—*Allie Blinder, Norcross, GA*

- -

PREP: 10 min.
BAKE: 10 min./batch
MAKES: 5 dozen

- 2 large eggs, room temperature
- ½ cup canola oil
- 1 pkg. butter pecan cake mix (regular size)
- 1 pkg. (10 to 11 oz.) butterscotch chips
- 1 pkg. (8 oz.) milk chocolate English toffee bits

1. Preheat oven to 350°. In a large bowl, beat eggs and oil until blended; gradually add cake mix and mix well. Fold in chips and toffee bits.
2. Drop dough by tablespoonfuls 2 in. apart onto greased baking sheets. Bake until golden brown, 10-12 minutes. Cool 1 minute before removing to wire racks.
1 COOKIE 95 cal., 5g fat (3g sat. fat), 10mg chol., 70mg sod., 11g carb. (3g sugars, 0 fiber), 1g pro

CANDIED CHERRIES

EASY MEXICAN
BROWNIES

EASY MEXICAN BROWNIES

I was hosting a Mexican-themed cocktail party and needed a quick dessert. Dressing up an ordinary box brownie mix made life easy and delicious!
—*Susan Stetzel, Gainesville, NY*

PREP: 10 min.
BAKE: 20 min. + cooling
MAKES: 2 dozen

- 1 pkg. fudge brownie mix (13x9-in. pan size)
- 2 tsp. ground cinnamon
- 1 tsp. ground ancho chile pepper
- ¾ cup dark chocolate chips
- 2 large eggs, room temperature
- ½ cup canola oil
- ¼ cup water

1. Preheat oven to 350°. Whisk together brownie mix and spices; add chocolate chips. In a separate bowl, whisk eggs, oil and water until blended. Gradually add dry mixture, mixing well. Spread batter into a greased 13x9-in. baking pan.
2. Bake until a toothpick inserted in center comes out clean (do not overbake), 20-25 minutes. Cool completely in pan on a wire rack.
1 BROWNIE 173 cal., 10g fat (3g sat. fat), 16mg chol., 92mg sod., 21g carb. (15g sugars, 1g fiber), 2g pro.

TEST KITCHEN TIP
You can prepare the dry ingredients ahead of time and use it like any other brownie mix! Whisk the brownie mix and spices; transfer to a 1-qt. glass jar. Top with chocolate chips. Store in a cool, dry place for up to 3 months.

SWEETHEART COOKIES

SWEETHEART COOKIES

These rounds filled with fruit preserves were blue-ribbon winners at the county fair two years running. A family favorite, they never last beyond Christmas!
—*Pamela Esposito, Smithville, NJ*

PREP: 25 min.
BAKE: 15 min./batch
MAKES: 2 dozen

- ¾ cup butter, softened
- ½ cup sugar
- 1 large egg yolk, room temperature
- 1½ cups all-purpose flour
- 2 Tbsp. raspberry or strawberry preserves
  Confectioners' sugar, optional

1. Preheat oven to 350°. Cream butter and sugar until light and fluffy, 5-7 minutes. Add egg yolk; mix well. Stir in flour by hand. On a lightly floured surface, gently knead dough for 2-3 minutes or until thoroughly combined.
2. Roll dough into 1-in. balls. Place 2 in. apart on greased baking sheets. Using end of a wooden spoon handle, make an indention in center of each ball. Fill each indentation with ¼ tsp. preserves.
3. Bake for 13-15 minutes or until edges are lightly browned. Remove to wire racks. Dust warm cookies with confectioners' sugar if desired. Cool.
1 COOKIE 102 cal., 6g fat (4g sat. fat), 23mg chol., 46mg sod., 11g carb. (5g sugars, 0 fiber), 1g pro.

DARK CHOCOLATE BOURBON BALLS

Here's an all-time chocolate classic made easy. The blended flavor of bourbon and pecans is always irresistible!
—Taste of Home *Test Kitchen*

- -

PREP: 30 min. + standing
MAKES: 4 dozen

1¼ cups finely chopped pecans, divided
¼ cup bourbon
½ cup butter, softened
3¾ cups confectioners' sugar
1 lb. dark chocolate candy coating, melted

1. Combine 1 cup pecans and bourbon; let stand, covered, for 8 hours or overnight.
2. Cream butter; continuing to cream, add confectioners' sugar, ¼ cup at a time, until crumbly. Stir in pecan mixture. Refrigerate, covered, until firm enough to shape, about 45 minutes.
3. Shape mixture into 1-in. balls; place on waxed paper-lined baking sheets. Refrigerate until firm, about 1 hour.
4. Dip balls into chocolate coating; allow excess to drip off. Sprinkle with remaining ¼ cup pecans. Let stand until set.

1 BOURBON BALL 124 cal., 7g fat (4g sat. fat), 5mg chol., 15mg sod., 16g carb. (15g sugars, 0 fiber), 0 pro.

TEST KITCHEN TIP
You can use less bourbon in this recipe, and replace it with another liquid like apple juice. If you're not a fan of boozy desserts and want them to be completely alcohol-free, replace all the bourbon with apple juice.

DARK CHOCOLATE BOURBON BALLS

MAPLE PRALINES

2. Remove from heat. Add butter; do not stir. Cool, without stirring, to 160°.

3. Stir in pecans. Beat vigorously with a wooden spoon until the mixture just begins to thicken but is still glossy. Quickly drop by spoonfuls onto waxed paper. Cool completely. Store in an airtight container.

1 OZ. 144 cal., 7g fat (3g sat. fat), 11mg chol., 4mg sod., 20g carb. (19g sugars, 0 fiber), 1g pro.

❄️

EASY CAKE MIX BARS

I take these bars to work for Friday pick-me-ups. I love to share them because they're so easy to eat, easy to make and easy on the wallet.
—*Amy Rose, Ballwin, MO*

- -

PREP: 5 min.
BAKE: 20 min. + cooling
MAKES: 3 dozen

1 yellow cake mix (regular size)
1 large egg, room temperature
½ cup 2% milk
⅓ cup canola oil
1 cup white baking chips
⅓ cup jimmies

1. Preheat oven to 350°. In a large bowl, combine cake mix, egg, milk and oil (mixture will be thick). Stir in baking chips and jimmies. Spread into a greased 15x10x1-in. baking pan.

2. Bake 18-20 minutes or until a toothpick inserted in center comes out clean. Place pan on a wire rack to cool completely. Cut into bars.

FREEZE OPTION Freeze bars in freezer containers. To use, thaw in covered containers before serving.

1 BAR 113 cal., 5g fat (2g sat. fat), 7mg chol., 102mg sod., 16g carb. (11g sugars, 0 fiber), 1g pro.

MAPLE PRALINES

This recipe rekindles memories of my grandfather and his love for making maple syrup. When I was in college, my mother would send me a package of her pralines during sugaring season. They were so popular with my friends that I barely managed to tuck away a few for myself!
—*Mary Beth Cool, Canajoharie, NY*

- -

PREP: 10 min.
COOK: 10 min. + cooling
MAKES: about 1 lb.

1 cup sugar
⅔ cup heavy whipping cream
½ cup maple syrup
2 Tbsp. butter
¾ cup coarsely chopped pecans, toasted

1. In a heavy 1-qt. saucepan, combine sugar, cream and syrup. Cook, stirring, over medium heat until mixture boils. Reduce heat to medium-low. Cook, uncovered, until a candy thermometer reads 234° (soft-ball stage), stirring occasionally.

PECAN MELTAWAYS

PECAN MELTAWAYS

These sweet, nutty treats are a tradition in our house at Christmastime, but they are delightful any time of year.
—*Alberta McKay, Bartlesville, OK*

PREP: 15 min. + chilling
BAKE: 10 min./batch + cooling
MAKES: 4 dozen

  1   cup butter, softened
  ½ cup confectioners' sugar
  1   tsp. vanilla extract
 2¼ cups all-purpose flour
  ¼ tsp. salt
  ¾ cup chopped pecans
     Additional confectioners' sugar

1. In a large bowl, cream butter and confectioners' sugar until light and fluffy, 5-7 minutes. Beat in vanilla. Combine flour and salt; gradually add to creamed mixture and mix well. Stir in pecans. Refrigerate until chilled.
2. Preheat oven to 350°. Roll dough into 1-in. balls and place on ungreased baking sheets. Bake 10-12 minutes or until set.
3. Roll warm cookies in additional confectioners' sugar; cool completely on wire racks. Roll cooled cookies again in confectioners' sugar.
1 COOKIE 73 cal., 5g fat (3g sat. fat), 10mg chol., 39mg sod., 6g carb. (1g sugars, 0 fiber), 1g pro.

PECAN MELTAWAYS TIPS

Do I have to chill the dough? Yes. Chilling the dough will make it easy to handle and also ensure the balls will keep their shape during baking.

How should I store these cookies? Keep them in an airtight container at room temperature for 3–5 days or freeze for up to 3 months. To use, thaw cookies overnight—you may need to re-roll them in confectioner's sugar before serving.

GIANT BUCKEYE COOKIE

I'm originally from Ohio, where we love our buckeye candy—a classic combination of peanut butter and chocolate. To make this skillet-cookie version, all you need is a few common pantry ingredients, and voila—you have a tasty dessert ready in under an hour. You can customize it by substituting other mix-ins for the chocolate chips. We serve it warm with ice cream or whipped cream.
—*Arianna Joy Harding, Sandy, UT*

PREP: 15 min. • **BAKE:** 20 min.
MAKES: 12 servings

- 1 pkg. chocolate cake mix (regular size)
- 2 large eggs, room temperature
- ½ cup canola oil
- 1 cup semisweet chocolate chips
- 1 cup creamy peanut butter
- ½ cup confectioners' sugar
  Optional: Hot fudge ice cream topping, vanilla ice cream, whipped cream and melted creamy peanut butter

1. Preheat oven to 350°. In a large bowl, combine cake mix, eggs and oil until blended. Stir in chocolate chips. Press half the dough into a 10-in. cast-iron or other ovenproof skillet. Combine peanut butter and confectioners' sugar; spread over dough in skillet. Press remaining dough between sheets of parchment into a 10-in. circle; place circle of dough over filling.
2. Bake until a toothpick inserted in center comes out with moist crumbs, 20-25 minutes. Serve warm, with toppings as desired.
1 PIECE 443 cal., 27g fat (6g sat. fat), 31mg chol., 372mg sod., 48g carb. (31g sugars, 3g fiber), 8g pro.

CHEWY MACAROONS

A perfectly made macaroon will be lightly crisp on the outside and chewy on the inside. Macaroons are primarily made with coconut but some varieties also feature nuts.
—*Herbert Borland, Des Moines, WA*

PREP: 10 min. • **BAKE:** 25 min.
MAKES: about 2½ dozen

- 2 large egg whites, room temperature
- ½ tsp. vanilla extract
  Dash salt
- 6 Tbsp. sugar
- 3 cups sweetened shredded coconut

1. Preheat oven to 300°. In a small bowl, beat egg whites, vanilla and salt on medium speed until soft peaks form. Gradually add sugar, 1 Tbsp. at time, beating until stiff peaks form. Fold in coconut.
2. Drop mixture by tablespoonfuls 2 in. apart onto well-greased baking sheets. Bake until just golden brown, about 25 minutes. Immediately remove from pan to wire racks to cool.
1 MACAROON 34 cal., 2g fat (1g sat. fat), 0 chol., 21mg sod., 5g carb. (5g sugars, 0 fiber), 0 pro.

GIANT BUCKEYE COOKIE

WHITE CANDY BARK

I use walnuts from our tree to make this quick and easy recipe, but you can use whatever fruits and nuts are on hand. Pecans always work well, and dried cherries are an easy swap for the cranberries.
—Marcia Snyder, Grand Junction, CO

PREP: 20 min. + chilling
MAKES: 2 lbs. (64 pieces)

1 Tbsp. butter, melted
2 pkg. (10 to 12 oz. each) white baking chips
1½ cups walnut halves
1 cup dried cranberries
¼ tsp. ground nutmeg

1. Line a 15x10x1-in. baking pan with foil. Brush foil with butter; set pan aside.
2. Microwave white chips on high until melted; stir until smooth. Stir in walnuts, cranberries and nutmeg.
3. Spread into prepared pan. Chill until firm. Break into pieces.
½ OZ. 46 cal., 3g fat (1g sat. fat), 1mg chol., 6mg sod., 5g carb. (1g sugars, 0 fiber), 1g pro.

ROSEMARY-LEMON SHORTBREAD SANDWICH COOKIES

These delectable shortbread sandwich cookies are always a welcome addition to our annual ladies holiday tea luncheon. The distinctive rosemary flavor, paired so well with the tangy lemon curd, has made them a favorite in our group for years!
—Jamie Jones, Madison, GA

PREP: 25 min. + chilling
BAKE: 10 min./batch + cooling
MAKES: about 2 dozen

ROSEMARY-LEMON
SHORTBREAD
SANDWICH COOKIES

1 cup butter, softened
¾ cup confectioners' sugar
2 cups all-purpose flour
4 tsp. minced fresh rosemary
¼ tsp. salt
½ cup lemon curd
Optional: Additional fresh rosemary and confectioners' sugar

1. Cream butter and confectioners' sugar until light and fluffy, 5-7 minutes. In another bowl, mix flour, rosemary and salt; gradually beat into creamed mixture. Divide dough in half. Shape each into a disk. Wrap and refrigerate until firm enough to roll, 30 minutes.
2. Preheat oven to 350°. On a lightly floured surface, roll each disk to ¼-in. thickness. Cut with a floured 2-in. round cookie cutter. Using a floured ⅞-in. round cookie cutter, cut out centers of half the cookies. Place solid and window cookies 1 in. apart on ungreased baking sheets.
3. Bake until set, 9-11 minutes. Remove from pans to wire racks to cool completely.
4. To serve, spread lemon curd on bottoms of solid cookies; top with window cookies. If desired, top with additional rosemary and confectioners' sugar.
1 SANDWICH COOKIE 144 cal., 8g fat (5g sat. fat), 25mg chol., 91mg sod., 16g carb. (8g sugars, 0 fiber), 1g pro.

HARD MAPLE CANDY

During the war, the women at my grandmother's church would donate sugar rations throughout the year to make candy as a fundraiser at Christmas. I'm lucky enough to have inherited this tried-and-true recipe.
—*Dorothea Bohrer,*
Silver Springs, MD

PREP: 5 min.
COOK: 30 min. + cooling
MAKES: 1¾ lbs.

1½ tsp. butter, softened
3½ cups sugar
1 cup light corn syrup
1 cup water
3 Tbsp. maple flavoring

1. Grease a 15x10x1-in. pan with butter; set aside. In a large heavy saucepan, combine sugar, corn syrup and water. Cook over medium-high heat until a candy thermometer reads 300° (hard-crack stage), stirring occasionally.
2. Remove from heat; stir in maple flavoring. Immediately pour into prepared pan; cool. Break into pieces. Store in an airtight container.

NOTE We recommend you test your candy thermometer before each use by bringing water to a boil; the thermometer should read 212°. Adjust your recipe temperature up or down based on your test.

½ OZ. 69 cal., 0 fat (0 sat. fat), 0 chol., 5mg sod., 17g carb. (17g sugars, 0 fiber), 0 pro.

ANISE HARD CANDY Use 2 tsp. anise extract instead of the maple flavoring. Add 6-9 drops red food coloring with the extract if desired.

HARD MAPLE CANDY

CHOCOLATE AMARETTI

CHOCOLATE AMARETTI

These classic almond paste cookies are like ones you'd find in an Italian bakery. My husband and children are always excited when I include these goodies in my holiday baking lineup.
—*Kathy Long, Whitefish Bay, WI*

PREP: 15 min.
BAKE: 20 min./batch
MAKES: 2 dozen

1¼ cups almond paste
¾ cup sugar
2 large egg whites
½ cup confectioners' sugar
¼ cup baking cocoa

1. In the bowl of a stand mixer, crumble almond paste into small pieces. Add remaining ingredients; mix on low until combined. Beat on medium until mixture is smooth, 2-3 minutes.

2. Drop by tablespoonfuls 2 in. apart onto parchment-lined baking sheets. Bake at 350° until tops are cracked, 17-20 minutes. Cool for 1 minute before removing from pans to wire racks. Store in an airtight container.

1 COOKIE 92 cal., 3g fat (0 sat. fat), 0 chol., 6mg sod., 15g carb. (13g sugars, 1g fiber), 2g pro.

CHOCOLATE PEANUT TREATS

When I was in high school, I took these sweet and crunchy squares to bake sales—they were the first to sell out. I still make them for family and friends who love the classic combination of chocolate and peanut butter.
—*Christy Asher, CO Springs, CO*

PREP: 20 min. + chilling
MAKES: about 2 dozen

- ¾ cup graham cracker crumbs
- ½ cup butter, melted
- 2 cups confectioners' sugar
- ½ cup chunky peanut butter
- 1 cup semisweet chocolate chips

1. In a bowl, combine cracker crumbs and butter. Stir in sugar and peanut butter. Press into a greased 8-in. square pan.
2. In a microwave or double boiler, melt chocolate chips and stir until smooth. Spread over peanut butter layer. Chill 30 minutes; cut into squares. Chill until firm, about 30 minutes longer. Store in refrigerator.
1 PIECE 148 cal., 9g fat (4g sat. fat), 10mg chol., 81mg sod., 18g carb. (14g sugars, 1g fiber), 2g pro.

HOMEMADE PEANUT BUTTER CUPS

I choose pretty mini muffin liners and colored sprinkles to coordinate with the holiday we're celebrating. These irresistible candies with gooey peanut butter centers are so easy to make!
—*LaVonne Hegland, St. Michael, MN*

PREP: 20 min. + chilling
MAKES: 3 dozen

- 1 cup creamy peanut butter, divided
- ½ cup confectioners' sugar
- 4½ tsp. butter, softened
- ½ tsp. salt
- 2 cups semisweet chocolate chips
- 4 milk chocolate candy bars (1.55 oz. each), coarsely chopped
- Colored sprinkles, optional

1. Combine ½ cup peanut butter, confectioners' sugar, butter and salt until smooth.
2. In a microwave, melt chocolate chips, candy bars and remaining ½ cup peanut butter; stir until smooth.
3. Drop 1 tsp. chocolate mixture into paper-lined mini muffin cups. Drop a scant teaspoon of peanut butter mixture into each cup; top with another 1 tsp. chocolate mixture. If desired, decorate with sprinkles. Refrigerate until set. Store in an airtight container.
1 PIECE 123 cal., 8g fat (4g sat. fat), 2mg chol., 76mg sod., 12g carb. (10g sugars, 1g fiber), 3g pro.

HOMEMADE PEANUT BUTTER CUP TIPS

What's the best peanut butter to use? Creamy peanut butter mixes best with the other ingredients. Use your favorite brand or make your own homemade peanut butter.

How do I store homemade peanut butter cups? Since they'll get too soft after more than a day at room temperature, store them in the refrigerator for a month or in the freezer for up to 3 months (if they last that long!).

HOMEMADE PEANUT BUTTER CUPS

BUCKEYES

CHOCOLATE CHUNK SHORTBREAD

Chocolate is a nice addition to shortbread, as this scrumptious recipe proves. The shortbread cookies are delicious served with a cold glass of milk.

—*Brenda Mumma, Airdrie, AB*

PREP: 20 min. + chilling
BAKE: 20 min./batch + cooling
MAKES: 2 dozen

- ¾ cup (340 grams) butter, softened
- ½ cup (60 grams) confectioners' sugar
- 1 cup (125 grams) all-purpose flour
- ¼ cup (40 grams) cornstarch
- 3 oz. (85 grams) semisweet chocolate, coarsely chopped
  Additional confectioners' sugar

1. Cream butter and sugar in a large bowl until light and fluffy, 5-7 minutes. Combine flour and cornstarch; stir into creamed mixture. Fold in chocolate.
2. Shape dough into 1½-in. balls. Place 2 in. apart on ungreased baking sheets. Flatten with a glass dipped in confectioners' sugar. Chill on baking sheets until firm, about 1 hour.
3. Preheat oven to 300°. Bake until edges are lightly browned, 20-25 minutes. Remove to wire racks to cool completely.
1 COOKIE 105 cal., 7g fat (4g sat. fat), 15mg chol., 46mg sod., 10g carb. (4g sugars, 0 fiber), 1g pro.

BUCKEYES

These chocolate peanut butter balls (no bake!) are always popular at my church's annual Christmas fundraiser. They resemble buckeyes, a type of chestnut—hence the name.

—*Merry Kay Opitz, Elkhorn, WI*

PREP: 30 min. + chilling
MAKES: 5½ dozen

- 5½ cups confectioners' sugar
- 1⅔ cups peanut butter
- 1 cup butter, melted
- 4 cups semisweet chocolate chips
- 1 tsp. shortening

1. In a large bowl, beat sugar, peanut butter and butter until smooth. Shape into 1-in. balls; set aside.

2. Microwave chocolate chips and shortening on high until melted; stir until smooth. Dip balls in chocolate, allowing excess to drip off. Place on a wire rack over waxed paper; refrigerate 15 minutes or until firm. Cover and store in refrigerator.
1 PIECE 127 cal., 6g fat (2g sat. fat), 0 chol., 29mg sod., 18g carb. (16g sugars, 1g fiber), 2g pro.

DID YOU KNOW?
Authentic Ohio buckeyes have a bit of chocolate-free space on each piece where the peanut butter shows, so that they resemble their namesake nuts.

CHOCOLATE CHUNK
SHORTBREAD

FRENCH BUTTER COOKIES

FRENCH BUTTER COOKIES

The Brittany region of France is known for its use of butter. These cookies, also known as sable Breton, shine the spotlight on the famous ingredient. This recipe is mildly sweet, rich, crisp and has a hint of salt. You won't be able to resist having a second—or third.
—Taste of Home *Test Kitchen*

PREP: 15 min. + chilling
BAKE: 15 min./batch + cooling
MAKES: 2 dozen

⅔ cup European-style salted butter, softened
½ cup sugar
3 large egg yolks, room temperature, divided use
1 tsp. vanilla extract
2 cups all-purpose flour
¼ tsp. salt
2 Tbsp. water

1. Cream butter and sugar until light and fluffy, 5-7 minutes. Beat in 2 egg yolks and vanilla. Gradually beat in flour and salt. Divide dough into 2 portions; shape each into a disk. Cover; refrigerate until firm enough to roll, about 30 minutes.
2. Preheat oven to 350°. Working with 1 portion of dough at a time, roll to ¼-in. thickness between sheets of parchment. Cut with floured 2-in. round cookie cutter. Place 1 in. apart on ungreased baking sheets. Whisk remaining egg yolk and water; brush over cookies. Create a cross-hatch design by dragging the tines of a fork across each cookie.
3. Bake until edges are light golden, 12-15 minutes. Cool on pans for 5 minutes. Remove to wire racks to cool completely.

1 COOKIE 107 cal., 6g fat (3g sat. fat), 37mg chol., 42mg sod., 12g carb. (4g sugars, 0 fiber), 1g pro.

CHOCOLATE BILLIONAIRES

Everyone raves about these chocolate and caramel candies. I received the recipe from a friend while living in Texas. When we moved, I made sure this recipe made the trip with me!
—*June Humphrey, Strongsville, OH*

PREP: 45 min. + chilling
MAKES: about 2 lbs.

- 1   pkg. (14 oz.) caramels
- 3   Tbsp. water
- 1½ cups chopped pecans
- 1   cup Rice Krispies
- 3   cups milk chocolate chips
- 1½ tsp. shortening

1. Line 2 baking sheets with waxed paper; grease paper and set aside. In a large heavy saucepan, combine caramels and water; cook and stir over low heat until smooth. Stir in pecans and cereal until coated. Drop by teaspoonfuls onto prepared pans. Refrigerate for 10 minutes or until firm.
2. Meanwhile, in a microwave, melt the chocolate chips and shortening; stir until smooth.

Dip candy into chocolate, coating all sides; allow excess to drip off. Place on prepared pans. Refrigerate until set. Store in an airtight container.
1 OZ. 172 cal., 10g fat (4g sat. fat), 4mg chol., 51mg sod., 20g carb. (17g sugars, 1g fiber), 2g pro.

DARK CHOCOLATE TRUFFLES

I learned to make these at a class at the local community college. I made them for my parents' 50th wedding anniversary, adding smoked salt and colored coarse sugars for garnish. The original recipe called for dipping them in dark chocolate. If you like, you can dust them with powdered sugar first before rolling them in cocoa powder—it helps sweeten the cocoa.
—*Shelly Bevington, Hermiston, OR*

PREP: 25 min. + chilling
MAKES: 5 dozen

- 1   lb. dark chocolate chips
- 1   cup heavy whipping cream
- 2   Tbsp. light corn syrup
- 2   Tbsp. butter, softened
- ¾   cup baking cocoa

1. Place chocolate in a small bowl. In a small heavy saucepan, heat cream and corn syrup just to a boil. Pour over chocolate; stir until smooth. Stir in butter. Cool to room temperature, stirring occasionally. Refrigerate until firm enough to shape, about 3 hours.
2. Place cocoa in a small bowl. Shape chocolate mixture into 1-in. balls; roll balls in cocoa. Store in an airtight container in the refrigerator.
1 TRUFFLE 56 cal., 4g fat (3g sat. fat), 6mg chol., 5mg sod., 5g carb. (5g sugars, 1g fiber), 1g pro.

DARK CHOCOLATE TRUFFLES TIPS

What kind of dark chocolate should I use?
This recipe was tested with Nestle dark chocolate chips, which are 53% cacao, but other dark chocolates of a similar percentage can be used. For a sweeter taste, use semisweet chocolate chips, which are typically 35% to 45% cacao.

What else can I roll these in besides baking cocoa?
Even with easy truffle recipes, changing up the look can be a lot of fun. Try rolling these candies in chopped nuts, sprinkles or confectioners' sugar, or try dipping them in melted chocolate.

How long will these last?
These goodies will last for about 2 weeks when stored in an airtight container in the refrigerator. But there's no guarantee they'll last that long if your family finds them!

DARK CHOCOLATE TRUFFLES

GRANDMA'S SCOTTISH
SHORTBREAD

GRANDMA'S SCOTTISH SHORTBREAD

My Scottish grandmother was renowned for her baked goods, and these thick shortbread bars are an example of why.
—*Jane Kelly, Wayland, MA*

PREP: 15 min.
BAKE: 45 min. + cooling
MAKES: 4 dozen

- 1 lb. butter, softened
- 8 oz. superfine sugar (about 1¼ cups)
- 1 lb. all-purpose flour (3⅔ cups)
- 8 oz. white rice flour (1⅓ cups)

1. Preheat oven to 300°. Cream butter and sugar until light and fluffy, 5-7 minutes. Combine flours; gradually beat into creamed mixture. Press dough into an ungreased 13x9-in. baking pan. Prick with a fork.
2. Bake for 45-50 minutes or until light brown. Cut into 48 bars or triangles while still warm. Cool completely on a wire rack.

1 BAR 139 cal., 8g fat (5g sat. fat), 20mg chol., 61mg sod., 16g carb. (5g sugars, 0 fiber), 1g pro.

PEANUT BUTTER
COCONUT COOKIES

PEANUT BUTTER COCONUT COOKIES

These four-ingredient cookies are easy to make, so you'll always have time to make a quick batch. Bonus: No flour means they're also gluten-free!
—Taste of Home *Test Kitchen*

TAKES: 30 min.
MAKES: 2½ dozen

- 1 large egg, room temperature, beaten
- 1 cup sugar
- 1 cup creamy peanut butter
- ½ cup sweetened shredded coconut

1. Preheat oven to 350°. In a large bowl, mix all ingredients. Scoop level tablespoonfuls; roll into balls. Place on ungreased baking sheets and flatten with a fork.
2. Bake until set, about 15 minutes. Remove to wire racks to cool.
1 COOKIE 82 cal., 5g fat (1g sat. fat), 6mg chol., 40mg sod., 9g carb. (8g sugars, 0 fiber), 2g pro.

★ ★ ★ ★ ★ **READER REVIEW**
"WOW! Since having to go gluten-free, I've been missing Ranger cookies. These are every bit as good and super easy to make. I may do a chocolate drizzle later, if there are any left by then."
—MOMSTAR3, TASTEOFHOME.COM

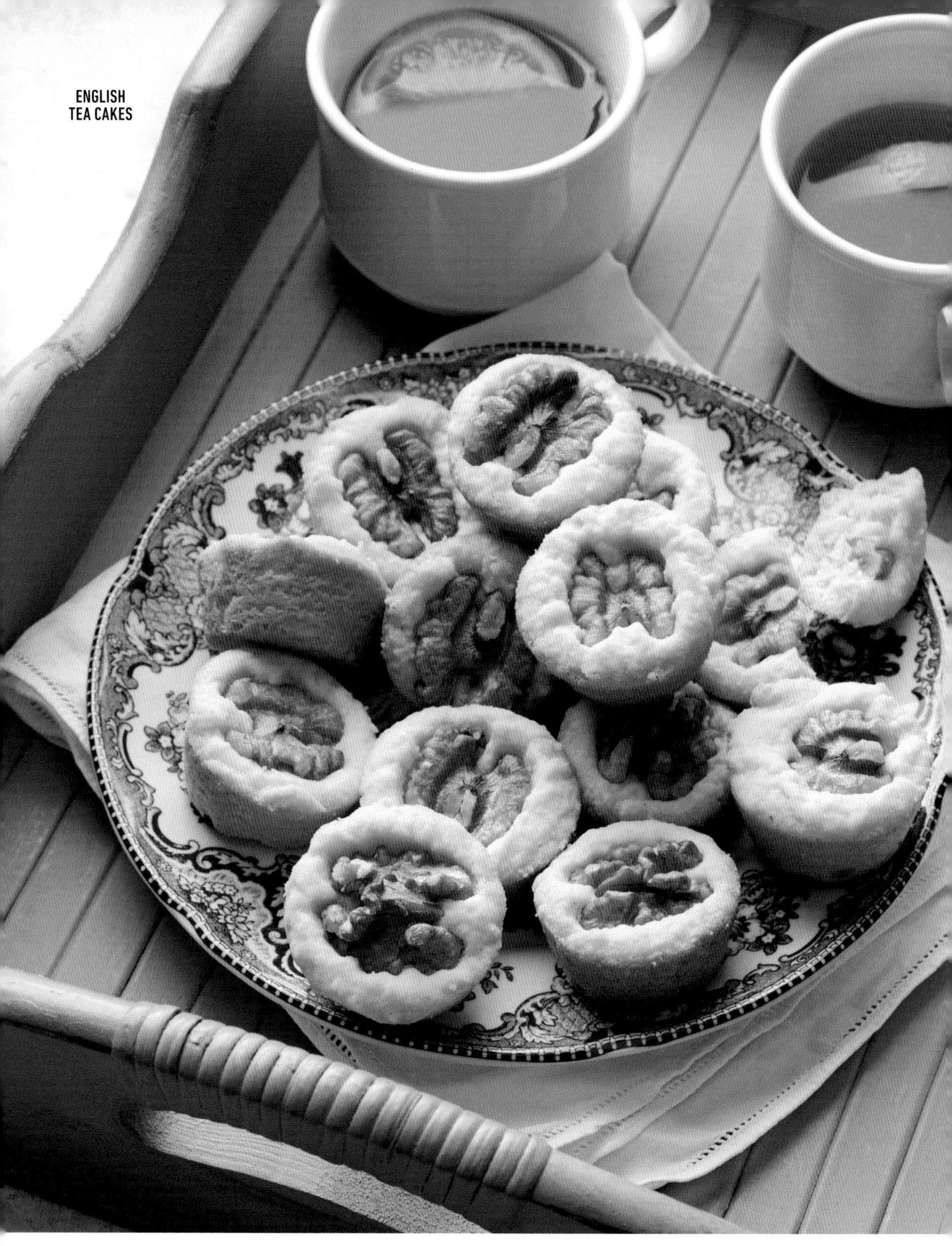

ENGLISH TEA CAKES

ENGLISH TEA CAKES

These unique cookies are baked in muffin cups, giving them a perfectly round shape. I will sometimes omit the nuts and decorate the cookies for holidays.
—*Beverly Christian, Fort Worth, TX*

PREP: 15 min.
BAKE: 10 min./batch
MAKES: 5 dozen

- 2 cups butter, softened
- 1 cup sugar
- 2 tsp. vanilla extract
- 4 cups all-purpose flour
- 60 walnut or pecan halves, toasted

1. In a large bowl, cream butter and sugar until light and fluffy, 5-7 minutes. Beat in vanilla. Gradually add flour and mix well. Drop by heaping tablespoonfuls into greased miniature muffin cups; flatten slightly. Press a walnut half into center of each.
2. Bake at 350° for 10-12 minutes or until edges are lightly browned. Cool 2 minutes before removing from pans to wire racks.
1 COOKIE 108 cal., 7g fat (4g sat. fat), 16mg chol., 49mg sod., 10g carb. (3g sugars, 0 fiber), 1g pro.

DID YOU KNOW?

Walnuts make these little cookies more authentically English, as pecans are native to the Americas and have been grown successfully in only a handful of places in Europe. However, either nut would make these cookies a treat!

FUNKY MONKEY
RICE KRISPIES TREATS

FUNKY MONKEY RICE KRISPIES TREATS

These crisp, delicious treats prove that bananas and peanut butter are truly a match made in heaven.
—*Taste of Home Test Kitchen*

PREP: 20 + cooling
MAKES: 2 dozen

- 1 pkg. (10 oz.) miniature marshmallows
- 3 Tbsp. canola oil
- 1½ tsp. banana extract, optional
- 5 cups Rice Krispies
- 1 cup dried banana chips, chopped
- 1 pkg. (10 oz.) peanut butter chips
- 1 cup dry-roasted peanuts, coarsely chopped, divided

1. In a microwave or a large saucepan over low heat, melt marshmallows in oil. If desired, add extract; stir until smooth. Remove from heat; stir in cereal, banana chips, peanut butter chips and ½ cup peanuts.
2. Press mixture into a lightly greased 13x9-in. baking pan, using waxed paper or a lightly greased spatula to press down; press remaining ½ cup peanuts on top. Cool to room temperature. Cut into bars.
1 BAR 206 cal., 10g fat (4g sat. fat), 0 chol., 126mg sod., 26g carb. (14g sugars, 1g fiber), 4g pro.

SALTED NUT SQUARES

A favorite of young and old, this recipe came from my sister-in-law. It's simple to prepare and delicious. There's no need to keep it warm or cold, so it's perfect for the potluck that has you traveling longer distances.
—*Kathy Tremel, Earling, IA*

PREP: 15 min. + chilling
MAKES: 32 squares

- 3 cups salted peanuts without skins, divided
- 2 Tbsp. plus 1½ tsp. butter
- 2 cups peanut butter chips
- 1 can (14 oz.) sweetened condensed milk
- 2 cups miniature marshmallows

1. Place half of the peanuts in an ungreased 11x7-in. dish; set aside. In a large saucepan, melt butter and peanut butter chips over low heat. Add condensed milk and marshmallows; cook and stir until melted.
2. Pour over peanuts. Sprinkle with remaining peanuts. Cover and refrigerate until chilled. Cut into squares.

1 SQUARE 194 cal., 12g fat (4g sat. fat), 7mg chol., 95mg sod., 16g carb. (13g sugars, 2g fiber), 7g pro.

CHOCOLATE CARAMEL BARS

CHOCOLATE CARAMEL BARS

Taking dessert or another treat to a church or school potluck is never a problem for me. I jump at the chance to offer these rich, chocolaty bars.
—*Steve Mirro, Cape Coral, FL*

PREP: 15 min. • **BAKE:** 25 min.
MAKES: 3 dozen

- 1 pkg. (11 oz.) caramels
- 1 can (5 oz.) evaporated milk, divided
- ¾ cup butter, softened
- 1 pkg. German chocolate cake mix (regular size)
- 2 cups semisweet chocolate chips

1. Preheat oven to 350°. In a small saucepan over low heat, melt caramels with ¼ cup evaporated milk; stir until smooth. Meanwhile, in a large bowl, cream butter until light and fluffy. Beat in dry cake mix and remaining evaporated milk.
2. Spread half the dough into a greased 13x9-in. baking pan. Bake for 6 minutes; sprinkle with chocolate chips.
3. Gently spread caramel mixture over chips. Drop remaining dough by tablespoonfuls over caramel layer. Return to the oven for 15 minutes. Cool and cut into bars.

1 SERVING 185 cal., 9g fat (5g sat. fat), 12mg chol., 161mg sod., 26g carb. (19g sugars, 1g fiber), 2g pro.

CHOCOLATE-COVERED PRETZELS

These chocolate-covered pretzels came from my grandmother who loves to make candy and treats for my students. I have followed in her footsteps and make these for people at my work and for other family members.
—*Aimee Worth, Fair Oaks, CA*

- -

PREP: 1 hour + chilling
MAKES: 20 pretzels

- 20 medium pretzel twists (about 5 oz.)
- 12 oz. milk chocolate candy coating disks, melted
  Colored sprinkles
- 12 oz. white candy coating disks, melted

1. Dip 10 pretzels in milk chocolate, allowing excess to drip off. Place on waxed paper. Decorate half the dipped pretzels with sprinkles. Chill until set, about 10 minutes.
2. Dip remaining 10 pretzels in white candy coating, allowing excess to drip off. Place on waxed paper. Decorate half the white-dipped pretzels with sprinkles. Chill until set, about 10 minutes.
3. Drizzle the plain white-dipped pretzels with milk chocolate. Drizzle the plain milk chocolate-dipped pretzels with white candy coating. Chill for 10 minutes or until set. Store in an airtight container.

1 PRETZEL 207 cal., 10g fat (9g sat. fat), 1mg chol., 143mg sod., 28g carb. (23g sugars, 0 fiber), 1g pro.
CHOCOLATE-COVERED SANDWICH COOKIES: Use an 18-oz. package of cream-filled chocolate sandwich cookies in place of the pretzels. Yields 4 dozen.

CHOCOLATE-COVERED PRETZELS

APPLE KUCHEN BARS

This recipe is about family, comfort and simplicity. My mom made this delicious sweet treat many a winter night and served it warm with some of her famous homemade ice cream. I like to make a double batch and pass on the love!
—Elizabeth Monfort, Celina, OH

PREP: 35 min.
BAKE: 1 hour + cooling
MAKES: 2 dozen

- 3 cups all-purpose flour, divided
- ¼ tsp. salt
- 1½ cups cold butter, divided
- 4 to 5 Tbsp. ice water
- 8 cups thinly sliced peeled tart apples (about 8 medium)
- 2 cups sugar, divided
- 2 tsp. ground cinnamon

1. Preheat oven to 350°. Place 2 cups flour and salt in a food processor; pulse until blended. Add 1 cup butter; pulse until butter is the size of peas. While pulsing, add just enough ice water to form moist crumbs.

2. Press mixture onto bottom of a greased 13x9-in. baking pan. Bake until edges are lightly browned, 20-25 minutes. Cool on a wire rack.

3. In a large bowl, combine apples, 1 cup sugar and cinnamon; toss to coat. Spoon over crust.

4. Place remaining flour, butter and sugar in food processor; pulse until coarse crumbs form. Sprinkle over apples. Bake until golden brown and apples are tender, 60-70 minutes. Cool completely on a wire rack. Cut into bars.

1 BAR 240 cal., 12g fat (7g sat. fat), 30mg chol., 106mg sod., 33g carb. (21g sugars, 1g fiber), 2g pro.

CHOCOLATE-COVERED ESPRESSO BEANS

Sweet chocolate pairs with rich, bitter coffee in a treat that is perfect as a garnish for a dessert or eating straight out of hand.
—Taste of Home *Test Kitchen*

TAKES: 30 min. • **MAKES:** ¾ cup

- ⅔ cup semisweet chocolate chips
- 1½ tsp. shortening
- ½ cup espresso beans
  Baking cocoa, optional

In a microwave, melt chocolate chips and shortening; stir until smooth. Dip coffee beans in chocolate; allow excess to drip off. Place on waxed paper; let stand until set, 10-15 minutes. If desired, roll in cocoa. Store in an airtight container.

1 TBSP. 50 cal., 3g fat (2g sat. fat), 0 chol., 2mg sod., 6g carb. (5g sugars, 1g fiber), 0 pro.

CHOCOLATE-COVERED ESPRESSO BEANS

CHERRY CRUMB DESSERT

SOFT & CHEWY CARAMELS

I made these caramels with my children when they were young, and now I enjoy making them with our eight grandchildren too!
—*Darlene Edinger, Turtle Lake, ND*

PREP: 5 min.
COOK: 30 min. + cooling
MAKES: 2 lbs. (108 pieces)

- 2 tsp. plus 1 cup butter, divided
- 2 cups sugar
- 1 cup light corn syrup
- 2 cups half-and-half cream, divided
- 1 tsp. vanilla extract

1. Line a 13x9-in. pan with foil; grease foil with 2 tsp. butter; set aside. Cube remaining 1 cup butter. In a Dutch oven, combine sugar, corn syrup and 1 cup cream. Bring to a boil over medium heat, stirring constantly. Slowly stir in remaining 1 cup cream. Cook over medium heat until a candy thermometer reads 250° (hard-ball stage), stirring frequently. Remove from heat; stir in cubed butter and vanilla until well mixed, about 5 minutes.
2. Pour mixture into prepared pan. Cool completely. Remove foil from pan; cut candy into 1-in. squares. Wrap individually in waxed paper; twist ends.
1 PIECE 45 cal., 2g fat (1g sat. fat), 7mg chol., 18mg sod., 6g carb. (6g sugars, 0 fiber), 0 pro.

CHERRY CRUMB DESSERT

Here's a sweet that's especially good with a dollop of whipped cream or a scoop of ice cream! The crumb topping has a sublime nutty flavor, and no one will guess this streusel started with a handy cake mix.
—*Ann Eastman, Santa Monica, CA*

PREP: 15 min. • **BAKE:** 30 min.
MAKES: 16 servings

- ½ cup cold butter
- 1 pkg. yellow cake mix (regular size)
- 1 can (21 oz.) cherry or blueberry pie filling
- ½ cup chopped walnuts

1. In a large bowl, cut butter into cake mix until crumbly. Reserve 1 cup for topping. Pat remaining crumbs onto the bottom and ½ in. up the sides of a greased 13x9-in. baking pan.
2. Spread pie filling over crust. Combine walnuts with reserved crumbs; sprinkle over top. Bake at 350° for 30-35 minutes or until golden brown. Cut into bars.
1 PIECE 294 cal., 11g fat (5g sat. fat), 15mg chol., 290mg sod., 46g carb. (26g sugars, 2g fiber), 3g pro.

MACAROON BARS

MACAROON BARS

Guests will never recognize the refrigerated crescent roll dough that goes into these almond-flavored bars. You can assemble these chewy coconut treats in no time.
—Carolyn Kyzer, Alexander, AR

- -

PREP: 10 min.
BAKE: 30 min. + cooling
MAKES: 3 dozen

3¼ cups sweetened shredded coconut, divided
1 can (14 oz.) sweetened condensed milk
1 tsp. almond extract
1 tube (8 oz.) refrigerated crescent rolls

1. Preheat oven to 350°. Grease a 13x9-in. baking pan; line pan with nonstick foil, allowing foil to hang over edges of pan. Grease foil; sprinkle 1½ cups coconut into pan. Combine condensed milk and extract; drizzle half the mixture over coconut. Unroll crescent dough into 1 long rectangle; seal seams and perforations. Place in pan. Drizzle with remaining milk mixture; sprinkle with remaining coconut.

2. Bake until golden brown, 30-35 minutes. Cool completely on a wire rack before cutting. Store in refrigerator.

1 BAR 103 cal., 5g fat (4g sat. fat), 4mg chol., 85mg sod., 12g carb. (9g sugars, 0 fiber), 2g pro.

BUTTERY LEMON SANDWICH COOKIES

BUTTERY LEMON SANDWICH COOKIES

My grandson approves of these lemony sandwich cookies made with crackers and prepared frosting. Decorate with whatever sprinkles you'd like.
—Nancy Foust, Stoneboro, PA

- -

PREP: 20 min. + standing
MAKES: 2½ dozen

¾ cup lemon frosting
60 Ritz crackers
24 oz. white candy coating, melted
Nonpareils, jimmies or sprinkles, optional

Spread frosting on bottoms of half the crackers; cover with remaining crackers. Dip sandwiches in melted candy coating; allow excess to drip off. Place on waxed paper; decorate as desired. Let stand until set. Store in an airtight container in refrigerator.

1 SANDWICH COOKIE 171 cal., 9g fat (6g sat. fat), 0 chol., 70mg sod., 23g carb. (19g sugars, 0 fiber), 0 pro.

COOKIES & CREAM FUDGE

COOKIES & CREAM FUDGE

I invented this confection for a bake sale at our children's school. Boy, was it a hit! The crunchy chunks of sandwich cookie soften a bit as the mixture mellows. It's so sweet that one panful serves a crowd.

—*Laura Lane, Richmond, VA*

- -

PREP: 25 min. + chilling
MAKES: about 3 dozen

16 Oreo cookies, broken into chunks, divided
1 can (14 oz.) sweetened condensed milk
2 Tbsp. butter
2⅔ cups white baking chips
1 tsp. vanilla extract
Crushed peppermint candies, optional

1. Line an 8-in. square dish with aluminum foil; coat with cooking spray. Place half of the cookies in pan.

2. In a heavy saucepan, combine condensed milk, butter and chips. Cook, stirring constantly, over low heat until chips are melted. Remove from heat; stir in vanilla.

3. Pour over cookies in pan. Sprinkle with remaining cookies and, if desired, peppermint candies. Cover and refrigerate at least 1 hour. Cut into squares.

1 PIECE 133 cal., 7g fat (4g sat. fat), 8mg chol., 64mg sod., 17g carb. (8g sugars, 0 fiber), 2g pro.

QUICK & EASY GUMDROPS

These homemade candies are sweet little gummy bites that are softer than store-bought varieties.
—*Leah Rekau, Milwaukee, WI*

- -

PREP: 25 min. + standing
MAKES: 64 pieces (1 lb.)

  3   envelopes unflavored gelatin
 ½   cup plus ¾ cup water, divided
1½ cups sugar
 ¼   to ½ tsp. raspberry extract
      Red food coloring
      Additional sugar

1. In a small bowl, sprinkle gelatin over ½ cup water; let stand for 5 minutes. In a small saucepan, bring sugar and remaining ¾ cup water to a boil over medium heat, stirring constantly. Add gelatin; reduce heat. Simmer 5 minutes, stirring frequently. Remove from heat; stir in extract and food coloring as desired.

2. Pour into a greased 8-in. square pan. Refrigerate, covered, 3 hours or until firm.

3. Loosen edges of candy from pan with a knife; turn onto a sugared work surface. Cut into 1-in squares; roll squares in sugar. Let stand, uncovered, at room temperature until all sides are dry, turning every hour, 3-4 hours. Store between layers of waxed paper in an airtight container in refrigerator.

NOTE For lemon gumdrops, use lemon extract and yellow food coloring. For orange gumdrops, use orange extract, yellow food coloring and a drop of red food coloring.

1 PIECE 19 cal., 0 fat (0 sat. fat), 0 chol., 1mg sod., 5g carb. (5g sugars, 0 fiber), 0 pro.

QUICK & EASY GUMDROPS

EASY CHERRY DUMP CAKE, PAGE 230

CAKES, PIES & DESSERTS

EASY CHERRY DUMP CAKE

1. Cherry Pie Filling
2. White Cake Mix
3. Butter
4. Almond Extract
5. Vanilla Ice Cream

ALL-AMERICAN SHEET CAKE

RIBBON PUDDING PIE

Cool, smooth and creamy, this pretty pie is a slice of heaven for diabetics and anyone who likes an easy yet impressive dessert. The lovely pudding layers feature a yummy combination of vanilla, chocolate and butterscotch.
—*Doris Morgan, Verona, MS*

PREP: 20 min. + chilling
MAKES: 8 servings

- 4   cups cold fat-free milk, divided
- 1   pkg. (1 oz.) sugar-free instant vanilla pudding mix
- 1   reduced-fat graham cracker crust (9 in.)
- 1   pkg. (1 oz.) sugar-free instant butterscotch pudding mix
- 1   pkg. (1.4 oz.) sugar-free instant chocolate pudding mix
      Optional: Whipped topping and finely chopped pecans

1. Whisk 1⅓ cups milk and vanilla pudding mix 2 minutes. Spread into crust.
2. In another bowl, whisk 1⅓ cups milk and butterscotch pudding mix 2 minutes. Carefully spoon over vanilla layer, spreading evenly.
3. In a third bowl, whisk remaining 1⅓ cups milk and chocolate pudding mix 2 minutes. Carefully spread over top. Refrigerate until set, at least 30 minutes. If desired, serve with whipped topping and pecans.

1 PIECE 183 cal., 3g fat (1g sat. fat), 2mg chol., 511mg sod., 31g carb. (13g sugars, 1g fiber), 6g pro.
DIABETIC EXCHANGES 2 starch, ½ fat.

ALL-AMERICAN SHEET CAKE

My sweet and tangy sheet cake piled with fresh whipped cream and juicy fruit is so good, you might just want to eat it for breakfast.
—*James Schend, Pleasant Prairie, WI*

PREP: 20 min.
BAKE: 25 min. + cooling
MAKES: 15 servings

- 1   pkg. white cake mix (regular size)
- 1   cup buttermilk
- ⅓   cup canola oil
- 3   large eggs, room temperature
- 2   to 3 cups sweetened whipped cream
- 3   to 4 cups assorted fresh fruit

1. Preheat oven to 350°. Combine cake mix, buttermilk, oil and eggs; beat on low speed for 30 seconds. Beat on medium for 2 minutes.
2. Pour into a 13x9-in. baking pan coated with cooking spray. Bake until a toothpick inserted in the center comes out clean, 25-30 minutes. Cool completely on a wire rack.
3. Spread whipped cream over cake; top with fruit. Store in the refrigerator.

NOTE To substitute for each cup of buttermilk, use 1 Tbsp. white vinegar or lemon juice plus enough milk to measure 1 cup. Stir, then let stand 5 min. Or, use 1 cup plain yogurt or 1¾ tsp. cream of tartar plus 1 cup milk.

1 PIECE 257 cal., 15g fat (5g sat. fat), 56mg chol., 261mg sod., 29g carb. (14g sugars, 0 fiber), 4g pro.

RIBBON
PUDDING PIE

CHOCOLATE BANANA BUNDLES

Banana with chocolate is such an irresistible combo that I make this quick dessert often. You can also top these tasty bundles with the butter and brown sugar mixture left over from coating the bananas, or sprinkle on a dash of sea salt.

—*Thomas Faglon, Somerset, NJ*

TAKES: 30 min.
MAKES: 4 servings

- 2   Tbsp. butter
- ¼   cup packed brown sugar
- 2   medium ripe bananas, halved lengthwise
- 1   sheet frozen puff pastry, thawed
- 4   oz. semisweet chocolate, melted
  Vanilla ice cream, optional

1. Preheat oven to 400°. In a large cast-iron or other heavy skillet, melt butter over medium heat. Stir in brown sugar until blended. Add bananas; stir to coat. Remove from heat; set aside.
2. Unfold puff pastry; cut into 4 rectangles. Place a banana half in center of each rectangle. Overlap 2 opposite corners of pastry over banana; pinch tightly to seal. Place on parchment-lined baking sheets.
3. Bake until pastry is golden brown, 20-25 minutes. Drizzle with chocolate. Serve warm, with ice cream if desired.

1 FILLED PASTRY 596 cal., 31g fat (12g sat. fat), 15mg chol., 249mg sod., 78g carb. (35g sugars, 8g fiber), 7g pro.

CARAMEL BANANA BUNDLES
Omit chocolate. Drizzle with caramel ice cream topping.

CHOCOLATE BANANA BUNDLES

CHOCOLATE TRUFFLE PIE

CHOCOLATE TRUFFLE PIE

I discovered a recipe for a quick chocolate mousse and thought it might make a good pie filling. My chocolate-loving family endorses this dessert, saying it melts in your mouth! Use a premade crust or make your own.

—*Keri Schofield Lawson, Brea, CA*

PREP: 15 min. + chilling
MAKES: 8 servings

- 2 cups semisweet chocolate chips
- 1½ cups heavy whipping cream, divided
- ¼ cup confectioners' sugar
- 1 Tbsp. vanilla extract
- 1 chocolate crumb crust (9 in.)
  Optional: Whipped cream and chocolate curls

1. In a large microwave-safe bowl, combine chocolate chips and ½ cup of cream. Cook on high until smooth, 1-2 minutes, stirring every 30 seconds. Stir in sugar and vanilla. Cool to room temperature.

2. In a large bowl, beat remaining 1 cup cream until soft peaks form. Gently fold into chocolate mixture, one third at a time. Spoon into crust. Refrigerate at least 3 hours before serving. If desired, garnish with whipped cream and chocolate curls.

1 PIECE 383 cal., 27g fat (15g sat. fat), 49mg chol., 99mg sod., 37g carb. (29g sugars, 3g fiber), 3g pro.

CHOCOLATE CRUMB CRUST (9 IN.) Combine 1½ cups finely crushed chocolate wafers (about 30 wafers) and ⅓ cup melted butter. Press onto the bottom and up the side of an ungreased 9-in. pie plate. Bake at 350° until set, 6-8 minutes. Cool on a wire rack before filling.

EASY CHERRY
DUMP CAKE

EASY CHERRY DUMP CAKE

Sweet, buttery and indulgent, this cross between a cake and a cobbler could not be easier to make—meaning dessert can be on the table even on busy nights.
—*Molly Allen, Ellensburg, WA*

PREP: 10 min.
BAKE: 45 min. + cooling
MAKES: 12 servings

1   can (21 oz.) cherry pie filling
1   pkg. white cake mix (regular size)
¾   cup butter, melted
1   tsp. almond extract
    Vanilla ice cream

1. Preheat oven to 350°. Spread pie filling into a greased 8-in. square baking dish. Sprinkle with cake mix; gently press into pie filling. Mix melted butter and extract; pour over cake mix.

2. Bake until top is set and filling is bubbly, 45-50 minutes. Cool on a wire rack for 10 minutes. Serve warm, with vanilla ice cream.
1 SERVING 297 cal., 13g fat (8g sat. fat), 31mg chol., 372mg sod., 44g carb. (26g sugars, 1g fiber), 2g pro.

CHERRY CREAM CHEESE TARTS

It's hard to believe that just five ingredients and few minutes of preparation can result in these delicate and scrumptious tarts!
—*Cindi Mitchell, Waring, TX*

TAKES: 10 min. • **MAKES:** 2 tarts

- 3 oz. cream cheese, softened
- ¼ cup confectioners' sugar
- ⅛ to ¼ tsp. almond or vanilla extract
- 2 individual graham cracker crusts
- ¼ cup cherry pie filling

In a small bowl, beat the cream cheese, sugar and extract until smooth. Spoon into crusts. Top with pie filling. Refrigerate until serving.

1 TART 362 cal., 20g fat (10g sat. fat), 43mg chol., 265mg sod., 42g carb. (29g sugars, 1g fiber), 4g pro.

HOMEMADE CHERRY PIE FILLING

Fresh tart cherries give this pie filling a homemade flavor that's superior to canned. Having this in your repertoire makes any recipe calling for pie filling even easier!
—*Taste of Home Test Kitchen*

TAKES: 15 min. • **MAKES:** 2⅓ cups

- ⅔ cup sugar
- ¼ cup cornstarch
- ¼ tsp. salt
- 4 cups fresh tart cherries, pitted
- 1½ cups water
- 2 Tbsp. lemon juice
- 6 drops red food coloring, optional

In a large saucepan, combine sugar, cornstarch and salt. Add cherries, water and lemon juice. Bring to a boil; cook and stir until thickened, 2 minutes. Remove from the heat; if desired, stir in food coloring.

ABOUT ¼ CUP 120 cal., 0 fat (0 sat. fat), 0 chol., 77mg sod., 30g carb. (23g sugars, 1g fiber), 1g pro.

NOTE This recipe makes enough for a 9-in. pie. To use in other dessert recipes, a 21-oz. can of commercial pie filling is equal to 2 cups.

CHERRY CREAM CHEESE TARTS

ARCTIC ORANGE PIE

❄ ARCTIC ORANGE PIE

This frosty pie is so easy to make. I have tried lemonade, mango and pineapple juice concentrates instead of orange, and my family loves each one.
—Marie Przepierski, Erie, PA

PREP: 20 min. + freezing
MAKES: 8 servings

- 1 pkg. (8 oz.) fat-free cream cheese
- 1 can (6 oz.) frozen orange juice concentrate, thawed
- 1 carton (8 oz.) frozen reduced-fat whipped topping, thawed
- 1 reduced-fat graham cracker crust (9 in.)
- 1 can (11 oz.) mandarin oranges, drained

1. In a large bowl, beat cream cheese and juice concentrate until smooth. Fold in whipped topping; pour into crust. Cover and freeze for 4 hours or until firm.
2. Remove from freezer about 10 minutes before cutting. Garnish with oranges.
1 PIECE 248 cal., 7g fat (4g sat. fat), 3mg chol., 298mg sod., 35g carb. (24g sugars, 0 fiber), 6g pro.

★ ★ ★ ★ ★ **READER REVIEW**

"We made the recipe as is—it tastes like a Dreamsicle. Yum! We also made a version with pineapple juice concentrate (which I liked even more)."

—BETH390, TASTEOFHOME.COM

BLUEBERRY COBBLER

BLUEBERRY COBBLER

This simple slow-cooked dessert comes together in a jiffy. If you'd like, substitute apple or cherry pie filling for the blueberry.
—Nelda Cronbaugh, Belle Plaine, IA

PREP: 10 min. • **COOK:** 3 hours
MAKES: 6 servings

- 1 can (21 oz.) blueberry pie filling
- 1 pkg. (9 oz.) yellow cake mix
- ¼ cup chopped pecans
- ¼ cup butter, melted
  Vanilla ice cream, optional

Place pie filling in a greased 1½-qt. slow cooker. Sprinkle with cake mix and pecans. Drizzle with butter. Cover and cook on high for 3 hours or until topping is golden brown. Serve warm, with ice cream if desired.
⅔ CUP 449 cal., 14g fat (7g sat. fat), 20mg chol., 343mg sod., 79g carb. (57g sugars, 3g fiber), 2g pro.

FROZEN GREEK
VANILLA YOGURT

✳ FROZEN GREEK VANILLA YOGURT

It's so simple and easy to make your own frozen Greek yogurt, you might even want to get the kids in on the fun.
—Taste of Home *Test Kitchen*

PREP: 15 min+ chilling
PROCESS: 15 min+ freezing
MAKES: 2½ cups

- 3 cups reduced-fat plain Greek yogurt
- ¾ cup sugar
- 1½ tsp. vanilla extract
- 1 Tbsp. cold water
- 1 Tbsp. lemon juice
- 1 tsp. unflavored gelatin

1. Line a strainer or colander with 4 layers of cheesecloth or 1 coffee filter; place over a bowl. Place yogurt in prepared strainer; cover yogurt with sides of cheesecloth. Refrigerate 2-4 hours.
2. Remove yogurt from the cheesecloth to a bowl; discard strained liquid. Add sugar and vanilla to yogurt, stirring until sugar is dissolved.
3. In a small microwave-safe bowl, combine cold water and lemon juice; sprinkle with gelatin and let stand 1 minute. Microwave on high for 30 seconds. Stir and let mixture stand 1 minute or until gelatin is completely dissolved; cool slightly. Stir gelatin mixture into yogurt. Cover and refrigerate until cold, about 40 minutes.
4. Pour yogurt mixture into cylinder of ice cream maker; freeze according to the manufacturer's directions.
5. Transfer frozen yogurt to a freezer container. Freeze 2-4 hours or until firm enough to scoop.

½ CUP 225 cal., 3g fat (2g sat. fat), 8mg chol., 57mg sod., 36g carb. (36g sugars, 0 fiber), 14g pro.

✳ STRAWBERRY-CITRUS FREEZER POPS

I knew that clementines and strawberries would create a luscious combination in a fruit pop, and I have to say these are delicious!
—*Colleen Ludovice, Wauwatosa, WI*

PREP: 20 min. + freezing
MAKES: 10 pops

- 2 cups fresh strawberries, sliced
- 6 Tbsp. water
- 1 Tbsp. sugar
- 10 freezer pop molds or 10 paper cups (3-oz. size) and 10 wooden pop sticks
- 2 cups clementine segments (about 10), seeded if necessary
- 6 Tbsp. orange juice

1. Place strawberries, water and sugar in a food processor; pulse until combined. Divide among molds or cups. Top molds with holders; if using cups, top with foil and insert sticks through foil. Freeze until firm, about 2 hours.
2. Wipe food processor clean. Add clementines and orange juice; pulse until combined. Spoon over strawberry layer. Freeze, covered, until firm.

1 POP 82 cal., 0 fat (0 sat. fat), 0 chol., 3mg sod., 20g carb. (16g sugars, 3g fiber), 1g pro. **DIABETIC EXCHANGES** 1 fruit.

STRAWBERRY-CITRUS FREEZER POPS

CREAMY RICE PUDDING

I was fortunate to grow up around fabulous cooks. My mother and grandmother taught me to experiment with recipes, and we tried a lot of variations on this one. No matter how we chose to embellish it, it was always tasty. Whenever I make this, it brings fond memories to mind.
—Laura German,
North Brookfield, MA

TAKES: 25 min.
MAKES: 2 servings

- 1 cup cooked long grain rice
- 1 cup whole milk
- 5 tsp. sugar
   Dash salt
- ½ tsp. vanilla extract
   Optional: Whipped cream, sliced almonds, raisins, ground cinnamon and cinnamon stick

In a small heavy saucepan, combine rice, milk, sugar and salt; bring to a boil over medium heat. Reduce heat to maintain a low simmer. Cook, uncovered, until thickened, about 20 minutes, stirring often. Remove from the heat; stir in vanilla. Spoon into serving dishes. Serve warm or cold, with desired toppings.
1 SERVING 220 cal., 4g fat (3g sat. fat), 17mg chol., 134mg sod., 38g carb. (16g sugars, 0 fiber), 6g pro.

EARL GREY PANNA COTTA

Panna cotta is a simple dessert that your guests will think is fancy! Earl Grey tea is one of my favorite flavors, so combining the two was a no-brainer.
—Judith Chow, Saugus, MA

PREP: 25 min. + chilling
MAKES: 6 servings

- 1 envelope unflavored gelatin
- 3 cups half-and-half cream
- ¼ cup sugar
   Dash salt
- 2 Earl Grey tea bags
   Fresh berries, optional

1. In a small saucepan, sprinkle gelatin over half-and-half; let stand 1 minute. Stir in sugar and salt. Heat and stir over low heat until gelatin and sugar are completely dissolved. Remove from heat. Add tea bags; steep, covered, 10-15 minutes according to taste. Discard tea bags.

2. Pour into six 4-oz. ramekins or custard cups coated with cooking spray. Refrigerate, covered, until set, about 5 hours. Unmold panna cotta onto plates. Garnish with fresh berries if desired.
1 PANNA COTTA 196 cal., 12g fat (8g sat. fat), 60mg chol., 87mg sod., 12g carb. (12g sugars, 0 fiber), 5g pro.

TEST KITCHEN TIP
This recipe is flexible, so try making it with other flavors like green tea (add matcha powder for stronger flavor) or chai. Or, omit the tea and serve it as vanilla, either using 2 tsp. vanilla extract or 1 vanilla bean. For a richer panna cotta, instead of half-and-half, use 2 cups heavy cream and 1 cup milk.

EARL GREY
PANNA COTTA

MAPLE MOUSSE

ALMOND PEAR TART

I had never seen a pie without a pan until my daughter brought back this wonderful recipe from a Rotary Club exchange program in Belgium. It's still a family favorite after all these years. If you like, you can make your own pie crust.
—*Sherry LaMay, Capitan, NM*

- -

PREP: 15 min.
BAKE: 20 min. + cooling
MAKES: 8 servings

1   sheet refrigerated pie crust or dough for single-crust pie
¾   cup plus 2 tsp. sugar, divided
3   Tbsp. all-purpose flour
4   cups sliced peeled fresh pears (about 4 medium)
3   Tbsp. sliced almonds

1. Preheat oven to 450°. On a lightly floured surface, roll dough into a 10-in. circle. Transfer to a parchment-lined baking sheet.
2. In a large bowl, combine ¾ cup sugar and flour; add pears and toss to coat. Spoon over the crust to within 2 in. of edges. Fold up edges of crust over filling, leaving center uncovered. Sprinkle with remaining sugar.
3. Bake until crust is golden and filling is bubbly, 15 minutes. Sprinkle with almonds; bake 5 minutes longer. Using the parchment, slide tart onto a wire rack to cool.
1 PIECE 269 cal., 8g fat (3g sat. fat), 5mg chol., 100mg sod., 48g carb. (29g sugars, 2g fiber), 2g pro.
DOUGH FOR SINGLE-CRUST PIE Combine 1¼ cups all-purpose flour and ¼ tsp. salt; cut in ½ cup cold butter until crumbly. Gradually add 3-5 Tbsp. ice water, tossing with a fork until dough holds together when pressed. Cover and refrigerate 1 hour.

MAPLE MOUSSE

I love to make this dessert with maple syrup produced in our area. It's a change from heavier cakes and pies, and a refreshing ending to a holiday meal.
—*Jane Fuller, Ivoryton, CT*

- -

PREP: 30 min. + chilling
MAKES: 6 servings

¾   cup plus 6 tsp. maple syrup, divided
3   large egg yolks, lightly beaten
2   cups heavy whipping cream
    Whipped cream, optional
2   Tbsp. chopped hazelnuts, toasted

1. In a small saucepan over medium heat, heat ¾ cup syrup just until it simmers. Reduce heat to low. Whisk a small amount of hot syrup into egg yolks; return all to the pan, whisking constantly. Cook and stir until mixture is thickened and reaches 160°. Transfer to a large bowl; set bowl in ice water and stir for 2 minutes. Cool to room temperature.
2. In a large bowl, beat cream until stiff peaks form. Gently fold into the syrup mixture. Spoon into dessert dishes. Chill for at least 2 hours. To serve, top with whipped cream if desired; drizzle with remaining 6 tsp. syrup and sprinkle with hazelnuts.
¾ CUP 441 cal., 33g fat (19g sat. fat), 215mg chol., 38mg sod., 34g carb. (32g sugars, 0 fiber), 3g pro.

RHUBARB CHERRY PIE

As a young girl, I dreamed of being able to make pies like my mother. Her rolling pin, which I inherited, is 2 feet long and 8 inches wide! This is Mom's recipe, although I substituted cherries for the strawberries in her original. I first made this pie for a church gathering 20 years ago, and everyone's looked for it at every potluck since!
—Eunice Hurt, Murfreesboro, TN

PREP: 10 min. + standing
BAKE: 40 min.
MAKES: 8 servings

- 3 cups sliced fresh or frozen rhubarb (½-in. pieces)
- 1 can (16 oz.) pitted tart red cherries, drained
- 1¼ cups sugar
- ¼ cup quick-cooking tapioca
- 4 to 5 drops red food coloring, optional
- 2 sheets refrigerated pie crust

1. In a large bowl, combine first 4 ingredients and, if desired, food coloring; let stand for 15 minutes. Line a 9-in. pie plate with crust. Trim to ½ in. beyond rim of plate. Add filling. Top with a lattice or other decorative crust. Trim and seal strips to edge of bottom crust; flute edge.
2. Bake at 400° until the crust is golden and filling is bubbling, 40-50 minutes.

1 PIECE 433 cal., 14g fat (6g sat. fat), 10mg chol., 206mg sod., 75g carb. (44g sugars, 1g fiber), 3g pro.

ROSE & RASPBERRY FOOL

I came up with this recipe when I was going through a floral phase, putting rose or lavender in everything! This dessert is easy to make, but it's also elegant to serve when company comes.
—Carolyn Eskew, Dayton, OH

PREP: 15 min. + chilling
MAKES: 8 servings

- 2 cups fresh or frozen raspberries
- 6 Tbsp. sugar, divided
- 1½ cups heavy whipping cream
- 1 tsp. rose water
   Fresh mint leaves

1. In a small bowl, lightly crush raspberries and 2 Tbsp. sugar. Cover and refrigerate 1-2 hours.
2. In a large bowl, beat cream until it begins to thicken. Add remaining 4 Tbsp. sugar and rose water; beat until soft peaks form. Gently fold in raspberry mixture. Spoon into dessert dishes. Garnish with mint leaves and, if desired, additional berries. Serve immediately.
½ CUP 206 cal., 16g fat (10g sat. fat), 51mg chol., 13mg sod., 14g carb. (12g sugars, 2g fiber), 2g pro.

RHUBARB
CHERRY PIE

MINI SWEET POTATO PIES

MINI SWEET POTATO PIES

My son Levi was only 2 years old
when he helped me create this
delicious recipe, and it was the
first time he told me "I love you"!
I'll always remember making
these with him.
—*Emily Butler,*
South Williamsport, PA

- -

PREP: 45 minutes
BAKE: 20 min. + cooling
MAKES: 2 dozen

2   large sweet potatoes, peeled
    and cut into ¾-in. cubes
2   sheets refrigerated pie crust
¼   cup all-purpose flour
3   Tbsp. cold unsalted butter,
    cubed
1   cup packed brown sugar,
    divided

1. Preheat oven to 400°. Place
sweet potatoes in a greased
15x10x1-in. baking pan; bake
until tender, 35-40 minutes.
2. Meanwhile, on a work surface,
unroll 1 crust. Using a 2½-in.
round cutter, cut out 12 circles.
Press circles onto bottoms and up
sides of 12 nonstick mini muffin
cups. Repeat with second crust.
Chill crusts until filling is ready.
3. In a food processor, pulse flour,
butter and ¼ cup brown sugar
until crumbly; set aside for
topping.
4. Add baked sweet potatoes and
remaining ¾ cup brown sugar to
food processor; pulse until almost
smooth. Fill crusts three-fourths
full. Sprinkle with topping.
5. Decrease oven setting to 325°.
Bake until crusts are golden
brown, 20-24 minutes. Cool 5-10
minutes before removing from
pan to a wire rack.
1 MINI PIE 156 cal., 6g fat (3g sat.
fat), 7mg chol., 67mg sod., 25g
carb. (12g sugars, 1g fiber), 1g pro.

25-30 minutes. Cool on a wire rack 1 hour before serving.

1 PIECE 294 cal., 21g fat (6g sat. fat), 20mg chol., 145mg sod., 26g carb. (13g sugars, 2g fiber), 5g pro.

BERRY RHUBARB FOOL

A fool is a British dessert that's usually made with custard. This is a modified, quicker version I created. My kids love it because it doesn't taste like rhubarb—so I guess it's well named!
—*Cheryl Miller, Fort Collins, CO*

PREP: 30 min. + chilling
MAKES: 6 servings

- 3 cups sliced fresh or frozen rhubarb (1-in. pieces)
- ⅓ cup sugar
- ¼ cup orange juice
  Dash salt
- 1 cup heavy whipping cream
- 2 cups fresh strawberries, halved

1. In a large saucepan, combine rhubarb, sugar, orange juice and salt. Bring to a boil. Reduce heat; simmer, covered, 6-8 minutes or until rhubarb is tender. Cool slightly.

2. Process rhubarb mixture in a blender until smooth. Transfer to a bowl; refrigerate, covered, until cold.

3. Just before serving, in a small bowl, whip cream until soft peaks form. In 6 parfait glasses, alternately layer whipped cream, berries and rhubarb mixture.

1 CUP 212 cal., 15g fat (9g sat. fat), 54mg chol., 42mg sod., 19g carb. (17g sugars, 2g fiber), 2g pro.

QUICK & EASY BAKLAVA SQUARES

I love baklava but rarely indulged because it takes so much time to make. Then a friend of mine gave me this simple recipe. I've made it for family and friends—they can't get enough. I'm always asked to bring these squares to special gatherings and parties, and I even give them as gifts during the holidays.
—*Paula Marchesi, Lenhartsville, PA*

PREP: 20 min.
BAKE: 25 min. + cooling
MAKES: 2 dozen

- 1 lb. (4 cups) chopped walnuts
- 1½ tsp. ground cinnamon
- 1 pkg. (16 oz., 14x9-in. sheets) frozen phyllo dough, thawed
- 1 cup butter, melted
- 1 cup honey

1. Preheat oven to 350°. Coat a 13x9-in. baking dish with cooking spray. Combine walnuts and cinnamon.

2. Unroll phyllo dough. Layer 2 sheets of phyllo in prepared pan; brush with butter. Repeat with 6 more sheets of phyllo, brushing every other 1 with butter. (Keep remaining phyllo covered with a damp towel to prevent it from drying out.)

3. Sprinkle ½ cup nut mixture in pan; drizzle with 2 Tbsp. honey. Add 2 more phyllo sheets, brushing with butter; sprinkle another ½ cup nut mixture and 2 Tbsp. honey over phyllo. Repeat layers 6 times. Top with remaining phyllo sheets, brushing every other 1 with butter.

4. Using a sharp knife, score surface to make 24 squares. Bake until golden brown and crisp,

CARAMEL CUSTARD

CARAMEL CUSTARD

My husband and I have enjoyed this simple dessert many times, especially after a Tex-Mex meal. In fact, I've made it so often I don't even look at the recipe anymore.
—*Linda McBride, Austin, TX*

PREP: 15 min. + standing
BAKE: 40 min. • **MAKES:** 8 servings

- 1½ cups sugar, divided
- 6 large eggs, room temperature
- 3 cups whole milk
- 2 tsp. vanilla extract

1. In a large heavy saucepan, cook and stir ¾ cup sugar over low heat until melted and golden. Pour into eight 6-oz. custard cups, tilting to coat bottom of each cup; let stand for 10 minutes.
2. In a large bowl, beat the eggs, milk, vanilla and remaining ¾ cup sugar until blended but not foamy. Pour over caramelized sugar.
3. Place the cups in two 8-in. square baking pans. Pour very hot water in pans to a depth of 1 in. Bake at 350° until a knife inserted in the center comes out clean, 40-45 minutes. Remove cups from pans to cool on wire racks.

4. To unmold, run a knife around rims of cups and invert onto dessert plates. Serve warm or chilled.
1 SERVING 259 cal., 7g fat (3g sat. fat), 172mg chol., 92mg sod., 42g carb. (41g sugars, 0 fiber), 8g pro.

❄ STRAWBERRY SORBET

I first made a raspberry sorbet with an abundance of raspberries I had growing, but this simple recipe is amazing with any kind of berry. Strawberry is one of my go-tos.
—*Karen Bailey, Golden, CO*

PREP: 5 min. + freezing
MAKES: 7 servings

¼ cup plus 1½ tsp. fresh lemon juice
3¾ cups fresh or frozen unsweetened chopped strawberries
2¼ cups confectioners' sugar

Place all ingredients in a blender or food processor; cover and process until smooth. Transfer to a freezer-safe container; freeze until firm.

½ CUP 181 cal., 0 fat (0 sat. fat), 0 chol., 2mg sod., 46g carb. (42g sugars, 2g fiber), 1g pro.

STRAWBERRY SORBET TIPS

Can I use other citrus juices instead of lemon? Definitely! Replace the lemon juice with the juice of a fresh lime or orange for a fun flavor twist.

Can I make this in an ice cream maker? You can! Simply pour the pureed berry mixture into the bowl of the ice cream maker and process according to the manufacturers' instructions. Transfer to a freezer-safe container and freeze until firm, 4–6 hours.

How long does this sorbet last in the freezer? Homemade sorbet generally lasts for 2–3 months when properly stored in the freezer. Ice crystals may develop after 1 month, so don't wait too long to enjoy it.

STRAWBERRY SORBET

PEACH BAVARIAN

PEACH BAVARIAN

Fruit molds are my specialty. This one, with its refreshing peach taste, makes a colorful salad or dessert.
—*Adeline Piscitelli, Sayreville, NJ*

PREP: 15 min. + chilling
MAKES: 8 servings

- 1 can (15¼ oz.) sliced peaches
- 2 pkg. (3 oz. each) peach or apricot gelatin
- ½ cup sugar
- 2 cups boiling water
- 1 tsp. almond extract
- 1 carton (8 oz.) frozen whipped topping, thawed Sliced fresh peaches, optional

1. Drain peaches, reserving ⅔ cup juice. Chop peaches into small pieces.
2. In a large bowl, dissolve gelatin and sugar in the boiling water. Stir in reserved peach juice. Chill until slightly thickened. Stir extract into whipped topping; gently fold into gelatin mixture. Fold in peaches.
3. Pour into an oiled 6-cup mold. Chill overnight. Unmold onto a serving platter; garnish with peaches if desired.

1 SERVING 249 cal., 5g fat (5g sat. fat), 0 chol., 53mg sod., 47g carb. (47g sugars, 0 fiber), 2g pro.

★ ★ ★ ★ ★ **READER REVIEW**

"This was super simple to make, and my family loved it. I couldn't find the flavor of gelatin in the recipe, so I used orange—and it was delicious."

—MISSCOFFEEPOT, TASTEOFHOME.COM

JELLIED CHAMPAGNE DESSERT

JELLIED CHAMPAGNE DESSERT

This refreshing dessert looks just like a glass of bubbling champagne.
—*Vickie McLaughlin, Kingsport, TN*

PREP: 20 min. + chilling
MAKES: 8 servings

- 1 envelope unflavored gelatin
- 2 cups cold white grape juice, divided
- 2 Tbsp. sugar
- 2 cups champagne or club soda
- 8 fresh strawberries, hulled

1. In a small saucepan, sprinkle gelatin over 1 cup cold grape juice; let stand 1 minute. Heat over low heat, stirring until gelatin is dissolved. Stir in sugar. Remove from heat; stir in the remaining 1 cup grape juice. Cool to room temperature.
2. Transfer to a large bowl. Slowly stir in champagne. Pour half the mixture into 8 champagne or parfait glasses. Add 1 strawberry to each glass. Refrigerate glasses and remaining gelatin mixture until almost set, about 1 hour.
3. Place reserved gelatin mixture in a blender; cover and process until foamy. Pour into glasses. Chill until set, about 3 hours.

1 SERVING 96 cal., 0 fat (0 sat. fat), 0 chol., 9mg sod., 13g carb. (12g sugars, 0 fiber), 1g pro. **DIABETIC EXCHANGES** 1 starch.

❄ BEST EVER VANILLA ICE CREAM

This ice cream is technically a custard since it contains eggs. I've found eggs are key to making a smooth and creamy treat that rivals the best ice cream shop.
—*Peggy Woodward, Shullsburg, WI*

PREP: 15 min. + chilling
PROCESS: 25 min./batch + freezing
MAKES: 4½ cups

- 2 cups heavy whipping cream
- 2 cups 2% milk
- ¾ cup sugar
- ⅛ tsp. salt
- 1 vanilla bean
- 6 large egg yolks

BEST EVER
VANILLA ICE CREAM

1. In a large heavy saucepan, combine cream, milk, sugar and salt. Split vanilla bean in half lengthwise. With a sharp knife, scrape seeds into pan; add bean. Heat cream mixture over medium heat, stirring to dissolve sugar, until bubbles form around side of pan.

2. In a small bowl, whisk a small amount of the hot mixture into the egg yolks; return all to the pan, whisking constantly. Cook over low heat, stirring constantly, until mixture is just thick enough to coat a metal spoon and temperature reaches 180°. Do not allow to boil. Immediately transfer to a bowl.

3. Place bowl in a pan of ice water. Stir gently and occasionally for 2 minutes; discard vanilla bean. Press waxed paper onto surface of mixture. Refrigerate several hours or overnight.

4. Fill cylinder of ice cream maker two-thirds full; freeze according to the manufacturer's directions. (Refrigerate remaining mixture until ready to freeze.) Transfer ice cream to a freezer container; freeze until firm, 4-6 hours. Repeat with remaining mixture.

½ CUP 310 cal., 23g fat (14g sat. fat), 188mg chol., 78mg sod., 21g carb. (21g sugars, 0 fiber), 5g pro.

CHOCOLATE ICE CREAM Melt 2 cups semisweet chocolate; cool to room temperature. Whisk melted chocolate into egg yolks before whisking a small amount of hot cream mixture into yolks. Proceed with recipe as directed.

STRAWBERRY ICE CREAM Crush 2 cups sliced fresh strawberries with ¼ cup sugar. Stir into cooked custard as it cools in a pan of ice water. Proceed with recipe as directed.

TEST KITCHEN TIP

You can still make this even if you don't have an ice cream maker! After chilling overnight, pour the custard into a frozen 13x9-in. dish. Cover and freeze for 30 minutes. Beat with a hand mixer until smooth; return to the freezer. Repeat the process, beating every 30 minutes or until desired consistency.

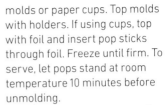

QUICK & EASY CHOCOLATE SAUCE

Mom made this fudgy sauce to drizzle on cake, and we like it over ice cream too. It will keep for several weeks in the refrigerator.
—*Janice Miller, Creston, IA*

TAKES: 15 min. • **MAKES:** 2¼ cups

- 12 oz. (2 cups) semisweet chocolate chips
- 1 cup heavy whipping cream
- ¾ cup sugar

1. In a small heavy saucepan, combine all ingredients. Bring to a boil over medium heat, stirring constantly. Boil and stir 2 minutes.
2. Store in airtight containers in the refrigerator. Warm gently before serving.

2 TBSP. 169 cal., 11g fat (6g sat. fat), 18mg chol., 7mg sod., 21g carb. (19g sugars, 1g fiber), 1g pro.

BLUEBERRY CREAM POPS

Blueberry and cream pops are such a fun afternoon snack. And they're simple to make!
—*Cindy Reams, Philipsburg, PA*

PREP: 15 min. + freezing
MAKES: 8 pops

- ⅔ cup sugar
- ⅔ cup water
- 2 cups fresh or frozen blueberries, thawed
- ¼ cup heavy whipping cream
- 8 freezer pop molds or 8 paper cups (3 oz. each) and wooden pop sticks

1. For sugar syrup, in a small saucepan, combine sugar and water; bring to a boil, stirring to dissolve sugar. Cool completely.
2. Meanwhile, in a bowl, coarsely mash blueberries; stir in cream and sugar syrup. Spoon into molds or paper cups. Top molds with holders. If using cups, top with foil and insert pop sticks through foil. Freeze until firm. To serve, let pops stand at room temperature 10 minutes before unmolding.

1 POP 112 cal., 3g fat (2g sat. fat), 10mg chol., 3mg sod., 22g carb. (21g sugars, 1g fiber), 0 pro.

SALTED CARAMEL SAUCE

Rich and delicious, this sauce is the perfect blend of sweet, salty and creamy all in one. I like to make a big batch and refrigerate it for up to 2 weeks.
—*Angie Stewart, Memphis, TN*

TAKES: 20 min. • **MAKES:** 1¼ cups

- 1 cup sugar
- 1 cup heavy whipping cream
- 3 Tbsp. butter, cubed
- 1½ tsp. salt
- 1 tsp. almond extract

Spread sugar in a large heavy saucepan; cook, without stirring, over medium-low heat until it begins to melt. Gently drag melted sugar to center of pan so it melts evenly. Cook, without stirring, until the melted sugar turns a medium-dark amber, 5-10 minutes. Immediately remove from heat, then slowly stir in cream, butter, salt and almond extract.

2 TBSP. 191 cal., 12g fat (8g sat. fat), 36mg chol., 388mg sod., 21g carb. (21g sugars, 0 fiber), 1g pro.

QUICK & EASY CHOCOLATE SAUCE

SLOW-COOKER CHOCOLATE LAVA CAKE

Everyone who tries this dessert falls in love with it. Using a slow cooker liner makes cleanup a breeze.
—*Latona Dwyer, Palm Beach Gardens, FL*

- -

PREP: 15 min. • **COOK:** 3 hours
MAKES: 12 servings

- 1 pkg. devil's food cake mix (regular size)
- 1⅔ cups water
- 3 large eggs, room temperature
- ⅓ cup canola oil
- 2 cups cold 2% milk
- 1 pkg. (3.9 oz.) instant chocolate pudding mix
- 2 cups semisweet chocolate chips
  Whipped cream, optional

1. In a large bowl, combine the cake mix, water, eggs and oil; beat on low speed for 30 seconds. Beat on medium for 2 minutes. Transfer to a greased 4-qt. slow cooker.
2. In another bowl, whisk milk and pudding mix for 2 minutes. Let stand until soft-set, about 2 minutes. Spoon over cake batter; sprinkle with chocolate chips. Cook, covered, on high for 3-4 hours or until a toothpick inserted in cake portion comes out with moist crumbs. Serve warm.
¾ CUP 215 cal., 10g fat (4g sat. fat), 28mg chol., 254mg sod., 32g carb. (22g sugars, 2g fiber), 3g pro.

POTS DE CREME

Looking for an easy dessert recipe that's still guaranteed to impress? Served in pretty glasses, this classic chocolate custard really sets the tone.
—*Connie Dreyfoos, Cincinnati, OH*

- -

PREP: 15 min. + chilling
MAKES: 5 servings

- 1 large egg
- 2 Tbsp. sugar
  Dash salt
- ¾ cup half-and-half cream
- 1 cup semisweet chocolate chips
- 1 tsp. vanilla extract
  Optional: Whipped cream and assorted fresh fruit

1. In a small saucepan, combine the egg, sugar and salt. Whisk in cream. Cook and stir over medium heat until mixture reaches 160° and coats the back of a metal spoon.
2. Remove from the heat; whisk in chocolate chips and vanilla until smooth. Pour into small dessert dishes. Cover and refrigerate, 8 hours or overnight. If desired, garnish with whipped cream and fruit when ready to serve.
⅓ CUP 246 cal., 15g fat (9g sat. fat), 55mg chol., 66mg sod., 28g carb. (25g sugars, 2g fiber), 4g pro.

POTS DE CREME

BLOOD ORANGE
UPSIDE-DOWN CUPCAKES

BLOOD ORANGE UPSIDE-DOWN CUPCAKES

When blood oranges are in season, this is one of my favorite ways to use them. I start with a cake mix and bump up the flavor with essential oil. No one ever knows these cupcakes are not from scratch.
—*Monica Chadha, Fremont, CA*

PREP: 20 min.
BAKE: 15 min. + cooling
MAKES: 2 dozen

- 4 medium blood oranges
- ¼ cup whole-berry cranberry sauce
- 1 pkg. orange cake mix (regular size)
- 1 cup water
- ⅓ cup olive oil
- 3 large eggs, room temperature
- 3 to 4 drops orange oil, optional
  Optional: Creme fraiche or sour cream

1. Preheat oven to 350°. Grease or line 24 muffin cups with paper or foil liners. Cut a thin slice from the top and bottom of each orange; stand orange upright on a cutting board. With a knife, cut off peel and outer membrane from orange. Thinly slice oranges; trim to fit muffin cups. Place 1 slice in each cup; top each with ½ tsp. cranberry sauce. Bake 8 minutes.

2. Meanwhile, in a large bowl, combine cake mix, water, olive oil, eggs and, if desired, orange oil; beat on low speed 30 seconds. Beat on medium speed 2 minutes. Remove pans from oven; fill with prepared batter.

3. Bake until a toothpick inserted in center comes out clean, 15-20 minutes. Cool in pans 10 minutes before removing to wire racks to cool completely. Remove liners, if used; serve with creme fraiche if desired.

1 CUPCAKE 130 cal., 5g fat (1g sat. fat), 23mg chol., 137mg sod., 19g carb. (11g sugars, 0 fiber), 2g pro.
DIABETIC EXCHANGES 1½ starch, 1 fat.

BLUEBERRY
LEMON TRIFLE

BLUEBERRY LEMON TRIFLE

A refreshing lemon filling and fresh blueberries give this sunny dessert sensation plenty of color. Don't worry about heating up the oven—this trifle doesn't require baking, making it perfect for the hot summer months.
—*Ellen Peden, Houston, TX*

PREP: 15 min. + chilling
MAKES: 14 servings

- 3 cups fresh blueberries, divided
- 2 cans (15¾ oz. each) lemon pie filling
- 2 cups lemon yogurt
- 1 prepared angel food cake (8 to 10 oz.), cut into 1-in. cubes
- 1 carton (8 oz.) frozen whipped topping, thawed
  Optional: Lemon slices and fresh mint

1. Set aside ¼ cup blueberries for garnish. In a large bowl, combine pie filling and yogurt.
2. In a 3½-qt. serving or trifle bowl, layer a third of the cake cubes, lemon mixture and blueberries. Repeat layers twice. Top with whipped topping. Cover and refrigerate at least 2 hours. Garnish with reserved blueberries and, if desired, lemon and mint.
1 SERVING 230 cal., 4g fat (3g sat. fat), 2mg chol., 235mg sod., 44g carb. (27g sugars, 1g fiber), 3g pro.

NEAPOLITAN CAKE

NEAPOLITAN CAKE

I received this easy recipe from a friend. It's a pretty cake for birthday parties. I like to add strawberry extract to the pink portion of the batter.
—*Marianne Waldman, Brimfield, IL*

PREP: 15 min.
BAKE: 40 min. + cooling
MAKES: 12 servings

- 1 pkg. yellow cake mix (regular size)
- 1 cup water
- ¼ cup canola oil
- 3 large eggs, room temperature
- 8 to 10 drops red food coloring
- ¼ cup chocolate syrup
- 1 Tbsp. baking cocoa
  Confectioners' sugar, optional

1. Preheat oven to 350°. In a large bowl, combine cake mix, water, oil and eggs; beat on low speed for 30 seconds. Beat on medium for 2 minutes. Divide batter into 3 equal portions.
2. Pour 1 portion into a greased and floured 10-in. fluted tube pan. Stir red food coloring into another portion; carefully spoon into pan. Stir chocolate syrup and cocoa into remaining batter; carefully spoon into pan. Do not swirl.
3. Bake until a toothpick inserted in the center comes out clean, 40-45 minutes. Cool 10 minutes before removing from pan to a wire rack to cool completely. If desired, dust with confectioners' sugar.
1 PIECE 222 cal., 7g fat (2g sat. fat), 47mg chol., 301mg sod., 37g carb. (21g sugars, 1g fiber), 3g pro.

FANCY FUSS-FREE TORTE

FANCY FUSS-FREE TORTE

Thanks to frozen pound cake and a can of pie filling, this torte is easy to make. If the layers slide, keep them in place with toothpicks around the edges as you build. Just remove before serving.
—*Joan Causey, Greenwood, AR*

TAKES: 15 min.
MAKES: 10 servings

1   loaf (10¾ oz.) frozen pound cake, thawed
1   can (21 oz.) cherry pie filling or flavor of your choice
1   carton (8 oz.) frozen whipped topping, thawed
½   cup chopped pecans

Using a long serrated knife, cut cake horizontally into 3 layers. Place bottom cake layer on a serving plate; top with half the pie filling. Repeat layers. Top with remaining cake layer. Frost top and sides of cake with whipped topping. Sprinkle with pecans.

1 PIECE 287 cal., 13g fat (7g sat. fat), 44mg chol., 122mg sod., 38g carb. (25g sugars, 1g fiber), 3g pro.

FUN & FESTIVE CAKE POPS

These delightful little nibbles are endlessly adaptable—you can change their flavor throughout the year and they're always delicious. Top them to match the occasion you're celebrating.
—Taste of Home *Test Kitchen*

PREP: 1 hour + chilling
BAKE: 35 min. + cooling
MAKES: 4 dozen

1 pkg. cake mix of your choice (regular size)
1 cup prepared frosting of your choice
48 lollipop sticks
2½ lbs. dark chocolate, milk chocolate, white or pink candy coating, coarsely chopped

Optional toppings: Nonpareils; crushed peppermint candies; finely chopped cashews; unsweetened coconut; assorted sprinkles; finely chopped crystallized ginger; crushed gingersnap cookies; melted caramels and coarse sea salt

1. Prepare and bake cake mix according to package directions, using a greased 13x9-in. baking pan. Let cake cool completely on a wire rack.
2. Crumble cake into a large bowl. Add frosting and mix well. Shape mixture into 1½-in. balls. Place on baking sheets; insert sticks. Freeze for at least 2 hours or refrigerate for at least 3 hours or until cake balls are firm.
3. In a microwave, melt candy coating. Dip each cake ball in coating; allow excess to drip off. Roll, sprinkle or drizzle with toppings of your choice. Insert cake pops into a foam block to stand. Let stand until set.

1 CAKE POP 213 cal., 11g fat (7g sat. fat), 13mg chol., 97mg sod., 28g carb. (23g sugars, 1g fiber), 1g pro.

FUN & FESTIVE CAKE POPS TIPS

My cake pops are bumpy. What did I do wrong? It could be that your cake mixture isn't compact enough. When forming the balls, tightly compact the scoop of cake crumbs and frosting in the palm of your hand and roll it into a very compact, round ball. Once it has chilled, if you still find it's a little bumpy, try gently rolling and compacting it again while it's cold. The problem could also be in the coating. When dipping the cake ball, stir the coating well first to make sure there are no lumps. If it seems a little thick, stir in a bit of vegetable shortening and reheat gently, stirring until smooth again.

Can I leave the cake pops in the fridge overnight before dipping?
Absolutely! Form the cake balls, place on a sheet pan or tray in a single layer, and cover them well so they don't dry out. Remove the cake balls the next day and let them sit at room temperature for 10 minutes before dipping.

FUN & FESTIVE CAKE POPS

RECIPE INDEX